CW00919650

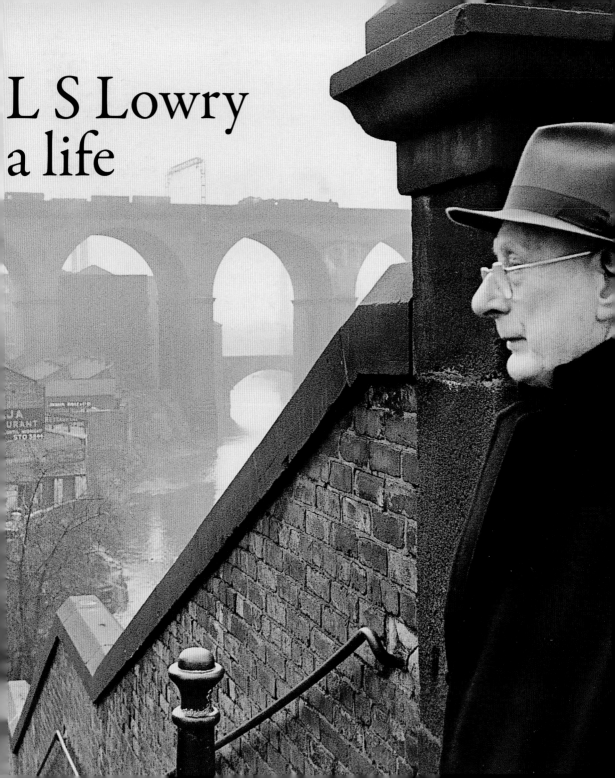

L S Lowry
a life

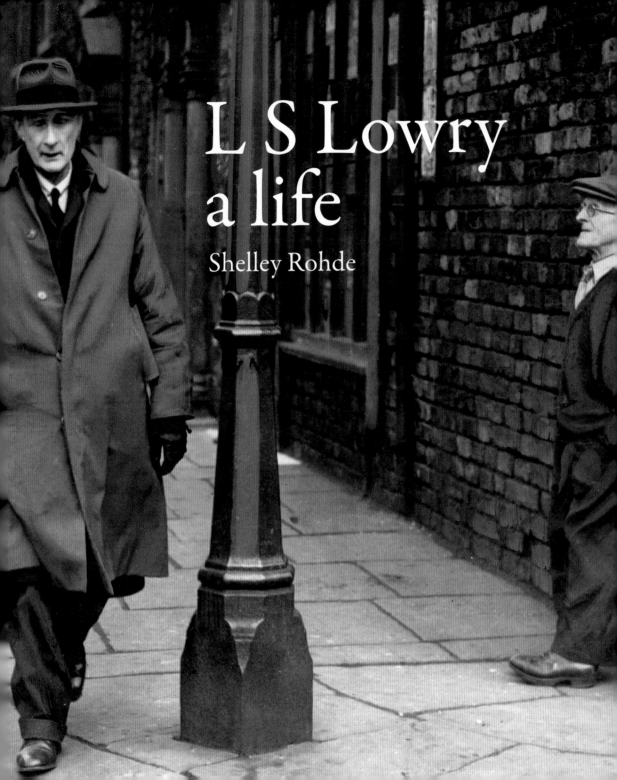

L S Lowry
a life

Shelley Rohde

Originally published in
Great Britain in 2007 by
Haus Publishing Limited
26 Cadogan Court
London SW3 3BX

Copyright © Shelley Rohde 2007

The moral right of the author has been asserted

A CIP catalogue record for this book
is available from the British Library

ISBN 978–1–90495–049–3

Designed in Adobe InDesign CS2 and typeset
in Adobe Garamond Premier Pro by Rick Fawcett

Cover image courtesy of Richard Green Gallery

Printed and bound in India by Replika Press Pvt. Ltd.

www.hauspublishing.co.uk

Contents

Prologue

Prologue

On the first day of March in the year 1995 the Bennett Collection of works by the artist Laurence Stephen Lowry came up for sale at Christie's Auction House in London. Lowry had been dead for nearly twenty years, the Rev. Geoffrey Bennett, a former bank manager who had taken Holy Orders late in life, a mere six months.

The Reverend Gentleman, as Lowry referred to him, had lived to see a steady rise in the value of the paintings which he had been collecting since they were both young men. Lowry would have been delighted at such an outcome of Bennett's patronage. He relished what he perceived as a kind of poetic justice that gave those who had faith in him when few others did, and bought for pleasure rather than for profit, what he would have deemed their proper reward; on more than one occasion he reacted vehemently when interrogators sought to elicit resentment from him when works that he had sold cheaply, or even given away, had commanded large sums. In the event, the Reverend Gentleman had left his estate in trust for the benefit of retired clergy and to help maintain Carlisle Cathedral–a state of affairs that Lowry, not a church-going man but a believer none the less, would undoubtedly have found appropriate. Had he been in a position so to do, he assuredly would have added the tale to his collection of anecdotes to be trotted out for the amusement of whatever audience he might be currently entertaining.

The auction was an event that, in retrospect, came to be regarded as something of a seminal moment in the English art world. In the words of Jonathan Horwich, Deputy Chairman of Christie's U.K., 'It was a sale that somehow, magically, reached parts that other sales could not reach. It took us all by surprise.'[1]

The sale attracted an unusual amount of publicity, both television and press coverage before, during and after the event and a high level of interest from the public that astonished the traditionalists in the art world.

The London saleroom that morning was packed–through the ante-room and down the wide staircase to the main foyer. The atmosphere was electric.

Unusually for an auction house as grand as Christie's, most of the buyers that day were people who were not collectors and who, possibly, had never been in a saleroom before. Even more surprising, many of the successful bidders paid in cash. One woman had travelled from Newcastle-upon-Tyne with £60,000 in notes in her bag and spent it all on works by Lowry.

She was so unsure of herself in such unfamiliar surroundings she brought cash with her because she 'didn't think you would accept a cheque from someone you didn't know.'[2] Christie's' cashiers reported later that they had taken more money in hard currency than ever they had taken before in one day.

Lowry's reputation as a chronicler of the aftermath of the industrial revolution, an English artist with a unique eye and a quirky view of life, was by that time well established. With reservations. He was as underestimated by the art establishment in death as he had been in life. It was almost as if he were too popular; too beloved of the general public, the ordinary people who inhabited his pictures–as if the simple fact that his work was liked, understood, recognised, collected, bought, issued as prints, put on mugs–though not as yet on tea towels–carried with it some sort of stigma, an indication of a lack of quality or class or

Left: Lowry at home in his chaotic workroom in Mottram-in-Longdendale. He refused to call it a studio; he thought that pretentious. He wasn't an artist, he said, he was a man who painted pictures.

3

I think he gets his hats
from Lincoln Bennett's
L.S.Lowry

Above: Lowry with Monty Bloom, a good friend and one of his most avid collectors, viewing a group of his grotesques in a Bond Street gallery. Lowry has written the caption himself: 'I think he gets his hats at Lincoln Bennett's' – a well known hatter of the day.

taste. Or whatever it is that makes great art.

As critic Waldemar Januszczak observed: '...the snobbish art establishment has never taken Lowry seriously...'[3] Januszczak had been to Salford to look at the pictures in the Salford City Art Gallery and had written: 'What emerges strongly...is that Lowry was anything but unsophisticated...He deserves to be seen alongside Stanley Spencer, Edward Burra, Lucien Freud as one of the edgy and independent urban realists of the century.'[4]

Jonathan Horwich put it rather more gently. 'The Art Establishment just don't get it. Or him. They find it embarrassing to be enthusiastic about how gifted he was. Quite simply, they underestimate him.'

Or as artist Harold Riley, who was at the Slade when Lowry was a Visiting Lecturer, said: 'His imagery is cast iron. Blue chip. Other artists appreciate his technique but they don't necessarily – if they are from the south or unfamiliar with Lowry's landscape – understand him. They understand the industry but not the imagery.' But then Riley is from Salford, and as he says,

that means he knows what Lowry is about. He adds: 'In my opinion he is head and shoulders above every English artist since Turner.'[5]

One of the unexpected results of the Bennett sale was that far from being the zenith of interest in Lowry, the peak of prices, it was simply a beginning of a greater interest, a greater rise in prices. 'Many of the pictures achieved prices which, we felt would not be exceeded,' says Horwich. 'But they have been exceeded and what, in fact, has happened is that the Bennett sale sparked an interest in people who had not previously considered Lowry. Some bought individual pictures, some started whole collections. Lowry has been discovered by people who thought he was...[...]...a none-too-serious painter and who have now realised he was something quite different. In a way the problem with Lowry may be that people who consider themselves knowledgeable about art feel uncomfortable about hanging Lowry with some others...'

In other words, the ugly issue of snobbism in art raises its unattractive head when it comes to the work of an artist who certain members of the cognoscenti consider to be no more than a *peintre de dimanche*[6] with an 'inability to draw the human figure'; or in the words of the *Evening Standard* critic Brian Sewell, 'a cloth-capped nincompoop.'

As if to prove Horwich's point, in 1999 Lowry's painting entitled *Going to the Match* sold at auction for a record price of nearly two million pounds. This was eight times as much money as Lowry left in his will when he died – though it should be noted that the Chief Executive of the Professional Footballers' Association (who bought the picture) was Gordon Taylor, who once played for Bolton Wanderers at Burnden Park, the club immortalised in this painting.

By the year 2002, when the writer Frederick Forsyth put his Lowry collection up for sale, the value of Lowry's work had in creased many times. Forsyth had been collecting since 1989 and had spent about half a million pounds on his Lowry works. They realised two and a half million pounds on the day.

According to Jonathan Horwich, speaking in 2005, Lowry is today's 'first buy'–the artist most frequently bought by first time buyers; in other words, beginners, newcomers to the art world who cannot be expected to know about the elitism rampant in such circles. They only know that they like his art, that since his death, weighty books and plays, have been written about him, a ballet commissioned and performed, a pop song sung about him and a grand new arts complex in his name built as an award winning millennium project on the banks of the Irwell in Salford. In other words most people today, whether they are collectors or not, have heard of L S Lowry. The word Lowryesque has even entered the English language.

'Art critics and historians have been unable to fit [Lowry] into a school of 'art,' says Lindsay Brooks, current Director of Exhibitions at The Lowry. '[They] have never been able to handle his popularity. Negative views about Lowry are largely the result of a prevailing view of the British art establishment that "if somebody is popular or accessible, they cannot be very good."'[7]

One of the most positive factors in Lowry's posthumous struggle for recognition has been–according to Mike Leber, a Keeper of the Lowry Collection at Salford City Art Gallery in the old man's lifetime–the attitude of the Lowry Estate and their handling of the legacy. 'The fact that they have hung onto the collection and have been so protective of his image has done nothing but good. They have not only allowed ready access to his work–loaning frequently to galleries for exhibition–which is paramount, but they have always been aware of the scholarship surrounding Lowry's work.

'I would go so far as to say that the way the Estate has handled things has been something of a case study in how such things should be done to best benefit the artist.

'If such a situation continues I firmly believe that it will happen one day–the recognition Lowry deserves and the establishment of a world wide reputation.'[8]

Curator, critic and art historian Julian Spalding is a self styled 'mad enthusiast' for Lowry. Giving the 2006 Lowry annual lecture at The Lowry he declared: 'As the twentieth century recedes and we can begin to assess the achievements of British artists in relation to those abroad, it is my belief that Lowry will emerge as the only painter of the period to have made a unique contribution to art on the world stage.

'Artists like Ben Nicholson, Graham Sutherland and Francis Bacon will come to be regarded as little masters working in the foothills of Picasso. Stanley Spencer, Lucian Freud and David Hockney will be valued for having added a personal note to the history on realism, but not for having broken through to anything really new.

'Lowry not only painted a subject area no-one had tackled in any depth before–the industrial scene and the lives of its people–but he also evolved a radically original language of art.

'One always recognises a Lowry, whether it shows a crowd going to a football match, a tramp sleeping on a park bench or just an empty seascape. His pictures range in mood from charmed delight to slapstick fun, from profound despair to eerie calm, from merry companionship to utter loneliness. But they are always Lowrys.

'He has been able to express this extraordinary range of feelings because he developed, doggedly over many years, a powerful and intensely personal artistic vocabulary.

'There has been nothing like it before in the history of art.'[9]

Or as Jonathan Horwich puts it: 'Lowry was neither a simple man nor a simple painter.'

Chapter One

'In case she should need to sit down.'

It was the year of the old Queen's Golden Jubilee, 1887, a year of excitement and celebration. A splendid year for Manchester in which the great Royal Jubilee Exhibition opened in May with its fairy fountains and fine bandstands and illuminated lake spread extravagantly across the greensward that was to become, the following century, home to a dog racing track called White City.

On Tuesday November 1st it was announced in the local press that a total of nearly four and a half million visitors–4,372,764 to be exact–had passed through the gates; not announced on that day was that a baby was born to Elizabeth Lowry, wife of the estate agent, Robert Lowry.* They called their son Laurence Stephen, their first born, their only born, a child of the Victorian age who would never lose the mantle of the time. He was a big boy; big hands, big feet, big head. And clumsy, too. Far from the delicate daughter on whom his mother had set her heart.

Elizabeth made no secret of her disappointment. She wept when the midwife told her: 'It's a boy.' According to her niece, she had wanted a girl and had never disguised the fact, wanted one so much in fact that she had convinced herself that it was indeed a girl she would have. Nor did she attempt to hide the fact from her son, telling him how much she admired her sister's girls and dressing the young Laurie, as they called him, in pretty white frocks, which,

although such frills were acceptable attire for a boy baby at the time, looked faintly incongruous on such a sturdy frame.[1] Laurie never could have been anything but a boy, no matter what he wore.

It has to be said that it was in Elizabeth Lowry's nature to be disappointed. She wore displeasure like a cloak. It was etched in the lines of her face, written in the downturn of her mouth. Life, for her, was one long let down and neither her husband nor her son succeeded in doing anything to fulfil either her hopes or her expectations of them.

The Lowrys, married just two years and a bit, lived in a modest semi-detached home, red brick and grey slate, identical to all the other semi-detached houses in Barrett Street, Old Trafford, at the meaner end of Deansgate.

Here, at this time, would drift on the evening breeze the 'rich aroma of Mexican cigars' and French perfume, overlaid with cheap cologne and rough cigarettes, from the heaving crowds of Jubilee merry makers who flocked to Old Trafford, half a mile up the Chester Road. They came from all parts of the city and all walks of life; this was a celebration for the common man as much as for the nobs.

Then there was the noise, of course, always the noise: the music of the bands, the laughter of the young, the rumbling of the carriage wheels and the clop of horses' hooves on cobble stones; and, all too often, the splatter of rain on upturned umbrellas. Manchester rain. Rain like stair rods. Not enough noise though (or so an older Lowry

Left: A uniquely revealing drawing of Elizabeth Lowry, a sickly woman who was housefast for the last twelve years of her life and bedfast for eight. 'A gifted pianist who became a hypochondriac,' as one of Lowry's cousins remarked with hindsight. *The Artist's Mother* (undated) from a student notebook.

*In truth, Robert was not exactly an estate agent although he liked to describe himself as such; he was more of a rent collector with aspirations.

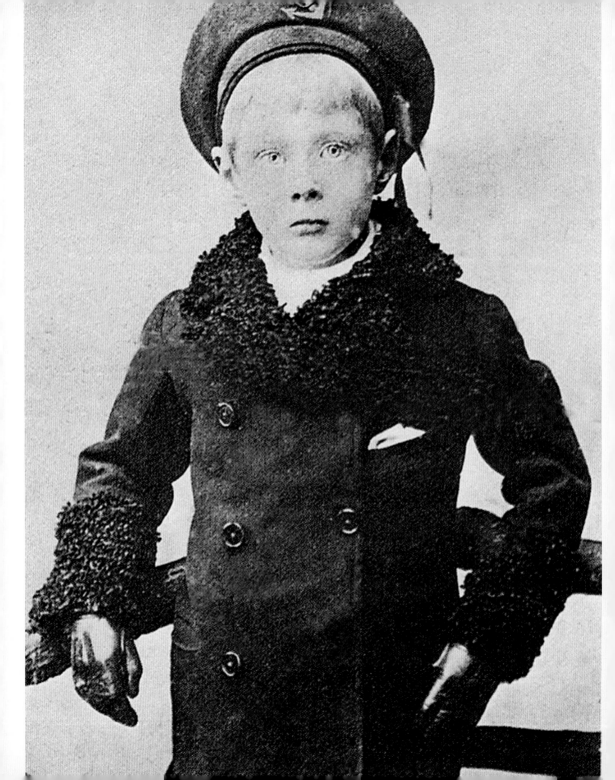

would relate) to drown the sound of his persistent crying which, at times, became so bad that his father 'threatened to throw me out of the window'. Enough none the less to bring on one of his mother's turns. Some days she felt so ill that she would de-camp, baby and all, to Anson Terrace where lived her sister Mary with her husband Tom Shephard (one of Robert's closest friends) and their two (soon to be three) pretty daughters. There Elizabeth would recline in the front parlour on a brocade covered *chaise-longue*, a moist handkerchief to her brow and a look of suffering on her face.

The Hobson girls, Elizabeth and Mary, had been well known and well liked in north Manchester, in the Oldham Road where their father William Hobson was a hatter by trade and a God fearing man by inclination. In later life some of the women who had been girls at the time remembered the family for their hats in particular. 'No-one ever saw any one of the Hobsons, nor indeed any of the folk within their circle, without an extremely fine hat'. Always a hat – whether it was to go to church on Sun-day or to a recital at the Gentleman's Con-cert Hall or even to a lesser venue where Elizabeth might have been invited to play the piano, sometimes as a soloist, more often as an accompanist to one of the great names of the day. On such an occasion the women would out-do each other in the exuber-ance of their *chapeaux*. All that, of course, the public recitals and the smart concerts, ended with the birth of Laurie as Elizabeth never ceased to remind him.

It was understood within the family that her constitution was fragile, and always had been, though there were some who assumed her frequent indispositions to be more of the mind than the body. As one of her nephews put it, she was 'a brilliant pianist who became a hypochondriac'. But as both her parents had died young – her father when she was only 11 – and both of consumption, she might have been excused

a certain preoccupation with her health. Mary, too, it seemed was 'chesty' although according to her youngest daugh-ter, 'she did not complain like Aunt Elizabeth.'

In the event Elizabeth lived to the age of 82 although the last eight years of her life were spent in bed, dutifully and lovingly tended by the son whom she once had wished had been a daughter.

All his life Laurie was devoted to his mother and, in due course, she came to be devoted to him; possessive, manipulative, control-ling, critical, demeaning, cruel even – but none the less devoted. In her final years, after Robert's death, it was he alone whom she would allow to tend her bed sores; he alone who would read to her until she fell asleep each night.

When she died it was the loss of her need for him, while his for her endured, that nearly destroyed him.

When Laurie first went down to Bennett Street Sunday School where Elizabeth played the organ, it was the rule that boys and girls were segregated. It was an estab-lishment that played an important part in the lives of all those within their immedi-ate circle; in fact, there were no friends within their immediate circle who were not involved with Bennett Street. By rights Laurie should have gone into a class with the other boys but because he was so pain-fully shy an exception was made and he was allowed to stay with his mother. 'He would stand by the organ, silently watching the ladies singing hymns,' and 'if anyone spoke to him he would hide behind her skirts.'[2] He was seven years old.

And when the scholars were required to walk round the parish, Laurie could be seen, smart in his sailor suit and leather gloves, or his fine coat with its astrakhan collar, trot-

Left: When the scholars of Bennett Street Sunday School were required to walk around the parish, Laurie could be seen, smart in his fine coat with its astrakhan collar, trotting a pace or two behind his mother, clutching in both hands a small wooden stool 'in case she should need to sit down.' *Photo from the Shephard family album.*

Above: The stern regard was there already, even at so young an age. The infant Laurie in the frilly white dress in which his mother liked to dress him, according to the custom of the time. *Photo from the Lowry family album.*

11

ting a pace or two behind his mother, clutching in both hands a small wooden stool 'in case she should need to sit down.'[3]

Sometimes during the week, Elizabeth would take her son to his Aunt Mary's house to play with his young cousins, Ruth and Grace both older than him, and May, one year younger. It was an outing he did not necessarily enjoy. 'Mother felt sorry for Laurie,' May recalled years later. 'She was always telling us to be kind to him and insisted on inviting him to all our parties and on every outing. "Oh no," we would say, but she would have it. "He's so lonely," she would tell us, pointing out that we girls were fortunate to have each other while Laurie had no brothers or sisters, nor could he invite companions to the house on account of his mother's sickness. We did find him difficult, though. As if he almost resented our invitations. Once he came on Halloween, which we made a fuss of because it was his birthday the next day, but as soon as he came in he kicked our turnip lanterns to pieces. My mother wanted him to say sorry, but he wouldn't. Grace was a bit aggressive, too, and the pair of them seemed to find it funny and sniggered in the corner for ages. Ruth went into the front parlour—we were in the cellar—and told his mother, but she just put her hand to her head and said nothing.

'She was a very different sort to my mother, although they were close in affection; my mother was a gentle sort and wanted to give Laurie the childhood pleasures she felt he should have.'[4]

Decades later, when Lowry produced haunting, desolate paintings of empty old houses, he insisted that such places held an enormous fascination for him. He would stand for hours staring at the dereliction, imagining, he said, the fun that had been had in them by the children who lived there years before. Conjuring up a childhood that was never his. 'I have no really happy memories of childhood,' he once said. 'It was not a nice time.'[5]

On rare occasions, when Elizabeth was in the throes of an 'attack', Laurie would be allowed to go with the Shephard family on holiday to Scotland, where they hiked and biked and went exploring. But more often, the whole family would go to Elizabeth's favourite guest house at Lytham St. Anne's on the Fylde coast where they would be joined by Elizabeth's cousin Annie and her two sons, Billie and Bertie, plus, of course, Mary and the girls. Young Billie, who was four years younger than Laurie, remembered those days well into his old age, telling his sons how he and Laurie tried to get on to the pier with only one ticket between them; as soon as one had been admitted, he would drop the ticket over the side to the other who waited below. '...Sometimes it would blow away and Laurie would have to chase it way across the sands before he could join me...'

The brash humour of the pier-end comics particularly appealed to the boys who would re-tell the same silly jokes to each other all the way home, and fall about laughing hugely as if it was the first time they had heard them. (Many years later, when a young friend[6] asked Lowry: 'How can you laugh so at those old jokes? He replied: 'Well child, I've been laughing at them for sixty odd years and I can't see why I shouldn't continue to laugh at them.' And he did.)

In 1889, when Laurie was eighteen months old, the family moved from Old Trafford to Longsight. The house at 4 Ellesmere Street was marginally larger than the one in Barrett Street. It had an extra bedroom for the live-in maid whom Elizabeth had persuaded Robert to employ, and was just around the corner from Rusholme Road where Mary Fletcher Lowry, Robert Lowry's sister, was Assistant Matron (and later Matron) of a charitable home for the children of widows.

Lucy Snarr, the 15-year-old parlour maid who worked at the Lowry's at the turn of the century, remembers Mary Lowry coming to the house at least once a week to 'sit'

with Elizabeth and thus give everyone else a bit of time to themselves. She was known as Aunt Lowry in order to distinguish her from Aunt Mary Shephard and was, by all accounts, 'rather jolly'. According to Lucy, 'she had a particular way with young people', a manner which contrasted greatly with Elizabeth's attitude of superiority.

Aunt Lowry would invariably find a kind word for the young maid, complimenting her either on her cooking or her skills as a laundress. Not at all like Elizabeth: 'I was always watching myself in her presence. She had a very refined air about her and never spoke without drawling her words. Her sentences would sort of fade away with a little flick of her cambric handkerchief...'

Long after she had married and had children of her own, Lucy remembered the time when, still virtually a child, while bending to lay the coal fire, she had pierced a breast with one of the whalebone stays that had worked loose from her corset. She suffered in silence for three days, intimidated by her mistress's stern demeanour, until finally the pain drove her to seek Elizabeth's help. Mrs. Lowry looked at the wound with ill-concealed distaste and dismissed the girl with the words: 'Go home to your mother to get it attended to.' Thus was Lucy dispatched a distance of some three miles on foot to have the injury bathed and dressed by her mother.

Robert Lowry seems to have impinged only minimally on the consciousness of his young son. 'He was a cold fish', was Lowry's assessment of his father. And yet memories of those within their circle differ widely from that of the young Laurie.

A Hobson cousin (the mother of Billie and Bertie) records in her diary: 'I went to town at noon and bought Laurie a needlework pinafore. Robert came to the works in the afternoon for some peat I had promised him and he took the pinafore back with him. How pleased he is in anything done for his child. I am fond of Robert Lowry. I do think he is good and kind and true...'

And Lucy – her recollections of the master of the house differ greatly from those of his son. 'They were so different, Mr and Mrs Lowry; he was very cheerful, always whistling; and he had an uproarious laugh that you could hear all over the house, even up in the attic where I used to sleep. He was very kind to me and often did the shopping to help out. When I look back on it I wonder how he stayed so cheerful with an invalid wife. I've wondered since, although I didn't think it at the time, if she were unhappy because she realized what a drag she was on them. It was obvious they had to be careful with their money and couldn't really afford having someone in to look after her. They were the only family in the cul-de-sac with a maid...'

It was in 1898, when Laurie was ten, that Elizabeth prevailed upon Robert to move yet again – this time to Victoria Park, a place of ultimate respectability, a remarkable private estate where, as the historian A J P Taylor wrote, 'Gothic palaces jostle each other and gardeners dust the soot from the leaves of the trees.'

There, within toll gates manned by uniform keepers, neither horse-drawn trams not the common electric ones that replaced them in 1902 were permitted to pass; the private motor-car was eventually admitted on sufferance and in the firm belief that 'only two or three of the inhabitants of the district would ever use them.'

Victoria Park was home not only to Manchester's intelligentsia, but also to some of its richest citizens. Ford Madox Brown, an artist whose work Lowry came to admire, once lived in Anson Terrace and the Pankhurst family had a house in Buckingham Crescent; the Shephard boys astride their tandems recall seeing the Pankhurst girls out on their own bicycles, 'and handsome young women they were too.'

Elizabeth Lowry's pretensions had been only minimally appeased by the move; their new home (where the rent was now £26 a year instead of the £16 it had been at Ellesmere Street) was only 'just inside the railings.' She still had to endure the sort of neighbours who 'sat in chairs on their front doorsteps and chatted away the afternoons.'

Life was as frugal as ever. 'If there was one thing Mrs. Lowry taught me,' said Lucy, 'it was to be an economical housekeeper, which was good for me. At home we were always poor because my mother spent too much on food for us.'

To Lucy, the Lowrys were middle class but 'very, very careful. The mistress instructed me in the art of building a fire so that it would burn for five or six hours, making it up systematically with little knuckles of coal at the front and slack at the back. The coal was delivered down a chute into the cellar where Mr Lowry would spend hours in the evenings sorting it out into graduated piles of big and little bits; they never had a fire in the front room except on Sundays.'

Above: Family photograph of the young Laurie looking neat and tidy, just the way his mother liked to see him. Even his hair has been persuaded to lie flat. *Photo from the Lowry family album.*

Right: A gentle watercolour – a rare medium for Lowry – of Elizabeth in her healthier, happier days. *Mother Sewing,* (undated)

Laurie, of course, was sent to a private school, while his cousins went to the local state schools. He hated it. For the rest of his life, whenever the subject arose, he complained of the teasing and ragging he endured there. The teachers, too, made him a butt of their humour. One day a master remarked: 'Lowry, you are a living example of Darwin's theory.' Puzzled, the boy returned home and asked what had been meant. Robert Lowry reacted with anger, not so much at the implied slur upon his son, but that the man, a teacher with influence over young minds, should even speak of such things. As Cousin Bertie observed: 'Robert was not a Darwinian. Elizabeth would not let him be.'

Homework was a constant struggle for him. 'He could never settle to it,' Lucy remembered. 'He was always slipping into the kitchen to talk to me: he never seemed to have any friends, which is probably why he spent time with me. I'd ask him about school–I was two years older than him and that seemed a lot to me–but he'd always shrug and grin as if I knew he was no good at it. I often wondered when he would settle down. He was so full of life, full of beans; he seemed like a lad who needed to let off steam but didn't because his mother wouldn't have liked it. He was very well behaved–as if he was continually holding himself in check. He'd come in from school and throw his cap at the hat-stand–he always missed–and his hair would be sticking up on end at funny angles. His mother was always on at him to brush it down'

In 1964 he told a group of students who were interviewing him: 'I've no brains, that's the trouble'. 'No brains? You've a very poor opinion of yourself, haven't you?' Lowry shrugged. 'No, I have no opinion at all. I'm only stating fact.'[7] By this time Lowry was in his seventies and the masks he wore were so much a part of his public persona that it was hard to tell who or what or where was the real man.

This was Lowry in the role of the Simple Man.

During the years at Pine Grove Elizabeth's health was noticeably deteriorating. Her breakfast, toast with marmalade and tea 'in her special pot', was taken to her in bed. At eleven when the dining room fire was burning well, Elizabeth would come down for a bowl of bread and milk, which Lucy would serve to her where she lay on the couch. According to Lucy: 'she never did anything but lie on the sofa, propped up by a few cushions, except when she got the urge to play the piano. But there was no heat in the front room and she never played for long. It seemed to exhaust her. I don't know what was the matter with her, but I got the impression it was something internal, probably from Laurie's birth.'[*]

'Despite it all they seemed happy enough. I never, never heard any words between them. They seemed in perfect harmony– he was such a gentle man, not rough in any way. They both adored her and she adored her son.'

'Sometimes Laurie would go to visit the Shephard cousins and I'd go too, to see my friend Pollie who worked there. Mrs. Shephard was a very kind lady, always worrying about whether Laurie was getting out enough and whether he had friends and a life of his own.

'He didn't, of course.'

Lowry professed to remember little pleasure in his youth. 'I've no really happy memories of my childhood...I've a one-track mind, sir. Poverty and gloom. Never a joyous picture of mine you'll see. Always gloom. I never do a jolly picture. You'll never see the sun in one of my pictures. No. Never see the sun, do you?'[8] Another role, another mask–one which ignored the knock-about humour in so many of his paintings, just as he could ignore, or deny, or forget, the incidental sunshine in the dark days of his

[*] Elizabeth Lowry died primarily of cardiac and respiratory failure; she also suffered from emphysema.

Left: This formal portrait of the artist's mother has apparently been done with considerably more care than that of his father made at much the same time – when Lowry was a student of the portrait painter Reginald Barber. 'Send the lad to me,' Barber told Lowry's Uncle Tom Shephard, 'If he has got anything, doing an office job won't stop him and he can still go to classes, part time.' Which is exactly what Lowry did. He kept the portraits of both his mother and his father on his sitting room wall until he died. In his will he left them to Salford, the art gallery that had by that time bought more than 300 of his works. *Portrait of the Artist's Mother*, 1912.

Above: One of the earliest of the derelict houses that so attracted Lowry. 'I seem to have a strong leaning towards decayed houses in deteriorated areas,' he said. *The Empty House*, 1934.

childhood. He avowed that he received neither birthday nor Christmas presents and yet, among his possessions when he died were found books and cards inscribed with good wishes, 'With Mother and Father's love, for Laurie'–which not only puts paid to the tale but implies, in the very fact of their long preservation, a sentiment that he would have strenuously denied.

In much the same way his later reported recollections of his father were somewhat at odds with the memories of others who judged Robert to be 'good and kind and true'. Said Lowry 'He was a queer chap in many ways...Nothing moved him. Nothing upset him. Nothing pleased him. It was as if he had got a life to get through and he got through it.'

Robert Lowry was the coach of the junior football team at St. Clement's Sunday School. He tried hard to enlist his son's support without much success. In later years Lowry claimed to have no sporting prowess whatsoever–though he frequently entertained the football fans among his friends with a faultless recitation of the names of each and every member of great teams of the past, rather like a child performing a party piece.

Billie and Bertie remember otherwise. 'One day when we were a man short we pressed Laurie, who was passing on his way home from school, into joining us. He really was jolly good. We had put him in goal and he threw himself all over the place, getting plastered in mud and thoroughly enjoying himself. Much to our surprise, we won. The other team didn't score once. He was very much the hero of the match, but, my goodness, did he look a sight. There was mud all over him, but he went off home with a beatific grin on his face. I don't think he realised what a mess he was in until he saw his mother's expression. I gather she practically had the vapours. He got in a frightful row; she was horrified to think that any son of hers could have walked through the streets in such a state. He never played with us again. We asked, lots of times, but he never would.'

No, he was no good at sport, said Lowry. More of a spectator than a player. Much as he was in life.

Above: This is a pastel drawing of a courting couple; or rather, this is a pastel drawing of what Lowry described as a courting couple. In his world even people in love don't touch; in fact, they barely communicate. In his world people stand alone, just as he stood alone. *Courting*, 1955.

21

Chapter 2

'All right for a hobby.'

Ever since he was a young boy Lowry had been fond of drawing, doodling away the days, filling bits of paper or cheap sketch books with leafless winter landscapes or pastel yachts on pastel seas or pigtailed girls in full skirts and pretty bows playing tennis or building sand castles on the beach at Lytham.

It was an idyllic world, the world of summer holidays. Long sunny days, pretty pictures, pleasant company. Laurie, pencil in hand, drawing, drawing, always drawing. Mother in a shady hat, sitting sedately in a deck chair; scones and jam for tea; post cards home to Father who 'wasn't interested in holidays at all.'[1] And the sea, always the sea, rough or calm, crashing in or ebbing out and fixing itself in his mind's eye to emerge, decades later, on the canvases of his old age.

An idyllic world indeed, and one in which for a brief time the young Laurie seemed to believe, without too deep an examination of his parents' ambitions for him, that he would be allowed to inhabit.

What he had failed to take into account was his mother's innate need, which was absolute, for convention and conformity, her desire for success on her terms, her father's terms, the terms of Manchester men. Success in business, success in commerce, success in the city that not so long ago had been universally known as Cottonopolis. If this, in itself, were not enough to frustrate his hopes, there were also at that time tales from Paris and from London, avidly reported by the press, of shocking goings-on in the world of art.

It was barely ten years since Van Gogh had shot himself in a corn field, not much more since Gauguin had abandoned his wife and children to go adventuring in the South Seas. Whistler had been declared bankrupt and his friend, Oscar Wilde, was languishing in Reading gaol having been convicted of sodomy. Artists were people who painted women with no clothes on and called it life; they fell in love with each other's wives or contracted syphilis and died; they wasted the nights in drink and the days in making daubs that no-one in his right mind would hang on his wall, far less buy. Their lives, or rather the popular image of their lives, was mocked by Gilbert and Sullivan and romanticised by Puccini. It was enough, more than enough, to make the Victorian that was Elizabeth Lowry retire to a darkened room with a cold compress and a large dose of smelling salts.

In other words there was no question of the young Laurie being allowed to follow the course in life that, according to his cousins, he most wanted to pursue. It must be said, however, that this version of the young Lowry's hopes for his future comes from contemporary recollections alone. By the time Lowry himself was called upon to talk of his beginnings the tale had been adapted by the teller to match the image he then presented to the world. It was the mask of insouciance he wore, the mask of the artist *malgré lui*, and it had become so much a part of his persona that even his beginnings had been tailored to fit. It is probable that he, himself, no longer remembered the

Left: After he left Manchester School of Art, Lowry enrolled as a part time student at Salford. When he left All Saints after ten years 'they tried not to look too happy.' This photograph, with Lowry standing before an easel, was discovered in the archives of the School of Art after Lowry's death. *Salford City Art Gallery archive.*

truth of it; or, if he did, he erased it.

Professor Hugh Maitland, an eminent bacteriologist, amateur artist and would-be Lowry biographer (who died before he could complete the project) frequently asked his friend about his beginnings. A session in November, 1970, was typical of the way of such conversations:

'How did you start to paint?'

'Because an aunt suggested I went to art school. I used to draw little ships when I was eight...'

'Didn't you want to go to the art school?'

'I wasn't particularly anxious to paint, ever...'

'You didn't pester your parents to go to the art school?'

'I didn't. No. I just went to the art school at my aunt's suggestion.'[2]

Only rarely did Lowry slip to reveal some point he later concealed, and that was usually, but not always, in the days when the act was in rehearsal. Asked if he had been influenced by the work of other artists as a boy, he replied: 'No, I did little books on the theme when I was eight. *And after that I tried to get into different places and couldn't.* And then an aunt of mine said, "I don't know what you are going to do with him. *If he is that fond of drawing,*[*] you had better send him to art school." I'll try anything once, you see. I got interested. That's how it happened. Because I wasn't fit to do anything else.'[3]

As early as 1955 he was telling writers Frank and Vincent Tilsley: '...Not brainy enough to do anything else. You don't need brains to be a painter, just feelings.'[4]

Ten years later he told Harold Evans on Granada Television: '...Started when I was fifteen. Don't know why. Aunt said I was no good for anything else, so they might as well send me to Art School. I didn't mind.'

Somehow, seamlessly, the story had come round once again to that of The Simple Man. The regular refrain: 'Not fit for anything else'. It was an image that fulfilled a double purpose: it forestalled the critics – there is no market in decrying a man who first decries himself. And it fostered the illusion that he had no other job, that he was, and always had been, a full time artist – which, given the lowly opinion of amateurs at the time Lowry was struggling for acceptance, was of prime importance to him. It was the most firmly, most successfully, fixed of all his masks; the secret of his other life, his business life, was revealed only after his death.

It was a good story, or would have been, had it been true. It was not, of course. Lowry did, indeed leave school at fifteen, much to Elizabeth's chagrin. She was mortified to realise that the expensive private school Laurie had attended had not, as she had hoped, prepared her son for greater things whereas, three of the cousins – Billie, Bertie and Ruth – who had gone to a local school, all went on to university and academic careers. (Grace joined the (National) Westminster Bank; May married (twice) and briefly became a chicken farmer.) Laurie had a good head for figures, a neat hand and fast, legible shorthand (as did his father); and that was about the sum of it.

'Mother and Father[**] knew he wanted to draw,' Cousin May recalled. 'He worried them. He was always sketching and doing little books of drawings and had his pockets crammed with bits of paper...But Aunt Elizabeth thought there was no future in it. She wanted him to do something proud. Even Uncle Robert didn't seem to think much of Laurie's ideas; they would have been all right for a hobby, but not for a career. There was no money in it and they needed the money – not that Aunt Elizabeth would ever have admitted *that*...'[5]

Above; Lowry told one collector that the boy in this drawing was a friend from school who enlisted in the First World War in 1914 and was killed in action. In earlier days he had been one of four companions who had gone regularly to Manchester City Gallery to absorb and admire the pictures. *Boy in a School Cap,* 1912.

[*] Author's italics

[**] Aunt Mary and Uncle Tom Shephard

The debates about Laurie's future had begun in the spring of 1903. Cousin Bertie remembered them well. 'She [Elizabeth] was always going on about how unfair it all was. The way she saw it she had given Lorry* the best and he had achieved nothing. From the beginning she would not have considered sending Lorry to the elementary school in Ducie Street where we went. It was a very good, but ordinary school and Aunt Lizzie was a fearful snob. Sometimes it was almost embarrassing, the way she would go

* Cousin Bertie invariably spelled Laurie's name *Lorry*.

on about it in front of him (and us) as if he were stupid or something. In fact he had been so repressed that it was a wonder he had any character at all. We all knew what he wanted to do, but she wouldn't hear of it. Father thought she was selfish, but Uncle Robert and Lorry adored her. We children couldn't understand it. She was so fretful and demanding.'[6]

Whatever Elizabeth's shortcomings, it would seem that she had qualities that others failed to see; all her life she inspired the unwavering devotion of both her husband

Above: Lowry as a young man standing in the back row, flanked on either side by his Shephard cousins, Billie and Bertie. Seated on the front row, wearing a bowler hat is the brothers' father W H Shephard and at the end on the right is his close friend and walking companion, Robert Lowry.

27

and her son. Robert went to great lengths to protect her from the knowledge of his true financial situation, and that it was exacerbated by the demands of her condition; he pandered to her every whim, no matter what the cost. There is no evidence that either father or son ever so much as hinted to the ailing woman what their devotion cost them: Robert his solvency; Laurie – a life of his own.

There is only one recorded instance of Lowry's recognition of the fact. 'Don't be like me,' he told a young man with a widowed mother. 'Don't build your life around your parents. Marry and make a life of your own.'[7] Not that Lowry took his own advice. He never married but stayed at home with her, alone after his father's death, caring for her and tending her, until her dying day.

Even after her death he had no words to say against her, no words to express or even acknowledge her failure to appreciate or accept what he wanted to do; what he wanted to be.

'Your mother was sympathetic to you in your work?'

'Sympathetic but not interested.'[8]

And again:

'Did your mother understand your work?'

'No, but she understood me and that was enough.'[9]

In the months that followed his fifteenth birthday it became apparent, even to Elizabeth, that there was no point in Laurie stay-

ing on at school. Robert had never doubted that this would be the case; he had always assumed that his son would follow his example and go into business, starting as a humble clerk and, with luck and application, working his way up in the properly prescribed manner. He had few illusions about the boy, only about himself. Elizabeth, of course, had neither the tact nor the perception to restrain herself from remarking that a 'job as a clerk' was not exactly what she had in mind for her son. She said it, repeatedly, in Robert's hearing, much to the embarrassment of his friends. He didn't like it but he accepted it as he accepted everything else.

Finally, in the summer of 1903, when Laurie was still some months shy of his sixteenth birthday, he was accepted for a post which had been advertised in the *Manchester Guardian*. He became a clerk with Messrs. Thomas Aldred and Son, Chartered Accountants, at 88 Mosley Street, Manchester. He stayed there for four years.

'On my leaving they were pleased to speak very highly of me,' he wrote in a later job application – a somewhat immodest remark from one much given to self denigration; the role of the brainless simple man had yet to be assumed; at this time there was no need; there was nothing to hide – and he needed a job to please his parents.

The fact remained, however, that Lowry was becoming increasingly frustrated by his parents' refusal to so much as consider his desire to pursue a career as an artist.

In later life he did suggest that at an early age he had applied for a place as a full time student at Manchester School of Art and had been rejected;[10] this may, however, be a part of the later mythology; he loved telling tales of rejection – though one might have thought that there were enough genuine instances in his life, without the need to invent more.

Moved by the boy's evident dissatisfaction with the role allotted him in life, Aunt

Left: Although this disturbing family portrait was done much later in Lowry's life, there is here a distinct resemblance to his two cousins and their father (see group photograph including W H Shephard and his sons on page 27.) Friends of his youth, Billie and Bertie, spent many seaside holidays with the young Laurie but found the forbidding Aunt Elizabeth hard to understand. *Father and Two Sons*, 1950.

Mary's husband—Lowry's Uncle Tom, father of the girl cousins—sought advice for his nephew from Reginald Barber, an artist from Ulverston living at that time in Fallowfield, Manchester, not far from Victoria Park. As a young man Barber had been a promising student at the Royal Academy and had been awarded a Silver Medal at the Paris Salon. Once past the first flush of youth, he had drifted into a kind of provincial obscurity, painting mediocre portraits and teaching a new generation of young hopefuls. He did not share the current disdain for the artistic amateur.

'Send the lad to see me,' he told Tom Shephard. 'If he has got anything, doing an office job won't stop him; and he can still go to classes—part time.'[11]

How Mary managed to persuade her querulous sister to go along with the suggestion is not recorded. But, for what was probably the only time in his life Lowry went against his mother's stated wishes, and began attending Barber's evening classes.

'I liked the sociability there,' he told Maitland, 'and I liked the class. They were all people who could draw quite decently. We just did heads. I kept on going until Barber died.'

If Lowry liked Barber it is probable that Barber liked Lowry, but whether the master, as Vice-President of the Manchester Academy of Fine Art, a stern and august body dedicated to upholding the principles of art in its most traditional guise, had any particular influence with the Manchester School of Art is not known; what is known, however, is that, in 1905, Lowry was finally accepted as an evening pupil in preparatory antique and freehand drawing at the school that had two years earlier (according to him) turned him down as a full time student.

At first he attended All Saints only occasionally. Then, no more than a year later, a Frenchman named Adolphe Valette was offered the post of master in charge of the life class. Valette accepted on the condition that he be allowed to teach by demonstration rather than by the customary lecture.

His students delighted in his methods: 'One Valette drawing was worth three hours of talking'.[12]

Valette, described as a 'brilliant pupil' at his local art school in St. Etienne,[13] brought with him the stimulus of new experience, the exhilaration of a personal knowledge of the French Impressionists and, surprisingly, an enthusiasm for the drab, smoky hues of the industrial north of England. He took up his duties just as Lowry, now nearly nineteen, joined the life class. 'Mr. Monsieur' as the students immediately dubbed their flamboyant master, was as puzzled as the rest of them by his strange pupil.

Just as they had at school, here they decided Lowry was 'an oddity'. His strangeness, however, came as much from his appearance as from his manner. He was a tall youth, well over six feet, and still remarkably thin, the gaunt lines of his face and figure as yet not softened by maturity. He had a large oval head and a thatch of sandy hair which, no matter how often he tried to smooth it, invariably stuck straight up from his head like a well-cropped field of hay, and which prompted one contemporary to described him as 'looking like a boiled egg with pepper on top.'[14] He didn't seem to walk as others did, rather he projected himself across a room or down a street as if he were a puppet manipulated by a hand too small for the glove, his head tilted in a way characteristic of those given to listening to the voices inside their heads rather than those around them.

'Many years later,' recalled Royal Academician James Fitton, a fellow student in Valette's life class, 'when I had become familiar with the odd idiosyncratic figures

Far left: 'I was going through my Impressionist period,' Lowry once said of this painting, done at a time he was attending art classes with the Frenchman Adolphe Valette. *Country Lane*, 1914.

Above: When Lowry came to the life class at Manchester School of Art in All Saints, the teacher was the Frenchman Adolphe Valette, known to his students as Mister Monsieur. He was, by all accounts, a fine teacher. 'One Valette drawing was worth three hours of talking.' *Albert Square*, 1906, by Adolphe Valette.

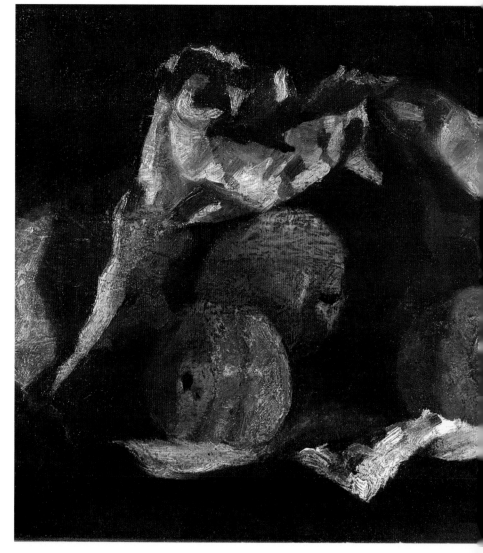

Right: One of the earliest of Lowry's works, this still life was made, in all probability, when he was attending classes with William Fitz, an American with a studio in Manchester. Fitz was, according to Lowry, 'a competent painter, but I don't think he was very distinguished. That doesn't matter. A teacher doesn't have to be distinguished.' In later years Lowry would frequently wonder aloud: 'Will I live?' He believed it took at least one hundred years before it could be said with any certainty if an artist's work would survive. This oil was painted one hundred years ago and, artistically, Lowry is still very much alive. In 2006 at Christie's in London, a thundering industrial panorama sold for one point four million pounds. *Still Life*, 1906.

that populated his canvases, I realised how very like they are to himself.'

Already he had developed an air of personal isolation. Paradoxically, however, he was gregarious as well as silent, friendly yet withdrawn – with others, but not of them. He was an enigma in a circle that accepted eccentricity on a grand scale but found minor peculiarities hard to understand.

'Lowry was regarded as an oddity because he was unteachable. Unteachable by anybody. He used to sit in front of a nude model and by the time he had finished – he made a swipe from the neck to the ankle more or less – it looked as if it had been carved with a meat axe.'[15]

Sam Rabin, artist, sculptor, teacher, wrestler and singer, arrived at the school on a

scholarship at the age of eleven, on his way to the Slade, the concert platform and the Olympics. He was a kindly man and had fond memories of his fellow student. 'Lowry wasn't a great figure draughtsman, but he would always try. Whatever else he lacked it wasn't enthusiasm.'

Lowry cannot, in truth, have been quite the 'joke' the more churlish among them called him; only the best students were allowed to join the life class.

In their early days together Valette would stop by Lowry's work and, as he did with the others, would draw in the corner of the pupil's paper a small sketch intended to demonstrate the balance of the figure or the drawing of a hand; he soon gave up doing this with Lowry's work. He would still stop, still look, but then, with a few almost unintelligible words in heavily accented English and a gentle pat on Lowry's shoulder, would pass on, his brow lightly furrowed.

On occasion he would declare: 'You will repent that,' which, allowing for his accent, the students took to mean 'You will *repaint* that.'

'Mr. Monsieur', who 'looked like all the Impressionists rolled into one, with a little black beard, black hair and a black cloak',[16] evoked in his students both gratitude and affection. As a result he was viewed by his colleagues with some suspicion and ill disguised envy. 'He was rather shunned by the other masters,' said Sam Rabin, 'and this, if anything, seemed to attract Lowry to him. And Valette, for his part, seemed to be drawn towards Lowry as a person. They had a warm regard for each other.'

Sir John Rothenstein, former director of the Tate Gallery on Milbank in London, records his recollection of Lowry's words: 'I cannot over-estimate the effect on me at that time of the coming into this drab city of Adolphe Valette, full of the French Impressionists, aware of everything that was going on in Paris. He had a freshness and a breadth of experience that exhilarated his students.'[17]

To Maitland Lowry expressed himself rather more simply: 'He gave me the feeling that life drawing was a very wonderful thing...I had not seen drawings like these before–for artistry. They were French life-class drawings...I was fascinated by it, and whilst I never drew in that way–I couldn't have done it, it wasn't my way of drawing–I greatly admired him and they helped me very much. They were great stimulants.'

After barely a year in the life class, it became clear that Lowry was looking for a greater commitment than he was later prepared to admit. He conceded only that he relished the company: 'It was good to meet people there. My temperament made me very unsociable although that was not my wish.'[18]

Given that he now spent most weekday evenings in the life class and half of every Saturday with Reginald Barber, it would seem that his needs were dictated more by artistic hunger than simple fraternity. Early in 1907 he went to Valette to ask for private lessons. Valette refused–without any offence or sense of rejection on Lowry's part–but recommended him to William Fitz of Alexandra Road. 'So I went,' said Lowry, 'and it did me a lot of good. Fitz was a very good painter, but I think he came down in the world.'[19]

Billy Fitz, as his students called him, was an American who had given up a professorship at the Cooper Institute in New York to study 'oil portraiture' in Germany and 'the old Dutch masters' in Holland. Arriving in Manchester after the turn of the century, he found his work much admired and, deciding at last to put down roots, took out English naturalisation papers. When Lowry went to him he was supplementing his income as an artist by giving lessons. His approach was very different to that of the gentle Valette. Lowry found him 'a rough, brusque man'[20] but said that he learned from him 'the German solidity, mass and weight.'

Ironically, despite the fact that once Lowry was called upon to give an account of his early studies he made no secret of his debt to his teachers, it was the persistent self denigration that caught the popular imagination. Not fit for anything else.

Once it had taken hold – the image of the naïve artist pushed into art by relatives who didn't know what else to do with him, and who painted matchstick men because he could do no other – paradoxically Lowry found the myth which was, after all, self propagated, both irritating and hurtful.

During a television interview in 1968, he could contain his annoyance no longer. 'I am tired of people saying I am self-taught,' he declared. 'I am sick of it. I went one day to Art School and I said, "Please I want to join," and so I went into the Freehand Drawing Class and then I took Preparatory Antique, light and shade, and then, after a time, the Antique Class, and when they thought that I was sufficiently advanced in Antique I went into the Life Class.

'I did the life drawing for twelve solid years as well as I could, and that, I think, is the foundation of painting. I don't think you can teach painting because everybody's colour sense is different. But drawing...the model is there and you either get it right or wrong, you see.

'And the strange thing is that you can tell whether people have drawn from life from their pictures.'

He was irritated, it transpired, less by the fact that the fiction had come to be accepted as fact, more by the inability of critics who should have known better to explode the myth for themselves – simply by looking at his figures. In this, the last decade of his life, he resented the labelling of the homunculi that peopled his later canvases as matchstick men – an epithet that, in mellower days, he had accepted with the words: 'Well, they've got to write something.'

Once, with uncharacteristic pride, he

Left:
In recent years Lowry's skill with the use of the colour white has won him great praise, this painting is a luminous example . *Snow in Manchester,* 1946.

confided in two companions who treated him as a friend rather than a well-known artist that Valette had gone to visit Robert Lowry – without his son's knowledge – to plead that the young man be allowed to continue his classes 'because he thought

36

I had something in me'.[21] It would seem from this story that there was, at one time, family pressure on Lowry to give up his art.

Giving it all up was certainly a recurrent refrain in Lowry's life. 'Whenever I was completely fed up something always happened. It made me think it was destiny.'[22] The truth, of course, had less to do with destiny, more with need. He was addicted to his art and was 'doomed to paint on compulsively.'

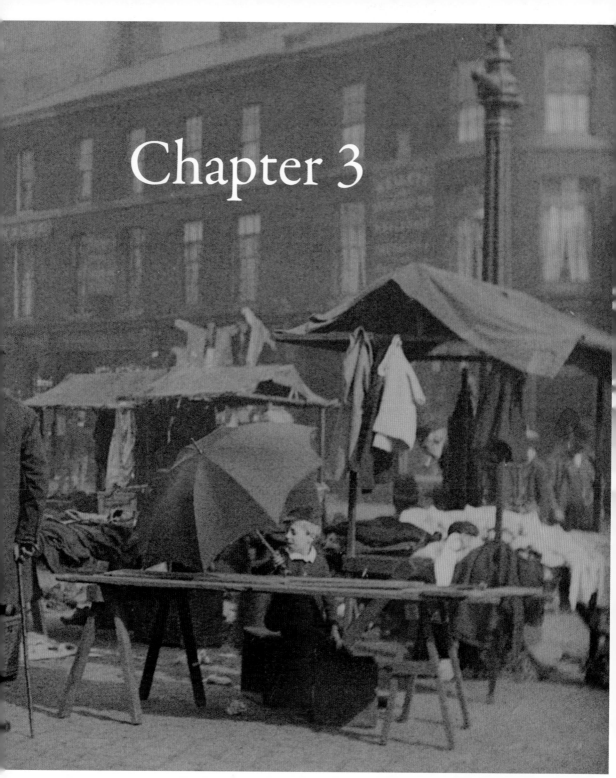

Chapter 3

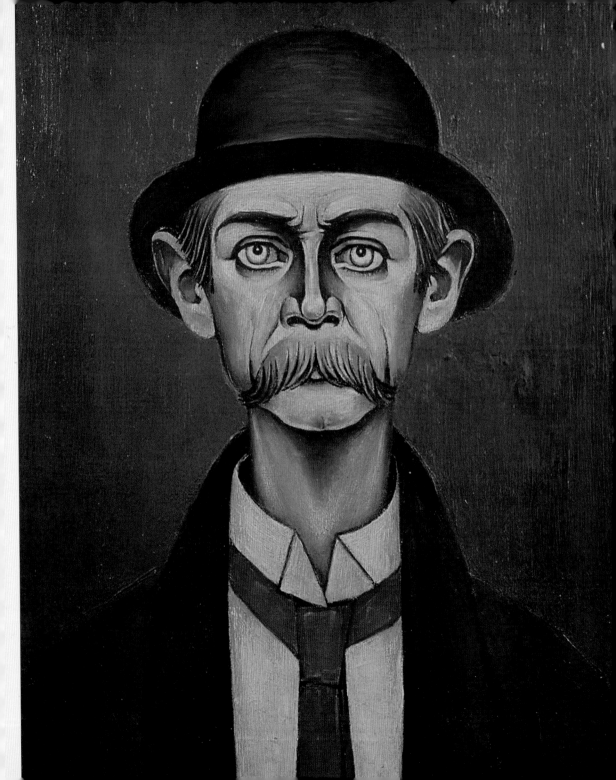

'Suddenly I saw it.'

Spring was unseasonably warm that year and on 4ᵗʰ May, 1909, the day that the Lowry family next moved home, from Victoria Park to the industrial suburb of Pendlebury, the area basked in 'brilliant summer like weather.'[1] It would seem, however, that postcard blue skies did nothing to reconcile the petulant Elizabeth to her descent – as she saw it – into the world of the common man.

The move from the smart to the shabby side of life had been dictated by Robert's failing finances, disguised as a desire to be closer to his friends, the Tophams. A bare three months later John Topham, the man who had been something of a surrogate brother to the orphaned Robert, was inconsiderate enough to die; his widow and three children promptly decamped to Hampshire which only increased the flow of Elizabeth's complaints. They were now alone in an alien land.

She hated their new home, spacious and bright (and ten per cent cheaper) though it might have been. She hated the mean streets, the terraced houses, the sight and sounds of the busy mills. No more did the daughters of the intelligentsia pass by on their bicycles, rather the mill workers clattered across the cobbles in their clogs; no more did the sounds of horse-drawn carriages taking top-hatted businessmen to the city annotate her day, rather the knockers with their poles banging the neighbours' windows woke her each dawn.

She hung thick net curtains at the windows and withdrew into the familiar comfort of her ill health; she got up later, went out less, entertained rarely; she played the piano hardly at all.

Some years later Ethel Ridgeway, the young maid of the time, remembered Elizabeth Lowry as a woman who always wore black. 'I was with them for four years and she went out once in that time and that was to her sister's funeral. She had a photograph taken of Mary in her coffin and kept it on the piano beside a photo of Laurie in a sailor suit.

'In the mornings she would sit on the sofa and in the afternoons she would go to bed where I would take her afternoon tea about 4 o'clock.

'Sometimes I would look at her and think she was just like a block of stone. The only times she got animated was when I did something wrong like bursting the sausages when frying them or not having my cap on straight.

'After she had gone to bed in the evening, Laurie would go up to his studio in the attic to paint and sometimes I would go in to put more coal on the fire. I don't think he ever noticed me. He was so absorbed in his painting that I don't think he even knew I had been in the room. There were paintings and drawings everywhere up there, but none anywhere in the house.'[2]

What the unhappy woman behind the heavy curtains of 117 Station Road was not to know was the dramatic effect the move was to have upon her son; it would be no exaggeration to say that this simple matter of location was to change Lowry's life for

Left: This savage portrait of a Mancunian businessman of the day is virtually a caricature of John Alfred Earnshaw, son and heir apparent to the man for whom Lowry's father worked as a rent collector until his death. Earnshaw Junior got the job on which Robert Lowry had been depending to solve his financial problems. *Manchester Man,* 1936/37.

Right: A landscape typical of the dark, sombre scenes that would have provided the backdrop to Lowry's long walks from Pendlebury to Bolton, Wigan and beyond. 'In those days there was a colliery at Kersley and there was the thump, thump, thump of the engines as you went past that colliery. And that was it. That's how it started. That's where the first idea came of doing it.' *Landscape in Wigan,* 1925.

Far right: This picture, dominated by the mill in the background, is almost an exact illustration of Lowry's description of seeing such a scene after missing a train: 'It would be about four o'clock and perhaps there was some peculiar condition of the atmosphere or something, but as I got to the top of the steps I saw the Acme Mill, a great square red block with the little cottages running in rows right up to it—and suddenly I knew what I had to paint.' *Street Scene,* 1935.

ever. His sudden exposure to the other side of life, the dark side, was to have as great an impact upon his art as anything the Dutchman Van Gogh might have experienced on his arrival in Paris and his introduction to the vivid colours of the Impressionists. This, coupled with the fortuitous arrival at All Saints of a teacher with the perception and sensitivity of Valette, went a long way towards making L S Lowry the artist he became. It took a particularly perceptive critic, writing more than a decade later, to recognise this fact: 'Mr. Lowry has refused all comfortable delusions. He has kept his vision as fresh as if he had come suddenly into the most forbidding part of Hulme or Ancoats under the gloomiest skies after a holiday in France or Italy.'

It was to be many years before Lowry, himself, recognised the fact; but when he did, he embraced the story with all the enthusiasm of a born raconteur and put it in his repertoire, a tale to be told time and time again with varying degrees of awe and wonder—depending always, of course, on the nature of his audience.

At first the young Laurie 'detested' their new home almost as much as did his mother. Or rather, it was the district he hated, cramped cottages grovelling in the shadow of tall chimneys and turbulent humanity, cowed by poverty and by toil, forever scurrying by their door; and over it all, night and day, winter and summer, a cloud of smoke that, dropping soot from darkened skies, insinuated grime into the very pores of those who lived beneath its pall. Here Laurie, lying in his bed, heard for the first time the sounds of his mother's childhood. He never forgot those sounds and in his old age he would recall them with the physical ache of nostalgia, and would hear again in his

43

imagination the imperious summons of the factory hooter in the wailing of the wind as it swept down from the Derbyshire hills.

But slowly, almost imperceptibly, his attitude changed. With familiarity came acceptance, then affection, and finally obsession. He was to conceive a personal vision in those squalid homes and sad lives, and was to paint them with a compassion that transcended mere understanding: his genius lay in his desire to reveal this vision, not as a social commentator, but as an artist–that others might see the beauty he saw.

To down-to-earth friends he told of his coming to the industrial landscape in down-to-earth terms: 'It was always a job to me. Always been a job. A laborious job.'[3]

To the romantics among them the tale of his artistic awakening became romanticised, encapsulated into one glorious moment of revelation much as if he were St. Paul on the road to Damascus. The most popular version of events (that has been repeated so often that it is now an integral part of Lowry mythology) was related first by the artist himself in a BBC television documentary made in 1957. He tells how, one afternoon in 1916, he missed a train from Pendlebury to Manchester. 'I remember that the guard leaned out of the window and winked at me as the last coach disappeared from the platform. I was very cross about that. I went back up the steps. It would be about four o'clock in the afternoon and perhaps there was some peculiar condition of the atmosphere or something. But as I got to the top of the steps I saw the Acme Mill, a great square red block with the little cottages running in rows right up to it–and suddenly, I knew what I had to paint.'[4]

Years later when a friend taxed him about the almost biblical revelation, Lowry laughed and said: 'Oh, you don't want to take any notice of that. I only did it to please them.'[5] As the critic Robert Wraight once put it: 'He is (and knows it and plays the part for all he's worth) God's gift to art

reporters.'[6] He was also, in his later days of fame, God's gift to reporters of any variety: the master of what came to be known as 'the sound bite.'

Sir John Rothenstein records the same event, as Lowry seemingly told it, even more poetically: 'One day he missed a train from Pendlebury and as he left the station he saw the Acme Spinning Company's mill. The huge black framework of rows of yellow-lit windows stood up against the sad, damp-charged afternoon sky. The mill was turning out, and hundreds of little pinched black figures, heads bent down (as though to offer the smallest surface to the whirling particles of sodden grit) were scurrying across the asphalt square, along the mean streets with the inexplicable derelict gaps in the rows of houses, past the telegraph poles, homewards to high tea or pub-wards, away from the mill without a backward glance. Lowry watched this scene (which he had looked at many times without seeing) with rapture: he experienced an earthly equivalent of some transcendental revelation.'[7]

On Tyne Tees Television Lowry produced yet another version and one which has a certain ring of truth: 'The whole idea started in m'mind on the walk Saturday night from Farnsworth to Bolton and that's how the idea came in m'mind to do it. And in those days there was a colliery at Kersley and there was the thump, thump, thump of the engines as you went past that colliery and that was it. That's how it started. That's where the first idea came of doing it…and that was about 1912 or '13.'[8]

Far left: *Oldfield Road Dwellings,* 1929.

Above: Lowry told one friend that this was a girl at art school he rather liked, a fellow pupil rather than a model. He told another that she was the mother of his god-daughter, Ann. In the corner of the drawing he wrote the initials M.C. which also appear on a later oil of a girl with a plait. *Woman in a Hat,* 1924.

Here he was placing the beginning of his industrial period much earlier than he had previously; it would seem that the vision, if vision it was, came to him gradually, over a period of years, rather than in one sudden flash of inspiration. His first *Mill Worker,* a delicate pastel, was done in 1910, within a year of the move, as were a pair of oils looking south to Pendlebury to a tentative horizon of factory chimneys: 'There are no figures in them – I was only then turning from landscape to pure factories. 1910 to 1920 – that was the period of genesis.'[9]

Critic Maurice Collis in his monograph *The Discovery of L S Lowry,* which is as much about the public's discovery of L S Lowry as the artist's discovery of his subject, records the artist's words to him: 'I was with a man

to look, to observe, to see 'with the eye of an artist'. Or even Fitz, instructing him to 'seek out the form of things'. Lowry may well have determined to record the industrial landscape for posterity at such a moment, although the idea had obviously been germinating in his mind almost since his arrival in Pendlebury. But the commitment to his vision, the decision to go ahead with his task, was not lightly made. As a student of masters who encouraged individuality, and an observer of public attitudes, Lowry was abundantly aware that, in order to command any sort of attention, an artist needed – if not genius which Lowry never *knew* he had – a personal theme, an originality of subject.

Lowry's problem was that his chosen theme was so far ahead of its time – so far *out* of its time – that it exposed him to ridicule and scorn.

As he explained to Frank Mullineux, Keeper of Monks Hall Museum, 'An artist can't produce great art unless he has a philosophy. A man can't say something unless he has something to say. He can see things that a camera cannot see. A camera is a very wonderful piece of mechanism but an artist has his emotions, he has his feelings and he puts those feelings into any work he is doing. If he feels strongly for his subject he will do it the better...a man can do it more vitally

and he said "Look" and, there, I saw it. It changed my life. From then on I devoted myself to it. I have never tired of looking. It is always fresh.'[10]

There may indeed have been such a man and such an incident. Or, perhaps, that man was Valette, not necessarily out walking with his pupil, but metaphorically at his side urging him, as he urged all his pupils,

Left: This is probably the first appearance of one of Lowry's mill workers – a woman in a shawl typical of her day. It is dated two years after he took a job as a rent collector. *Mill Worker,* 1912.

Far Left: Critics were to call Lowry's figures 'matchstalk men'. This irritated Lowry who (he once announced to a television crew) 'spent twelve solid years' studying life drawing... 'And the strange thing is, you can tell whether people have drawn from life.' *Returning from Work,* 1929.

than a photograph.'[11] Such an examination of the well spring of his industrial vision was unusual for Lowry; highly unusual. It was something he normally shunned, almost as if he feared that too close an investigation into the nature or source of inspiration might kill it. But Frank Mullineux, although not an artist himself, was in the business; he not only curated a fine 'Tribute' exhibition for Lowry in 1964 but also wrote perceptive notes to a variety of catalogues over the years. In other words, he understood; Lowry was preaching to the converted and, as ever, adapting his history to his audience.

Had Robert Lowry been a successful business man, and prosperous, and had they not moved to the city of Salford, had they stayed in Victoria Park with the nobs – would his son have painted as he did? 'That is a question I have often wondered about,' Lowry

L.S. LOWRY 1920

told Hugh Maitland. 'But I don't know. I lived in the residential side of Manchester–a very nice residential side–and then I went to live in Pendlebury–one of the most industrial villages in the countryside mid-way between Manchester and Bolton. At first I detested it. And then, after a few years, I got pretty interested in it and began to walk about. Vaguely in my mind I suppose pictures were forming, and then for about thirty-odd years after that I did nothing but industrial pictures. That is how it all happened. I wasn't brought up in it.'[12]

Began to walk about. This was said in 1965 and to a group of students from a northern art college who had taken the trouble to research their subject and prepare their questions; they were well informed and at all times appeared properly interested in, and sympathetic to, their subject. There was no reason for Lowry to deceive them by default except that the role he was playing was so much a part of his persona and, at the age of 77, so firmly fixed as to be immovable. But what, in truth, had happened by the time Lowry 'got pretty interested in' the industrial landscape of the north is that he had acquired a new job. A nine to five job, not exactly an office job, sitting five days a week behind a desk, but a job none the less–and one he kept hidden from the art world all his life.

He had become a rent collector.

In January, 1910, Lowry had received a letter from Charles Collin, the Resident Secretary at his then current employers, General Accident in Manchester. '...It is with great regret I have to inform you that your services will not be required...' After two and a half years as a claims clerk in their Cross Street branch, Lowry had been made redundant. It was, he assured his anxious father, no fault of his. He was not the only one to go in the present 'reduction of staff.' As Mr. Collin, softening the blow of dismissal, wrote: 'I have no complaints to make against you. Should you require a

Previous spread: Lowry's fascination with the behaviour of crowds when confronted with an accident or sudden illness is nowhere better illustrated than in this early oil. It may well have been one of the pictures shown in the October 1921 exhibition on Mosley Street. Then titled *Man Taken Ill,* it remained unsold at fifteen guineas, and sold years later, in the '50s, to the collector Monty Bloom. In 1972 Bloom sold it in a London gallery for £4000; two days later, finding he 'missed it too much' he bought it back again for £6000. *Sudden Illness,* 1920.

Left: One of the Reverend Geoffrey Bennett's early acquisitions, painted before Lowry had fully explored the versatility of flake white. *Pit Tragedy,* 1919.

reference any time I shall be happy to give you one, and assist you in obtaining another situation.'

Laurie did require a reference; his father demanded it. As Elizabeth said: 'You can't just do nothing.' 'Nothing' to her was his art, as indeed it was to Robert.

A week after his notice had expired, Lowry was given a testimonial to the effect that he had 'fulfilled his duties satisfactorily...He is honest, straightforward, willing and a good worker.' One could hardly have asked for more for an employee whose mind was more often concerned with the finer points of line and form than with estimates of loss.

It took until March that year for him

to find himself another position. Answering, once again, an advertisement in the *Manchester Guardian*, he applied and was accepted for the post of rent collector and clerk with the Pall Mall Property Company in Brown Street. They started him at 22 shillings a week and, after he had collected his train fare from the petty cash, he was dispatched that first day on his rent rounds. His duties soon took on a regular pattern: Longsight and Old Trafford on Mondays, Hulme and Higher Broughton on Tuesdays, Withington on Wednesday mornings, and the remainder of the week employed as a cashier in the front office.[13]

Although it was some time before Lowry fully appreciated the fact, this was a propitious change of employment; he was no longer condemned to the monotony of five days a week confined behind a desk – and he had landed with a firm of exceptional indulgence. 'As long as his work was done, no one ever queried the hours he kept or the time he spent out of the office. No one ever remarked on the fact that it took him nearly three days to collect rents which could have been gathered in less than two; or that he was frequently late; or that he spent much of his time drawing portrait heads on the backs of office notepaper.'[14] After the impersonal bustle of General Accident, the Pall Mall Property Company was, for a man of noted shyness and little dedication to the world of commerce, a particularly pleasant place to work. 'When you started they told you that, as long as you didn't fiddle the books or pocket the rents, you had a job for life.'[15]

And that is exactly what Lowry got: a job for life. He stayed with the company until 1952, retiring at the age of sixty-five with a pension of £200 a year. He gave his colleagues no opportunity for an emotional send-off. 'I'll not be in tomorrow,' he announced casually after forty-two years. And he was not.

Left: Berwick-on-Tweed was a favourite stopping off point for Lowry, often on the way to Scotland. He once even thought seriously of buying a house on the windier sea front of the town. Today they celebrate his interest with a 'Lowry Walk' which takes in all the places he chose to draw or paint. *Market Place*, 1935.

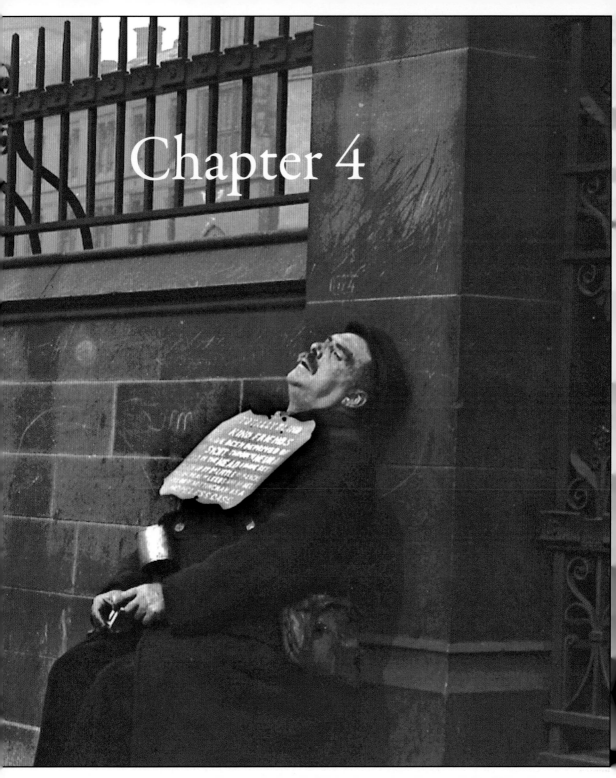

Chapter 4

'Right there on his doorstep'

By the time Clifford Openshaw, a lad of fifteen, arrived in the offices of the Pall Mall Property Company in Brown Street, Manchester, Lowry was well established as what was described as 'the office character'.

The year was 1928. Lowry was forty years old and the task of showing the new boy the rent rounds fell to him. It was a job he did with remembered kindness and courtesy.

Openshaw, who lived with his widowed mother, had grown up in the district, his awareness of his surroundings dulled by familiarity. Now he saw it with new eyes; Lowry's eyes. He found himself moved by his companion's almost boyish enthusiasm and curiosity and intrigued by the way he, Lowry, was constantly looking behind and beyond the superficial landscapes of their journeys. Impressed by the mutual respect between Lowry and his tenants, Openshaw determined, in those early days, to try to emulate the older man's tolerance and understanding in his own dealings; he had expected to be despised, feared even, and was astonished to find that the people they called upon each week were not, as he had supposed, begrudging of demands for their hard earned cash; they accepted the rent men as an integral part of hardship, an integral part of life. If they had no money, as was most often the case, they would say so. 'I've nothing for you but will you come in and have a cup of tea?' If they had it, they would hand it over with a simple enquiry after the collector's health; almost as if they cared. And Lowry, it seemed, would

remember who had an illness in the family, or a death, or more particularly if they had a new arrival and finances were particularly stretched.[1]

For nearly a decade now Lowry had been not simply living within sight and sound of his emerging vision, but working in it, tramping the streets, entering the homes of his people, talking with them, observing their problems, their expressions, their ways, and fixing them in his mind's eye with an accuracy and a compassion that was to remain with him for half a century. When he saw a sight that appealed to him, he would stop in his tracks and sketch on any piece of paper that came to hand – the back of an envelope, a rent book or the wrapping from his lunchtime sandwiches. As John Read commented in a film tribute to Lowry, a year after his death: 'He painted what he did because its character was stronger than anything else he knew, and it was right there on his doorstep.'[2]

Two and a half days a week he sat behind mounds of ledgers in the front office. There, within immediate view, he fell prey to clients and peddlers alike. If a customer chanced to call at lunchtime he might find Lowry, alone, feet on desk, eating his sandwiches. 'We're all at lunch,' Lowry would say. 'You'll have to come back later.'

The peddlers – the shabby, careworn characters who were to appear so often in his later work – he greeted almost like old friends. Invariably he bought something from them, taking a mischievous delight in expending the petty cash on extra pencils for the office

Far left: A young cloth-capped Lowry looking, according to BBC film maker, John Read, 'like the hero of a working class play.' *Self-Portrait 1925.*

59

and, once in a while purchasing, with his own money, matches or bootlaces, shoving them hurriedly into his pocket with a muttered excuse: 'Never know when they might come in handy'; almost as if, without such an explanation, his actions might be considered rashly charitable. All his life he cherished–even fostered–a reputation for parsimony. In the affluent '60s, faced with a 1d* weighing machine he was asked by a companion when he had last weighed himself. He replied, 'About forty years ago, I don't have money to throw around on weighing myself you know.' Years later a waiter at a hotel in Sunderland remembered Lowry as a generous tipper. The money, however, would be handed over surreptitiously and with the muttered injunction not to tell anyone–'I have my reputation to protect, you know,'[3] he would say with feigned ill temper.

Above: Photograph of the artist as a young man–a studio portrait that, according to a contemporary friend, Lowry rather liked. He thought it made him look handsome, despite Jim Fitton's description of him as looking 'like a boiled egg with pepper on top' –a reference to his high forehead and sandy coloured hair that he often wore close cropped.

Another mask. Another role. At the same time as he was declaring an aversion to feeding a penny into a weighing machine, he was enthusiastically bidding thousands of pounds (by proxy) for the works of Rossetti and other Pre-Raphelites at auction.

In truth, he could be enormously generous, not only with his money, but with his time and emotional support, putting more than a few young art students through college at his own expense and buying the works of struggling artists whom, he felt, needed encouragement. In the '40's, when he heard that the artist Joseph Herman, with whom he was sharing a London exhibition, had sold nothing whereas Lowry himself had sold several, on his next visit to the show he

* One penny in old coinage is less than half a pee in today's money.

bought a work by Herman and presented it to Salford City Art Gallery. After his death, the artist Sheila Fell said: 'If he had not come into [my] first exhibition and bought, it would have been a total flop. He was the one person I could rely upon to buy and to keep on buying.'[4]

Human behaviour was a source of constant fascination for him, and the greater the peculiarity, the harsher the circumstances, the stranger the appearance, the more Lowry was intrigued–not with mawkish curiosity but with an empathy that amounted almost to self-identification. He seemed to recognise that in every man, himself included, are the seeds of his own destruction. 'I always have to curb the grotesque in me,' he once remarked, faced with a little collection of his own drawings of Manchester's misfits, the down-and-outs who peopled Piccadilly Gardens and the back alleys of the city. 'There but for the grace of God go I.'[5] It was as if he saw himself, with them, as one of life's misfits, the oddity his colleagues thought him to be or the clumsy, lumbering lummox his mother made him feel. In the last twenty years of his life, when his people had emerged to stand alone, independent of the mills in which they worked or the houses in which they lived, he was to devote himself to painting and drawing the strange, the deformed, the derelict. In the office, when such a caller had left, he would ponder aloud: 'There's a tragedy for you. What a terrible thing. To see a man once so rich, now so poor. What do you think went wrong? How did he get like that?'[6] The question was invariably rhetorical. The teenage Clifford could think of nothing to say. Forty years later, Lowry was still wondering. '... all the time I'm thinking about what happened to them and how they got into that state. Some people shoot themselves, some people drink themselves to death and other people go like that, taking the line of least resistance. The sad thing is we can't do anything about it. And this could happen to any of us

if we were faced with a crisis. I feel certain all of them had a crisis of some sort which they weren't quite proof against. In some cases it could be drink alone but I think in many cases it's more than that–shock, very often, I should say. Well, I am very sorry for them. I wonder about them. And when you talk to them, very often, in most cases in fact, they're very interesting people.'

Never one to lack a sense of the ironic, Lowry particularly admired the innate humour of people for whom life was far from easy and, as Openshaw observed on their travels, relished the fatalistic philosophy of the tenants. He remembered them with warmth even into the '70s–'I am sure those people were a darn sight happier than I was; and far happier than many today who have far more'; he did not, of course, reveal that the people of whom he spoke were his tenants; his life as a rent collector was, as ever, a closely guarded secret.

He never sought to analyse their attitudes, any more than he sought to analyse his own; he simply observed them and portrayed their idiosyncrasies with naked candour.

It was this honesty in his work that made it, initially, so distasteful to those to whom such people and such places were most familiar. It was as if, in his pictures, they were suddenly confronted by a mirror that stripped their illusions and exposed them to the reality of their own lives. Lowry never tried to romanticise the industrial north, nor to imbue it with 'Turneresque hues' as Valette had done–and as his mother might have wished. 'It's bad enough having live among it, Laurie,' she would say in a sad little voice, 'without you bringing it into the house'

Many years later, when his work had received the beginnings of recognition in the

South, John Rothenstein, art historian and Director of the Tate on Milbank, found himself 'simply riveted by the sheer likeness with which Lowry had captured certain aspects of the industrial North...he had extracted from this appalling wilderness pictures of surpassing beauty.'[7]

But in those days, the early days at Pall Mall, the vision lived, as yet, in his mind alone. Ahead lay the years of distillation from eye to canvas. He had already conceived the set; now he had the cast: 'The buildings were there and I was fascinated by the buildings. I had never seen anything like them before...but an industrial set without people is an empty shell. A street is not a street without people – it is as dead as mutton. It had to be a combination of the two – the mills and the people – and the composition was incidental to the people. I intend the railways, the factories, the mills to be a background.'[8]

The particular style that has made Lowry's characters as instantly identifiable as his chimneys was not a spontaneous development despite all his retrospective talk of '... suddenly I saw it'. There was nothing sudden about it. It evolved painfully, over many years of disciplined experimentation, acute observation and constant exposure to the influences of his new environment. 'The scenes were all around me. I could see them every time I went out of the house...'

Once the vision had been distilled, its sharpness captured in his mind's eye, he became fascinated and absorbed by it 'until it had him almost enslaved.' Lowry was, according to Rothenstein, 'to an extraordinary degree, dependent upon it.'[9] He was also extraordinarily faithful to it. From 1910 to 1939 he painted on without recognition or understanding. Despite the derision of his peers, the revulsion of his mother and the apathy of his friends, he never compromised. He continued to work in his own way 'sustained only by his vision and the conviction that what he was doing was

worth while.'[10] He might have been deeply hurt by his repeated rejection, but he never allowed himself to become bitter or disillusioned or resentful.

'I was hoping that people would get to like these things sooner or later, ' he said in 1968, 'but I didn't feel I could expect them to buy them. Nobody asked me to paint.'

At Art School he found little appreciation of the style he was developing. He only once showed them to Valette. 'We didn't see eye to eye at all about my paintings – I didn't show them to him again.'[11]

Lowry, being the man he was, continued in exactly the same way, developing his theme in his own fashion and in his own time. If he had made no adjustments to his style in the face of his mother's rejection, he was certainly not going to do so to please his teachers. Or his peers.

He still attended class regularly, observing, absorbing and, according to his own recollections, enjoying the company.

When James Fitton first joined Manchester School of Art he had just started work as an office boy in the Manchester branch of the *Daily Citizen*, Britain's first Labour newspaper; he was 14 years old. 'I immediately palled up with Lowry, because he was a very silent man and, in those days, I was very shy,'[12] Fitton, by then a Royal Academician, recalled half a century later. Unlike Lowry, the new student had been awarded a scholarship and was thus relieved of the payment of fees: 7s 6d a term. Lowry was now earning £2 a week, his wages having been increased that year from £78 per annum.

An indication of the peculiarly relaxed atmosphere of the school, at a time when Victorian mores were alive and well, is evident in the fact that Fitton, despite his youth, was quickly allowed into life classes. Only minimally awed, and certainly unaware of the assumed threat to his virtue, Fitton worked on, happily oblivious of the concern his presence was to cause the guardians of

Far right: Down the left hand side of this art school study from the life are faint drawings that may well have been done by Adolphe Valette. The Frenchman preferred to illustrate a point to his students rather than lecture them. 'I did not draw the life very well,' said Lowry years later. 'I was competent. But I did find it valuable, and I still believe that long years of drawing the figure is the only thing that matters.' *Seated Male Nude,* c. 1914.

the city's morals. He was spotted eventually by the Bishop of Manchester on a surprise visit to the school and was summarily ejected, together with Bert Wilson, a student of the same age. Valette apparently exerted his influence, and once the fuss had died down the pair were quietly permitted to return to the life class. It was not until 1918 that a new rule was introduced that 'students under 18 should not be admitted...for drawing from the nude female model.'

The basis of the comradeship that was to develop between the seemingly ill matched pair was their mutual unease in company. Fitton's shyness was no more than adolescent self-consciousness; Lowry's, of course, went deeper–an innate isolation of spirit that was to be mistaken, in later years, for the loneliness of the recluse. In reality Lowry was never a recluse: he simply kept his friendships–and there were many–separate from his public image. He habitually compartmentalised his relationships; he rarely spoke of one friend to another, nor did he introduce them. He actively disliked chance meetings with one when he was in other company. At his funeral one of his older friends greeted a couple from Cheshire–whom she had never met–with the words: 'Oh, so you're Boxing Day!' To which someone else in the crowd piped up: 'And we were Sundays.'[13]

Lowry valued his friends; they were important to him. In his seventies and eighties he was to maintain that they were one of the few remaining pleasures in life, that they sustained and comforted him in his declining years. It was not, in truth, that such friends were particularly close–although they might have thought themselves to be–or that they knew him particularly well; but they were as close to Lowry as it was possible to be and they knew him as well as Lowry would allow. And, because of his knack of adapting his behaviour and his attitudes to the company of the moment, the Lowry each set of friends or acquaint-

Far left: One of the most familiar of Lowry's mill scenes. Done first in pastel more than a decade earlier, this 1930s oil was bought by Salford City Art Gallery, at which point Lowry declared: 'It gives me great pleasure that Salford have bought [this] picture–for I have always thought it was my most characteristic mill scene.' *Coming from the Mill*, 1930.

ances knew was not, necessarily, the Lowry known to another. Thus some thought him mean, others found him generous; some thought him funny, others found him sad; some thought him shy and reclusive while others knew him to be gregarious and fond of company. All things to all men. A paradox. Or as the artist Harold Riley (who came to know him as well as any) put it: 'He shut himself quite firmly into his own box...it was as if he felt that, if he was open, people would climb into him and see what he was–and he really didn't think he was very much.'

In their background Fitton and Lowry could not have differed more. Fitton was born in Oldham; his mother was a weaver, his father a planer in the iron works. 'My father was a sensible man who found out what I wanted to do and helped me to do it.'[14] On a Friday evening, on his way home from work, his hard-earned pay packet in his pocket, James Fitton Senior would stop at the local Penny Bazaar to buy his younger son a roll of sugar-paper on which to draw.

In the evenings, after class, the odd couple–Fitton still a gangling youth, Lowry a lurching, uncoordinated man nearing thirty–would stroll to the docks where Fitton had now taken a job. They would walk mostly in silence, each deep in his own thoughts, pausing sometimes at a dockside stall to take a cup of cocoa or, in summer, a beaker of Vimto, a curious brown liquid whose origins remained a mystery to them. Ahead of them both lay a night's work: Jim loading great bales of goods for Hong Kong or Batavia, Lowry alone in his attic painting until his father dimmed the light. The following morning Jim would sleep until ten and spend the day drawing; Lowry was awake by seven for a day at the office where he would arrive sometimes late, frequently bleary-eyed. At the weekends they would meet in the porticoed entrance to the school in All Saints for a day's sketching at the Cathedral, or Daisy Nook or Boggat Hole

Clough. Jim would draw the trees, Lowry the chimneys.

Once when it was raining, Lowry suggested they went to the theatre. Making assumptions, as so many did, about the tastes and preferences of his friend, Fitton 'assumed we would be going to Miss Horniman's.' Instead he took me down to Hulme Empire to see Fred Karno's troupe, where he laughed until the tears ran down his face.'

As Fitton matured, he concluded that his friend lacked the ambition with which he himself was now fired. Fitton left Manchester in 1922, in tears and clutching a bundle of his drawings, lured from the North by the greater opportunities of London. He was twenty-one years old; Lowry was thirty-four and, Fitton observed, 'quite unmotivated by ambition.' It seemed to him that his friend's world was encompassed by his mother's wishes and that nothing during her life-time would induce Lowry to leave her side; which is not, of course, to say that he had no ambition, simply that his feelings for his mother overwhelmed anything and everything else; except his need to paint.

'The more I came to know him, the more I became aware of his mother's dominance of him. She came into his conversation at all times. My own mother was so very different, a bustling active woman who got up to make the tea as soon as I came in. When I went to Lowry's home it was the opposite. Lowry went to make the tea while his mother sat in a sort of invalid chair. She was not a frail woman, nor pale, nor sickly-looking, but my overriding impression of her was of an invalid. I never knew what was the matter with her, simply that she was not well. She was not dominant in the aggressive, suffragette way, but she obviously had control of him. His father was a recessive figure...She seemed to dominate him through her weakness, by her dependence upon him,

*A classical British repertory theatre that specialised in the latest plays by up and coming writers; it was here that Lowry first saw Stanley Houghton's *Hindle Wakes* which dealt on stage with the same subjects that Lowry was putting onto canvas.

by her need. She absorbed his interests and his time."[15]

In Clifford Openshaw's early days at Pall Mall he was attending evening art classes and would arrive in the office the next morning eager to talk of the previous night's lesson. But, he said, not once did Lowry suggest that he himself went to classes nor even hint that he was an artist '...possibly because he never seemed to believe himself to be one.

'He listened to me with interest and looked at my work with only the kindest criticism. Even when we did become aware of his life outside the office, he always implied that his painting was merely a way of passing the time, and that he never took it seriously...'

In all his years at Pall Mall and with office friends, Lowry rarely referred to his art. When he did, it was so casually and with such apparent insouciance, that they

Right: In middle age Lowry confessed to a fascination with the misfits of the world, the down-and-outs. 'I feel more strongly about these people than ever I did about the industrial scene,' he once said. 'There but for the grace of God go I.' And again, 'I think that this is my best period. I think I am saying more, going deeper into life than I did.' *A Beggar*, 1965.

Far right: A mother in child in which there is absolutely no contact. The woman who owned this picture for nearly forty years said of it: 'I believe this is Lowry's archetypal woman, Ann, and the little boy is Lowry himself.' Carol Ann believes the mother figure to be Lowry's own mother, Elizabeth. The woman who bought the picture at auction in 1998 has a very different view. She calls it Lowry's Madonna and Child. *Mother and Child,* 1956/57.

accepted at face value the minimal importance he put upon such activities; for nearly fifty years they regarded him as a rent collector who painted, rather than a painter who collected rents. In his younger days he had pretended that such work that they did chance to see was not his, but that of his 'brother Tom'.

'He would bring in a canvas on its way to the framers and prop it carelessly against his desk, leaving it there so long that we had to warn him to move it in case a cleaner stuck her broom through it. If we asked to see it, he would show it as the work of his brother; whether this was so that we would feel uninhibited enough to comment honestly–which we did–or because he had so little confidence in himself, we never knew...' said Openshaw.

'Looking back on it I wonder if he were

not deeply hurt by so many dismissive attitudes; why else would he have pretended that it meant so little to him?

'What do you think of that?' he would ask. 'Not much,' they would say. 'No,' Lowry would reply, deadpan, 'Neither do I.'

Thus Openshaw ascribed Lowry's reluctance to present himself as an artist as the result of a lack of self-confidence. Others, who encountered it in his later life, called it modesty. John Rothenstein believed it to have been humility: 'No painter whom I have known has been more consciously aware of a sense of privilege, amounting almost to a sense of wonder, at being a painter.'[16]

The more perceptive members of his family, the cousins who had grown up with him, believed his life-long habit of self-deprecation to be based on deep-seated feelings of inadequacy induced by his mother's continual criticism. 'More than anything it was embarrassing–to hear Elizabeth going on about the ugliness of what her son was doing, how sordid it was, how devoid of beauty and how unnecessary. She never seemed to have a good word to say for them. It was the only time we ever saw Lorry oppose her–oh, not in anything he said. He sat there and accepted it all while we blushed for her. No, it was in his continuance of his work that his defiance lay. In the face of such exquisitely displayed distress we would have expected him, as the dutiful son that he undoubtedly was, to have abandoned the mills and returned to the landscapes and the yachts. It was, after all, as she kept repeating, only a little hobby.'[17]

The truth, of course, as with most truths, lies no doubt somewhere in between; in all these factors, all these causes, and others as yet unknown.

Lowry spoke of his mother's inability to see the beauty he saw, only in abstract terms. 'All the relations laughed at them. But the family were very good: they said, 'He can't help it, you know, and it keeps him out of

mischief. He's not fit to do anything else, so he paints pictures.'[18]

His artistic achievements impinged so minimally on the family consciousness that they were hardly mentioned; they were not considered worthy of comment. It was only after Lowry's death that Denys, the son of Ruth, one of the girl cousins, became aware, much to his surprise, that he was in any way connected with an artist whose work he greatly admired. The family solicitor, Alfred Hulme, recalls being in the Western Desert during the Second World War when he received a letter from his father which said: 'Your friend Laurence Lowry is becoming quite successful—as an artist of all things.'

And in 1977 a contemporary of Lowry's who had known the family intimately, searching her long memory for a recollection of him, remarked: 'Oh yes, Laurie. His mother was a brilliant pianist, but he never amounted to anything.'

Far left: The steep roads leading to Brindle Heath Road, Salford, were bordered by stepped houses, the church in the valley is similar to St Thomas'. In typical fashion they have been moved from their actual settings. *The Church In The Hollow,* 1944.

Top left: Lowry's first version of *Coming from the Mill* was done in pastel more than a decade before this version painted in oil. One feature the pictures have in common is that the horse in the foreground is half hidden behind a wall. Lowry always claimed he could not draw horses and, on occasion, would invite the children of his friends to draw a horse for him. One such woman remembers doing a horse for Lowry when she was about twelve years old and being astonished to receive by post the next morning, a cheque for two guineas. *Coming from the Mill,* 1930

Bottom left: Lowry was taken by a photographer to tramp these very streets – little knowing it was his rent round.

Chapter 5

'Why do you keep on?'

When Lowry died and the truth about his double life came out, the loftier end of the English art establishment reacted with a disdain that made a kind of sense of his deception. Such was the scorn in some quarters – quarters that had never been exactly admiring of Lowry in the first place – that if it did not precisely justify his almost phobic obsession with secrecy, it certainly explained it. It made the role he had opted to play in life both comprehensible and acceptable to those with the sensitivity to look beyond and beneath the disappointment at having been among the deceived; in other words, those of his friends who examined the deception from his point of view, rather than their own, were able to see it for what it was: a part of the armour he wore – the armour he wore for survival.

His old friend James Fitton was shocked at the reaction at the Royal Academy where he was now a venerable, senior member. This was in 1977 and Lowry had been dead no more than a year. 'I had often mentioned his job here, in the Academy, and certainly when he was elected, but they didn't believe me. They said it was only rumour. But when it all came out they immediately revised their opinion of him; and some of the criticism was very, very dodgy. Some said: "Ah, now we know why he never painted shadows – because he painted by electric light". That is the stupidest thing I ever heard. It is rubbish. Others said: "Ah, we knew he was only an amateur". This is really the most foolish kind of criticism. And it was,

I think, one of the reasons why he kept his job quiet.'

This response to the revelation by the art establishment was far from atypical. There were many among his peers who seemed to feel somehow cheated that they had not been party to the big secret; and yet everything they said or did after the truth came out, only went to emphasise exactly what Lowry feared.

One couple with a long acquaintance, both professional and personal, with Lowry, were discussing the disclosure that had shocked them so much: 'I can't think why he didn't tell me,' remarked the husband. 'It wouldn't have made any difference.' 'Oh, I don't know,' replied his wife, 'remember when we first met him, what you used to say about amateurs?' 'You have a point there,' came the reply. And then, after a short pause for reflection, 'Perhaps Lowry had a point.'

Those who counted themselves among his friends were rather more understanding although there were some who took umbrage to learn that they had not been trusted with the truth; what they failed to see was that *no one* was trusted with the truth; anyone who knew the secret by virtue of their long acquaintance with him was simply put in a box and isolated from those who did not know.

Some time after Lowry's death, Tilly Marshall, a gallery owner who with her husband Micky had promoted Lowry with enthusiasm and sympathy for the last fourteen years of his life, wrote: 'We had certainly sensed that there was a well-guarded secret in the artist's life. He was forever on hostile guard

Far left: The annual Whit Walks with the children in their Sunday best and the bandsmen playing their hearts out might have been a regular feature of northern life, but they were a source of endless fascination for Lowry. Each year he would find something new, a different angle, a fresh perspective. He painted at least half a dozen versions, and nearly all of them with the inevitable suited man in the foreground, facing the scene and talking it all in. The artist as observer. *The Procession*, 1937.

Right: An early example of one of the characters who was to dominate Lowry's later works, the people he called the grotesques. 'I'm fascinated by the grotesque...I feel like them.' *An Old Lady,* 1942.

Far right: No happening in a city street was too insignificant, too ordinary, for Lowry, be it a procession, an illness or an accident. A quarrel was just too tempting to ignore. One version of just such an event – or it may even have been the same one – Lowry gave to Howard Spring in 1942 after the writer had displayed a rare understanding of the artist in something he had written. In his thank you letter, Spring wrote: 'It is all that I could have wished and more than I cd have deserved. If I had personally gone through all your pictures, I feel I cd not have found one that wd more vitally express what I take to be your view of Manchester and Manchester people.' *A Quarrel,* 1935.

with the press. But it certainly never entered any of our heads that he was successfully hiding a full working life as a rent collector and cashier...it was not the work for which we condemned him but the deception...Our efforts in his cause were not enough for him to trust us, apparently. I doubt if he ever trusted a human being in all his life.'

With the Marshalls, who had promoted him energetically and given him several shows, he had certainly been dogmatic about his lack of a job. They had been at his side and heard him tell a television film maker: 'I couldn't go out in the morning ever after and get down at half-past nine with an attaché case and an umbrella in my hand and a bowler hat on my head. I couldn't do it.' And yet, that was exactly what he did do; without the bowler hat – he usually wore a trilby.

It had all begun, according to Clifford Openshaw, Lowry's young colleague at Pall Mall, in 1933. On June 7th that year there appeared in the *Manchester Evening News* a photograph of Lowry – presumably taken

with his consent – under the headline 'Academy Honour for Stockport.' The cause for congratulation was the acceptance by the Royal Academy of two of Lowry's paintings – *A Street in Stockport* and *The Procession.* The piece was highly complimentary, but in his enthusiasm to give the reader every detail, the reporter had revealed something that had never before appeared in print. 'Mr. Lowry is the Assistant Secretary to a well-known Manchester firm of property and estate agents, and he does much of his work in the evenings...Art to Mr Lowry is the antidote to a day of strain at a city desk.'

Having sent out for the first edition of the paper, the force of the artist's anger when he read the offending article was remembered by his Pall Mall colleagues long after he had retired. 'He was furious,' recalled Openshaw, 'absolutely raging. He grabbed his coat and threw it across his shoulders, jammed his hat hard on his head, took his stick and stormed down to the newspaper offices as if he was going to set about them physically. What he said to them when he got there, we don't know, but when he returned he instructed us that never, *never* again, was anyone to mention his job in connection with his art. He had told the paper people, he said, that he wanted no such details to appear again. They were irrelevant to his painting.'

After Lowry had recovered from his anger, he and Openshaw laughed to think that he had been elevated in print to the position of Assistant Secretary to the company; he was still a book-keeper and cashier and was to remain so. After Lowry's death, Openshaw described him to a journalist as the 'Chief Cashier' – 'but' as Openshaw explained with an embarrassed smile, 'only because I thought it would make him sound more important.' The former clerk seemed oblivious of the irony implicit in an assumption that the status of the artist L S Lowry, R.A., would be elevated – even in 1976 – by a moderate position in commerce; or that his of-

fice work might, by definition, be considered more 'important' than his art.

Never again in Lowry's lifetime was his rent collecting, nor indeed any of his previous jobs in Manchester offices, mentioned in print. The *Evening News* honoured the artist's request and, curiously, no other newspaper, either then or subsequently, picked up the information from their cuttings libraries.

'Until that time I had not realised how strongly he felt about it,' recalled Openshaw. 'It seemed he feared – and quite rightly – that many professional artists would use the fact of his job to label him an amateur, a so-called Sunday Painter.'

In old age, Lowry was to become adept in the preservation of his secret. Once he had retired, he shut the memory of those business years so far into the recesses of his mind

that it was as if they had never happened. He cut himself off from those who might have reminded him of them and manoeuvred friends and acquaintance into specific compartments. Those who did not know never met those who did; and those who did were apt to find they could no longer count Lowry among their friends.

In the days that Lowry had first come upon the Manchester art scene, the role of the amateur was indeed a lowly one. It was part of the constitution of the Manchester Academy of Fine Arts – a body founded in an atmosphere of cultural enthusiasm engendered by the Great Art Treasures Exhibition – that only those men who earned their living either as artists or architects were permitted to join. It is a measure of the strength of the disdain for the amateur that women – who, in those days, were still with-

out the vote and had no status in society apart from that afforded by their husbands or fathers—were admitted long before men who worked otherwise for their living.

The subject of the admission of amateurs was first mooted in 1865 and speedily dismissed; the matter was to be raised again many times before their eventual acceptance half a century later. The Academy was, in those early days, complacent in its non-parochial image, with the proud inclusion among their members of Sir Edward J Poynter, who became President of the Royal Academy in 1896; Alfred Waterhouse, who designed the Manchester Town Hall and painted pictures that were much to Lowry's liking; and Ford Madox Brown, who decorated the Town Hall walls with his

Above: Family holidays –cousins, aunts and uncles included–were usually spent at Lytham St. Anne's, a popular seaside resort on the smarter side of Blackpool. The scenery was typical of the gentle

landscapes of Lowry's childhood, before he moved with his parents to industrial Pendlebury in 1909, before he succumbed to the lure of the mills and the misfits. *Country Road near Lytham*, 1920.

frescoes–and whom Lowry described as 'the greatest artist Britain has produced outside Turner.'[3]

But, by 1913 so many had left, drawn by the bright lights of London, that the Academy's annual exhibition could no longer attract work of great merit. Again it was proposed that amateurs might be invited to join 'to help with the work' but the suggestion caused such an outcry that the idea was shelved. At last, in 1917 the constitution of the Academy was changed: amateurs were to be admitted. The decision was greeted with ill-concealed dismay by members who regarded such a step as a devaluation of the establishment.

Lowry, now over thirty, applied for student membership. His work was examined and in the winter of 1918, he was accepted into the life class. Upon payment of his two guineas subscription he was permitted to attend classes two evenings a week. The fact that he was accepted at all is some indication that his life drawings, a compulsory part of his submitted portfolio, were not as weak as some of his fellow students remembered them to be; these were not men who would look with indulgence upon the work of a rent collector. Lowry had earned his place.

At these classes, however, Lowry found none of the joyful enthusiasm or reciprocal respect he had enjoyed with Valette. The students were disgruntled, the studio was cold and, according to the students, the room smelt bad.

But the predominant reason for Lowry joining the hallowed realms of the professional was undoubtedly the fact that, at the age of thirty-one, he had yet to exhibit or, more important, to make a public sale–factors that had not gone unnoticed or unremarked upon at home. 'In those days I was constantly trying to justify myself to my parents.'[4]

As a student member of the Academy, Lowry now had a right to present his work for inclusion in the Annual Exhibition at Manchester City Art Gallery. Accord-

ingly, in February 1919, he submitted three works. All were accepted: *Portrait of an Old Woman,* priced at 15 guineas, *Landscape* at 6 guineas, and *Pencil Drawing* at 4 guineas.

In the catalogue Lowry's forename was spelt 'Lawrence' not 'Laurence', and in a later exhibition his surname was printed 'Lowrey' rather than 'Lowry'–a mistake that was to persist into the '60's on some of the Gallery post cards. It is unlikely that such trivialities upset Lowry; instead he incorporated them into his saga of life's bitter blows. When, in the '30's the French press recorded his name variously as 'Lowsky', 'Lowny' and even 'Lowsy', rather than trumpeting the fact that the French critics were talking about him at all (which they were, and in glowing terms) he seized upon the errors with mock dismay and included them in his burgeoning repertoire of self-deprecatory anecdotes with as much delight as if they had been the warmest of compliments. 'They called me "Lowsy"–do you think they might have a point, Sir?'[5]

Only the *Manchester Guardian* mentioned Lowry by name. Their critic, Bernard D Taylor (later to become one of Lowry's teachers), was not on the whole enthusiastic about the show; but in his review of the picture he mentioned, in passing, that there were 'good portrait heads by Messers Barber, Lowry and Roberts.' It was the first recorded praise for Lowry's work.

Unhappily, Lowry's nominal acceptance into the ranks of the professionals did little to increase his standing at home. He might have received an honourable mention but he had failed to make a sale. (*Portrait of an Old Woman,* 1910, not exactly a pretty picture and unsold at 15 guineas, is now in a private collection and valued at more than £30,000)

And worse–according to later recollections of surviving Academicians, his work was not well received by his contemporaries. While some merely sneered, others laughed out loud. Indeed, one member of the Art

Above: 'Isn't it bad enough having to live among it without you bringing it into the house,' Elizabeth Lowry complained to her son. 'What would you like me to paint, Mother?' he asked. 'Little yachts at Lytham,' she replied. *Yachts at Lytham*, 1924.

Gallery Committee of the time, was remembered less as an artist more as The Man Who Laughed at Lowry.[6] He was by no means alone–although another member of the derisive clique, James Chettle, earned Lowry's grudging respect when he became the first amateur to become President of the Manchester Academy.

Lowry's fund of apocryphal yarns is littered with tales of the amateur triumphing over the professional. It was one of his favourite themes–hardly surprising in retrospect. 'They have a naïveté and an approach that the professional or the amateur that becomes professional, loses after a time. I find far more pleasure in the amateur's work, or a local art society, than I do in a proper show. With the amateur you don't know what you are going

to see…but in the art trade you've a pretty good idea.' In Newcastle-upon-Tyne in 1968 he dragged a television crew (who were supposed to making a film about Lowry) to the town's public convenience to see the paintings of Sam West, the attendant there. 'I don't care if he's the lavatory man or the King of Siam,' Lowry announced. 'His pictures have got something.' There is always the possibility, of course, that Lowry had done what he did purely out of mischief: playing the role of the eccentric. But whether he was looking to deflate pomposity on this occasion or simply having fun, it is undoubtedly true that if an artist's painting 'had something' that was good enough for him. And Sam was, of course, an amateur.

Much of the Academy's derision and

laughter may have come later in Lowry's association with this august body, when his commitment to his industrial vision was total. But whence and whenever it came, there is no doubt that it was real and open; there seems to have been no effort to protect Lowry from the poor opinion of those around him. Rather to the contrary; they revelled in it; it became something of a local sport.

Presumably because of the way his work was received in 1919, Lowry did not apply for membership the following year. He was not to exhibit with the Academy again until 1932 – and, even then, it had taken a direct invitation to accomplish this; it was no longer Lowry applying to be shown, rather the reverse.

By this point in his still struggling career, his resistance to scorn had been buttressed both by limited acceptance in London and Paris and by the acquisition of the protective carapace he now wore. But he was enough of a name locally to be included in a contemporary novel about an itinerant artist by the writer Howard Spring. In the novel, *Shabby Tiger,* the hero remarks: 'There are only two painters in Manchester with any guts at all: L S Lowry and myself.'[7] Spring, who came to enjoy a 'comradeship' with Lowry, was the first to publicly credit Lowry with courage. He made his character express such an opinion because it was his own and he knew it to be quite out of tune with popular opinion; the remark, in fact, was regarded as a piece silly sentimentality by many of Spring's readers who had not the slightest conception of the truth of it.

If he knew of Spring's admiration, Lowry never spoke of it. He knew only that the Academy laughed at him, his friends laughed at him, his family laughed at him (though maybe slightly more kindly) and his mother, who could so easily have cushioned him from the humiliation of that first

exposure to the world of the professional artist, only reacted with embarrassment when anyone was misguided enough to offer money for the fruits of her son's curious hobby. '*Oh no, dear, he'll give it to you.*'

There is no record of Lowry ever having spoken specifically about the early reception of his work. He appeared, in fact, to have banished the memory of the experience from his mind, consistently referring to 1932 as the year in which he first showed with the Academy. He never consciously exposed his emotions. He merely stated fact: 'My friends all laughed at me and asked, "Why do you keep on painting those ridiculous pictures?"'

Such comments were made with no visible sign of rancour or bitterness; it was as if he wore the mask of the artist doomed to derision with something verging on pride.

As John Read, the BBC arts critic commented in his 1997 film tribute to Lowry: 'Even though he was the recipient of three honorary degrees, had the Freedom of the City of Salford, and sold a picture to the Queen, his secret was undiscovered until he day he died…Lowry was quite happy to contribute to all the false assumptions. Possibly he feared that if he were caught out, he might still be regarded as an amateur – a weekend painter not to be taken seriously.

'Perhaps, secretly, he feared that that was the truth, in spite of all his fame.'[8]

One of Lowry's young protégées, an artist with a deep affection for her mentor, commented: 'I find is so sad, so very sad, to think that he felt the need to go to so much trouble to hide the truth. It is tragic to think he lived his life in constant fear of discovery… and for what? What had he done that was so very shameful?'[9]

Above: Lowry's headgear of choice, throughout his life, was a well-worn trilby. Occasionally a cloth cap. Despite this it is generally believed that the tall man with a walking stick and wearing a bowler who frequently appears on the edge of frame, looking in rather than out, is the artist himself: Lowry as an observer of life, rather than a participator. *Studio portrait of Lowry.*

Chapter 6

'Didn't sell one'.

Lowry was 33 years old before he risked his first exhibition, and then in the company of amateurs. The date was October 21ˢᵗ, 1921.

Although he always insisted that he did not sell a single picture–'Not one!'–from that show, if any single event in his artistic life could be said to be the start of it all, the start of recognition, the start of his career as an artist, rather than the more usually remembered first London exhibition of 1939–this was it. And what is more, it gave him his first personal and highly perceptive review.

It would be dramatically neat to be able to relate that, from this time on, his reputation was made, his future secure. It was not to be. There is no indication that it made so much as the tiniest ripple on the complacency of the Manchester art establishment. It was to be another eleven years before he was invited to show again with the Academy.

But in 1970, half a century on, he was to relate the events to his friend Hugh Maitland, with what in anyone else might be regarded as pride. It would seem that the impact on Lowry himself was indelible. He was to remember the details and to keep a copy of the catalogue recording the prices at which his pictures were offered all his life.

The exhibition was held in the offices of 'a very clever architect,'¹ Rowland Thomasson, at 87 Mosley Street, Manchester. Thomasson and his friend Tom H Brown, both water colourists, exhibited thirty pictures between them. Lowry showed twice as many: twenty-five oils and two pastels. 'It was,' he told Maitland categorically, 'the first time I was ever shown in public.'² The debacle of 1910 had been erased from his personal history with all the efficiency of a keeper of Soviet records.

On the morning of the opening–the eve of Lowry's 34ᵗʰ birthday–there appeared in the *Manchester Guardian* a review by their critic, Bernard D Taylor, who devoted more than three-quarters of his allotted half-column of space to Lowry alone. Having dealt sympathetically with both Thomasson and Brown, he went on:

'The third contributor, Laurence S. Lowry, has a very interesting and individual outlook. His subjects are Manchester and Lancashire street scenes, interpreted with technical means as yet imperfect, but with real imagination. His portrait of Lancashire is more grimly like than a caricature, because it is done with the intimacy of affection. He emphasises violently everything that industrialism has done to make the aspect of Lancashire more forbidding than of most other places. Many of us may comfort ourselves a little with contemplating suburban roads, parks, or gardens in public squares, or with the lights and colours of morning or sunset. Mr. Lowry has refused all comfortable delusions. He has kept his vision as fresh as if he had come suddenly into the most forbidding part of Hulme or Ancoats under the gloomiest skies after a holiday in France or Italy. His Lancashire is grey, with vast rectangular mills towering over diminutive houses. If there is an open space it is of trodden earth, as grey as the rest of the

Far left: Lowry always said that he never painted happy pictures. Perhaps so, but he certainly painted pictures to bring a smile to the face, pictures of humour. He had a great knack of spotting the incongruous or the eccentric in a situation, and translating it to canvas. This incident he said he saw outside a lodging house in Manchester. 'I only paint what I see.' *A Fight*, c. 1935.

landscape. The crowds which have this land-scape for their background are entirely in keeping with their setting; the incidents in the drama of which they are the characters are also appropriate. "A Labour Exchange", "The Entrance for Out-Patients", "A Main Street in a Small Town", "A Quarrel in a Side Street", "Ejecting a Tenant" are titles which will give a clue to the subjects of the pictures. We hear a great deal nowadays about recovering the simplicity of vision of the primitives in art. These pictures are authentically primitive, the real things, not an artificially cultivated likeness to it. The problems of representation are solved not by reference to established conventions but by sheer determination to express what the artist has felt, whether the result is according to rule or not. The artist's technique is not yet equal to his ideas. If he can learn to express himself with ease and style and at the same time preserve his singleness of outlook he may make a real contribution to art.'[3]

It is hardly surprising that Lowry was to retain the memory of this review all his life. Here, at last, was one man who not only liked his work but, quite evidently, understood it; not only understood it, in fact, but understood the artist's vision. He was the first among critics so to do; there was to be nothing as perceptive written for more than twenty years. Taylor was the first to recognise the 'intimacy of affection' – an affection that a later critic, Eric Newton, was to compare with the love of a devoted mother for a disabled child. 'It is her physical imperfections that bring out the insight and the tenderness in him, and give him the power to turn ugliness into beauty.'[4]

The Manchester Guardian review was, failing a sale, exactly what Lowry most needed at that time. 'That's what gave me the confidence to carry on,' he told Maitland. 'That was very important to me. It was all I had got. The Guardian was very marvellous to me for years and years.' Then, in an aside that was less of a non-sequitur than it might

have seemed, he added: 'My father took the Guardian.'

It should be pointed out, however, that Lowry's personal history was littered not only with tales of the amateur triumphing over the professional, but also with a host of, quite possibly apocryphal, stories of turning points in his life; moments when something happened just as he had been thinking of 'giving it all up'. Whatever it was invariably 'gave me the confidence to carry on.' He frequently ascribed such an event to 'fate'; it was more likely to have been Lowry's reading of the incident; or his recollection of it. Almost as if he needed an excuse, a reason, a justification not only to the outside world but to himself for persisting in painting 'those ridiculous pictures.'

It was as if, believing his life to be mundane, he had to make the ordinary, extraordinary; the insignificant, significant. There are too many such 'seminal' events in his long life for his reading of them not to have been deliberate; and on each occasion when the human so-called catalyst was told of its importance in Lowry's iconic memory, he was astonished.

The exhibition continued for two week. 'I didn't sell one,' said Lowry. 'Not one'.[5] The largest of the oils were priced at £25, the smallest was 5 guineas. For many years now most, if not all, of those unsold Lowry works form a valued part of collections the world over.

Item No. One in the catalogue, 'A Lodging House,' was bequeathed to Salford Art Gallery (and now forms part of The Lowry Collection on permanent display at Salford Quays) by a Mr J H Aldred. He left no information as to how or when it had come into his possession, but Lowry's first job was with the firm of Thomas Aldred and Sons of 88 Mosley Street, directly opposite the office where the exhibition was held. Thus, it is conceivable that the picture, a lyrical pastel of a typical Manchester scene, did in fact sell, was in fact bought – by one of his colleagues from his other life. The possibility of such a lapse of memory, deliberate or otherwise cannot be dismissed; other, equally important events, were forgotten–or erased for effect–by Lowry in his later telling of his progress in what he liked to call the Battle of Life. (Originally priced at 10 guineas, the value insurers put on *Lodging House* in 1986 was £10,000; by 1997 it had risen to £40,000.)

Many of these early exhibits were to be shown again and again before they found a home; many Lowry worked on over the years, re-dating them and re-titling them. 'I never waste anything,' he told Maitland.

Item No Two was a poetic oil originally called *Man Taken Ill* and re-named *Sudden Illness*. Priced originally at 15 guineas, it was bought by the collector Monty Bloom from the artist in the '50's. *Hawker's Cart* is in the Royal Scottish Academy, Edinburgh, *Pit Disaster* went to Lowry's friend Geoffrey Bennett and *Coming Out of School* was bought by the Duveen Fund for the Tate.

The Quarrel in a Side Street Lowry gave to Howard Spring, who had not only mentioned Lowry in his book *Shabby Tiger* but had also written sympathetic articles about him. When the artist first offered Spring a picture, he replied: 'I don't like accepting as a gift the thing by which a man earns his bread; yet, when such a thing is offered in the spirit of comradeship which I detect in your letter, it becomes the most intimate and precious gift of all. As to the choice, may I leave that to you? Whatever you send I shall deeply value it, both for itself and because it will be a link in comradeship.'[6] A month later Spring received *The Quarrel* and wrote to Lowry: 'It is all that I could have wished and more than I cd. have deserved. If I had personally gone through all your pictures, I feel I cd. not have found one that wd. More vitally express what I take to be your view of Manchester and Manchester people.'

It cannot have been co-incidence that Bernard Taylor, the understanding reviewer at

Above: Steps and footbridges were another familiar theme in Lowry's works, particularly when he was working in pencil. *Footbridge,* c. 1935.

Over page: Variation on a theme. Another Whit Sunday, another Whit Walk. *A Procession,* 1938.

this early exhibition, was a teacher at Salford School of Art where Lowry had enrolled as a part time pupil in 1915. Whether the two had actually met by this time is not on record, but being in the same school at the same time, even if not in the same class, they must have been aware of each other.

In the months between the débâcle of 1919 and the 1921 exhibition (and between Taylor's first public mention of Lowry's work and his *Guardian* review) all Lowry's efforts were devoted to the communication of his vision in art. 'I wanted to get a certain effect on canvas. I couldn't describe it, but I knew it when I had got it. My painting is all a question of fiddling about until you get it right. It is not an intellectual reaction, it just comes.' Lowry spoke these words to Monty Bloom

LOWRY 1935.

decades later, but there is no doubt it was an effect for which he had been striving all his artistic life.

By 1915 he needed more from his teachers than he was getting. The brusque Billy Fitz had died. Barber was no longer teaching. The influence of Valette was waning; his wife had died, he was ill and his preoccupation was more with own painting than with his teaching. Lowry had now been doing 'the life' at Manchester for twelve 'solid' years. 'They didn't think much of me there,' said Lowry without visible rancour, 'and when I told them I was going to leave they tried hard not to look too happy about it.'[7] At other times, paraphrasing an old music hall cliché, he would say: 'I left by popular demand'.[8] And so 'for the benefit of a laugh' as he put it—lest his audience might feel too high a sense of purpose implicit in his desire for continuing instruction—Lowry started at Salford School of Art.

It was to Taylor, who for some years taught the life class at Salford, that Lowry took 'one or two pieces I had done of crowds in the streets in front of an industrial scene.'[9] They were, as the artist conceded to Maitland, 'very confused, with the group and the figures getting rather mixed up together.' He was aware of their shortcomings but he had 'worked very hard on them' and was not prepared for Taylor's dismissive reaction. 'This will never do,' declared Taylor. He held the pictures up for Lowry to see against a dark background where their dingy confusion was immediately apparent.

'You'll have to do better than that,' said Taylor.

'How do I do that?' asked Lowry.

'That's for you to find out,' came the reply.

Lowry was irate. He picked up the pictures and trundled off. 'I didn't like it a bit. I went home and I did two pictures of dark figures on an absolutely white ground. Just plain flake-white ground. I was very an-

91

Above: Yet another scene of dereliction, yet another of the empty houses that so fascinated the man. 'They are symbols of myself. They are symbols of my mood.' *Derelict Building,* 1941.

noyed. Very cross. I said to myself: "That'll show the old bird." I took them to him and plonked them down in front of him. And do you know what he said? He said: "That's what I meant. That's right. That's perfectly right".'

Lowry, ever the raconteur, couldn't help but add: 'I could have killed him'–which, as usual, turned a simple incident into an entertaining anecdote; it was no longer a small event in the history of his artistic development, but a story in his repertoire of events in the Life of a Simple Man ('*Not fit for anything else...*' '*Suddenly I saw it...*') to

be repeated again and again, and delivered with the immaculate timing of the pier end comics he so enjoyed as a boy.

Whether this particular encounter happened as Lowry related, and whether it happened before or after the Brown Street show no-one can say. But *Sudden Illness,* dated 1920, certainly shows considerable evidence of experimentation with flake white–which has now dropped to such an extent that the background is a beautiful creamy grey which gives the picture an almost dreamlike quality.

If Lowry was indeed laying down a white

Left: No pictures might have sold at that first exhibition in Mosley Street in 1921, but this moody pastel was bought soon afterwards for £5 by 'a friend of my father's' who had seen it in the show. Lowry once said that his was his first sale. Originally called *A Lodging House for Men* and priced at ten guineas, it was bequeathed to Salford City Art Gallery years later by Mr J H Aldred – significantly Lowry's first job was with the firm of Thomas Aldred and Sons of 88 Mosley Street, directly opposite the office where the exhibition was held. *The Lodging House,* 1921.

base for his oils by 1920, it would mean, of course, that Taylor's advice was given and acted upon before the 1921 show–and before Taylor wrote his review. Or, then again, it might have been Taylor's review, with talk of 'technical means as yet imperfect' that spurred Lowry on to take his pictures to the master. Or, then again, it might have been Taylor's words of praise for *Portrait of an Old Woman* in the Academy show of 1919.

This new technique was one Lowry was to use all his life. He explained: 'My job, first of all, was to get these figures standing out from the background, because the interest in the picture was in the figures and you had got to do the background artificially light to throw the figures up. You had to keep it very white, almost chalky white if you want, because the picture was worthless if the ground and the figures merged together ... You can always drop white a little but you can't lift up, you can't paint white on black but you can always drop a white ground, and in time you know that it won't be chalky white, it will be a cream colour. But my job in those early days–and it was a job–was to paint these figures–and I have done a lot of them in my time–on a ground that would always be distinct.'[10]

Whichever was the real sequence of events, there is a story about Lowry's further experimentation with white which he, himself, dated as 1924. He described it in the '60's to the critic Edwin Mullins: 'I remember I got a little piece of wood and painted it flake white six times over. Then I let it dry and sealed it up; and left it like that for six or seven years. At the end of that time I did the same thing again on another piece of board,

Above: A battered, well-thumbed copy of the catalogue of Lowry's first exhibition in October–November, 1921 at 87 Mosely Street, Manchester. and at which he sold 'not one single' picture.

opened up the first piece I'd painted and compared the two. The recent one was, of course, dead white; but the first had turned a beautifully creamy grey-white. And then I knew what I wanted. So, you see, the pictures I have painted today will not be seen at their best until I'm dead, will they?'

The 1921 exhibition might not have brought Lowry the longed for public sale (there is evidence that he sold several drawings privately before this date)–but it did attract the attention of several people with influence in the right places. Taylor was so impressed with the originality of Lowry's work that he had mentioned the Mosley Street show to James Bone, the London editor of the *Manchester Guardian* and brother of the artist Muirhead Bone. As a critic himself Bone had experienced some difficulty in coming to terms with the work of the Post-Impressionists but, making a visit to Mosley Street on Taylor's recommendation, he found no such problems: he liked what he saw and said as much both to Taylor and to Lowry. From that time on the *Guardian* was virtually constant in its support of Lowry. When, in 1926, the newspaper produced a prestige supplement to celebrate Civic Week they asked Lowry for permission to reproduce three of his pictures. The Literary Editor, Arthur Wallace, was so taken with them that he asked the artist if he might buy one: 'And he did buy one–so I threw in another'[11] with a note asking him to accept it 'as a souvenir'.[12] Only a man of Lowry's humility would have responded to a sale, at the age of thirty-nine, with the offer of a free souvenir to celebrate the event.

After Wallace's death the picture came up for sale at Christie's and Lowry was asked, during the making of a television documentary, if he was not bitter that the man's family should receive a large sum of money for something that had been presented as a gift. Lowry denied any such resentment with vehemence. 'It was no sacrifice to me,' he retorted. 'No one would

give tuppence for them. Mr Wallace enjoyed that picture all his life-time. I'm very pleased if his family will be helped by the sale. He was a nice chap, very helpful to me. Good luck to his family with it. I'd like them to do well out of it.'[13]

Wallace was not the only enthusiast to have been introduced to the artist by the first exhibition. A certain Mr W H Berry, at that time director of Oldham Art Gallery, had also been along to the Mosley Street show and thereafter made it his business to keep in touch with the artist and his work. By 1923 the relationship had become such that Berry invited Lowry to his home for Sunday lunch. It was there that Lowry

met Berry's wife, a striking woman deeply involved with the art world of London. She commuted each weekend between Manchester and the capital. Her name was Daisy Jewell and she was head of the framing department of James Bourlet and Sons, fine art agents extraordinary. The effect of their ensuing friendship and Miss Jewell's unswerving faith in this unheralded artist was to be greater than either of them could have hoped; the results of her systematic efforts on his behalf were not to be fully realised for a whole decade but there is no doubt that this one woman was almost single-handedly responsible for Lowry's eventual emergence on the London art scene.

Above: Yet another lyrical landscape of Lowry's childhood holidays, illuminated with a rare joyous splash of red. *Regent Street, Lytham*, 1922.

95

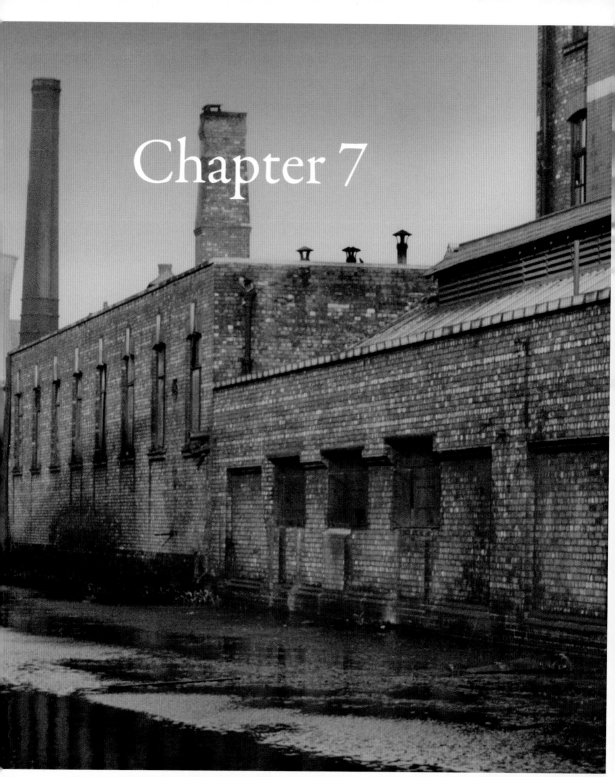

Chapter 7

'Pictures that nobody wanted'

'For thirty years I painted pictures that nobody wanted,' Lowry reprised in old age. It was, as one friend remarked, a familiar song.

By the time the journalists and the art critics came in any number to his door, Lowry was well past middle age; old age fast approaching, he would say complaining of rheumaticky limbs.

As was not unusual in those days, the days before the cult of celebrity, little had been written of him, less remembered, despite his burgeoning renown. Now he was being asked for an account of his life to date. It was as if he had been presented with a blank canvas on which to paint a self portrait in words and, being the raconteur he was, a man with a love of a finely tuned tale, that was what he gave them. Of a sudden he had the freedom to relate his version of events which, although it might not have been strictly accurate, it was either the way he perceived it or the way he chose to perceive it.

He might have been well exhibited but he was, indeed, little bought; which was to him an indication, abundantly clear, that people did not like what they saw of his work. They did not appreciate his vision of the industrial north; they turned away and, in rejecting it, they rejected him; in laughing at *it*, they laughed at *him*.

And so the uncomfortable truth, the uneasy reality, was expunged from his personal history. The rent collecting, the jobs in the city, the days behind a desk, the demands of nine to five – all were omitted from the chronicles of Laurence Stephen Lowry. It was less the telling of lies, more – to use a later idiom – an economy with the truth.

At the time, in the '30s when he was in his vigorous forties, he would talk of such success as he did achieve – later to be dismissed or forgotten – openly and with tempered pride. Asked to provide a brief synopsis of his career to date he wrote that he was 'a regular exhibitor at the Paris Salon des Indépendents, the Salon d'Automne, the New English Art Club, an exhibitor by invitation at many corporation galleries, had been invited to submit a picture for the Canadian National Exhibition in Toronto, had drawings and paintings illustrated in various periodicals, a picture bought by the Duveen Fund for the Tate and one oil painting bought by the Rye Art Gallery'. Hardly a catalogue of failure – and this written in July, 1931.

And still he could talk of the days before the '40s in terms of unrelieved gloom. 'He did have a rough time,' recalled Edith Timperley, a close and supportive friend of the '20s and '30s . 'He had no emotional support at home and negligible recognition in the town. The only thing he wanted to be was an artist; it was the only thing that roused him to animation. He would say bitterly that he wasn't appreciated. He craved to be appreciated.'[1]

Although he had come to know Harold Timperley in their early days at Manchester School of Art it was not until the '20s that Lowry became a regular visitor to the flat Harold shared with his wife, a writer

Left: A story Lowry often told was how his father had been virtually responsible for 'one of my best pictures.' It was Robert who had directed his son to St. Simon's Church with the comment that it was 'right up your street.' Lowry ignored him. 'Never do today what you can put off 'till tomorrow.' Some weeks later Lowry Senior repeated: 'You'll really have to go and see that St. Simon's Church. It's your cup of tea and it's going to come down very soon.' *St. Simon's Church,* 1928.

Right: By the time Lowry had completed his drawing of St. Simon's, the church had been demolished. *St. Simon's Church*, 1927.

Lower right: Warned by his father that this Salford church was about to be demolished, Lowry made a preliminary sketch on the back of a used envelope, which for him was enough to enable him to make a more detailed study later. *Preliminary sketch of St. Simon's Church.*

Far right: A thundering composite of everything that, at the time, most fascinated Lowry, an essay in desolation painted when his mother was sinking fast. A foul swampland, a drowning boat, rubbish, waste, gravestones, a broken fence, a crooked pole and overlooking it all a vast metropolis of stinking chimneys and satanic mills. *The Lake*, 1937.

ing highly coloured labels for bales of brilliantly decorated cotton for the African market. I would play the piano, Harold the fiddle and Neville and Thomas would sing; Lowry just listened, but with obvious enjoyment. Even then he was a restless man and, unless there was music, he would be up and down, pacing the room with his lolloping stride, wielding his stick and pounding at things for emphasis. Sometimes he would arrive and order: "Now Edith – knit," as if he craved the semblance of domesticity. I remember him once being very annoyed because he had asked Neville to arrange for him to go into the press box for a big cricket match at Old Trafford and Neville had said: "If he wants to go, he can go on his own." I got the impression that Lowry wanted to be made something special of, but Neville wouldn't do it: he didn't want his beloved cricket made into something grotesque.' Cardus was at the time one of the country's leading cricket commentators, a man of fine reputation.

Lowry did eventually paint a picture of a cricket match at Old Trafford. In fact he painted several. In no respect were they grotesque, and in 1996 one of them was sold at Sotheby's for £133,500. Years before, that same painting had been bought by a collector called Fritz Pachd who did not dare take it home to his family 'where they hung nice bourgeois pictures'; he took it instead to his office where his colleagues wondered audibly if he were 'going off his head.' Another cricket painting was commissioned by the art collector and Treasurer of Lancashire County Cricket Club, Alick Leggat, for which Lowry was paid £350. Not long afterwards, Lowry took a sharp blade to the canvas and cut it into two; artist and patron were agreed that the field of play and the children milling round the sight screen worked better as separate pictures. In 1998 they were insured for £120,000 and £60,000 respectively by Manchester City Art Gallery to whom they were on loan. In

called Edith Brill, in Whalley Range. 'We knew all the nice people in Manchester,' Edith related, 'the literary ones and the people who did things. Lowry seemed to relish the atmosphere, the conversation, the gaiety. He would turn up at our musical evenings with Neville Cardus, the *Manchester Guardian* critic and Thomas Bird, another dear friend, who earned his living produc-

November, 2004, they sold as a pair for well over half a million pounds.

There were outings together—to the pantomime 'where the boys would laugh until the tears fell down their cheeks' and to the City Art Gallery where they would gaze for hours at the paintings of Rossetti and the Brotherhood and joke about 'all those daft ladies laying about in their baths with all that hair'.[2] The discussion continued in the Gallery tea room until 'waitresses fidgeted for us to leave, then we would go home and talk the hours away—for art was all that mattered.' The two men were, according to Edith, so fascinated by the Pre-Raphaelite women and studied them so avidly that 'they could have both gone away and reproduced them without ever looking at them again.' But, while Jim Fitton declared Lowry's affection for Rossetti's women to be an extension of his 'evasion of reality', Edith believed it to have been based on an admiration for the 'technical excellence' of the artist and nothing more. Lowry, himself, said he had no idea why he liked Rossetti ('the only man I have ever wanted to possess'[3]) but that it had something to do with the 'potential poetry' of the work.

All this time the Timperleys' paradoxical friend was presenting himself to his business acquaintances and his colleagues at Pall Mall as a man for whom art was no more than a casual pass-time, a hobby, if, in fact, he mentioned it at all. And yet, in the easy intimacy of the Timperleys' social circle he relaxed enough to reveal something of the ambition that was devouring him. It would seem, however, that although Edith appreciated Lowry's yearning, her understanding was tempered by a natural loyalty to her husband. 'Harold was a giver; Lowry was a taker. All Lowry really wanted was to be encouraged. He yearned for success although when it came it did not do for him what he had hoped it would do; it was too late. In those days he would get enormously depressed. On one such occasion, when he was particularly low, I persuaded Harold to ask Lowry to do the drawings for his Cotswold book. Harold was reluctant; he wanted someone who knew and loved the country to do them[3]

Harold's instincts were well founded; the Cotswold landscape was not the kind of beauty that attracted Lowry the artist, nor indeed Lowry the man. 'To my loss, country lanes have been foreign to me somewhat for quite a while past – for alas my recreation seems to have developed into drifting amongst all the back streets etc., I can come across. I don't know what your naturalistic nature will think of an outlook like that!' he wrote to Timperley in 1929 – and from the way he talked of walking the backstreets as if it were for his amusement alone, it seems

102

Left: From earliest boyhood Lowry was fascinated by the sea. 'It's all there,' he would say. 'The Battle of Life.' *Ship Entering Princess Dock, Glasgow,* 1947.

Right: One of the many meticulous drawings that Lowry did in 1931 to illustrate *The Cotswold Book* by his friend, Harold Timperley. The book had only modest sales and when Timperley came to do his next book the publisher rejected Lowry's drawings in favour of photographs. *The Guide Post on Crickley Barrow,* 1930

clear that he knew the Timperleys were among those who were ignorant of his job.[5]

Despite Lowry's apparent failing in qualification for the task, Edith got her way with her husband. 'I talked him into it. I wanted to give Lowry some tangible encouragement. I wanted to help him—you know how you are when you are young, I hadn't realised then that this was an old song, that he sang it to everyone: nobody loved him, nobody wanted his painting, nobody understood him.'[6]

With Harold, if not with Edith, Lowry maintained the bantering attitude of insouciance, placing the emphasis of his ambition upon financial success rather than artistic recognition; it was an attitude he was frequently to adopt with men, less so with women who in his experience proved rather more sympathetic; Mother excepted.

'I hope the LSD* side of things is turning out all right,' he wrote later that same year. 'It's the very devil is the LSD side of all this, don't you think?'[7] And again, in 1931, when *The Cotswold Book* was published: 'We must pray for 1000s of sales for you and then you'll get fat and try a Rolls Royce or two!'[8] Timperley joined in the game; he replied: 'Beware! Soon you will be going about wearing two fur coats, smoking two cigars, having two wives–!! Your Lancashire scenes may even become popular, and then what would you do?' It is interesting to note, in retrospect, that the prospect of Lowry's Lancashire scenes, as Harold called them, becoming popular was as ridiculous as the artist wearing two fur coats or driving two cars. Timperley was aware, incidentally, that a few years previously Lowry had had a brief and quite unexpected flirtation with the idea of a motor car. As he told one interviewer: 'I was very bothered about a car in 1924. "Mother," I said, "if you'll buy a car I'll drive you out." But she didn't take to the idea. Oh no, not at all: "We'll wait until your father comes in." When Father came

*LSD was the abbreviation in current use for the Latin term for pounds, shillings and pence.

104

home he just said three words: "The man's mad!"'–which, given the Victorian convention of unquestioning obedience to the dictates of a parent, was enough to close the matter for good. Lowry never did learn to drive, nor did he buy a car. 'It bothered me at the time, but I don't think I should have made a driver, no, I don't think I should.'[9]

After a few years in Manchester, the Timperleys moved to a more rural spot, to Romiley in Cheshire where they rented an old stone cottage with low ceilings and heavy beams where they proved to be as hospitable as ever. The musical evenings and Lowry's visits continued into the '30s although he invariably left in time for the bus that would get him to town for the Pendlebury connection and home in time to see his mother to bed; and, or so Edith believed, to read to her before she slept. Often he took with him bunches of flowers which Edith had gathered for Elizabeth from their garden. Mrs Lowry's reception of them was hardly the most gracious. 'Mother was greatly pleased with all those flowers,' her son once wrote, 'but said it was a shame to cut all that number...'[10]

Lowry was now in his early forties, the compartmentalism of his friends and acquaintances already well established. It had, in fact, become a part of his normal way of life, not solely, it would seem, in order to keep the secret of his job but simply because this was in his nature. Edith found such behaviour hard to accept; she could not understand it–not the deed, not the reason. She was deeply hurt, even angered, when having believed Lowry to be friendless she arrived with Harold to spend an evening at the home of a certain professor at Manchester University, to find Lowry happily ensconced in the best armchair eating macaroni cheese. 'We had assumed he had no friends at all, because that was what he had led us to believe; not in so many words, but by implication. He had never spoken of them to us. He didn't like us finding him

there. He didn't want to be discovered. He was like a little boy with treasures that mustn't be exposed, as if only so long as they were kept secret did they retain any value.

'His deceptions were all part of his queer sort of protection against the world. Even if you had been quite intimate with him, you couldn't ask him personal questions. He wouldn't have it. He must have spent a lot of time covering up–and for what?'

At much the same time as he was fostering a friendship with the Timperleys, Lowry embarked upon a relationship that, although at first no more than casual, became one of the most enduring of all. It was in 1926 that Lowry, then thirty-eight years old, and Geoffrey Bennett, thirteen years his junior, first came together. Bennett was a clerk in the Foreign Department of the Manchester city centre branch of the London and County Westminster Bank where Lowry's cousin Grace also worked. Curiously, Cousin Grace was one of the few who did on occasion meet others in his life; possibly because she was as meticulously as was Lowry at keeping her counsel. As Doreen Sieja, an office girl at the Pall Mall Property Company remarked: 'Of all the people I heard [Lowry] talk about over the years, so that I felt I almost knew them personally, [Cousin Grace] was the only one I ever met.'[11]

Regularly once a week Lowry would arrive at the bank at lunch-time to take Grace for a meal. 'He would come in through the rotating doors, his mac billowing behind him, his trilby pulled hard on to his head, and stand, shuffling his feet, until she was ready. He was a friendly soul and would chat to us who worked in that part of the bank. We knew he was something of an artist...' But, astonishingly, they did not know he was also something of a rent collector. Lowry may well have assumed, quite understandably, that Bennett did know, as the Reverend Gentleman was to suffer from a degree of compartmentalisation in the later

years of their friendship.

If Grace's dismissive attitude towards her artist cousin, who was at the time enjoying a not insignificant measure of success, seems surprising in the light of modern conceptions of celebrity, it was not in the least astonishing to Bennett. 'We, at the bank, would talk of Lowry's work, but we were interested simply because he was Grace's cousin...When we went together to look at his paintings in a gallery, she had no pride in him at all. Why should she? His work was considered a joke. It had not been accepted. In those days the accepted subjects for art were nice views, portraits, maybe groups of people, but posed not casual—very formal. Lowry's work was nothing of the kind; it was totally unconventional and, as such, more of an embarrassment to his family than a source of pride, even had they been the sort to feel such a thing. They found nothing in his artistic endeavours to make a noise about.'[12]

The young clerk was, at that time, living with his sister in Levenshulme, Manchester. In 1933 he married Alice, a beautiful young mezzo-soprano whom he had loved for nearly a decade, ever since he had heard her at a lunch time concert in the Houldsworth Hall. When Alice met Lowry she was, like Edith Timperley, intrigued by this strange man and, according to her husband 'quickly achieved a total sympathy with him'. She always made him welcome in whatever house they were living, and made no objections when her husband chose to spend their meagre savings on a Lowry painting. And so their friendship—based, as it was, not on compatibility alone but equally on Bennett's steadfast admiration of Lowry's work—blossomed and endured.

After Lowry's death Bennett explained the basis of their relationship as he saw it: 'Mr Lowry and I had an affinity which is rare between two people. It was a sympathy, an understanding. I could understand him perfectly, and I think he understood me,

Left: Preliminary drawing for a subsequent oil entitled *Cranes and Ships, Glasgow Docks*, 1947.

because our background, our upbringings were so similar. There was no fuss about our friendship. We simply accepted each other. He liked my views and I admired what he did. I recognised in him many of the influences that had so affected my own development. We were both born in a generation of parental rule. Parents had enormous control over their children, a control that young people today can hardly conceive. You had to obey your parents, despite the fact that, at this time, parents had a scathingly poor view of their own progeny. I experienced it, just as he experienced it: nothing he did gained the admiration of his parents in the same way that nothing I did gave any seeming pleasure to my father (my mother was already dead). This is one of the pathetic aspects of the early Edwardian days, an aspect that gave me, and I am sure gave Lowry, an awful inferiority complex. If Lowry's parents gave him no due for any achievement, they were not special in that.'

But, by Lowry's standards, these were happy days. In retrospect he was often to say: 'The years from 1924 to 1932 were the happiest of my life.'[13] He had hope, he had faith in his vision, he had friends and he had his art. When once he was asked what he was doing when he was not painting, he replied: 'Thinking about painting'. Not strictly true, of course. He may well have been in the office or collecting rents, but he enjoyed the riposte and the way it tripped neatly off the tongue and so it was absorbed into his fund of well-honed phrases that made up the contemporary saga of his life.

In much the same way when, in 1927, the local press announced that *Coming Out of School* had been acquired by the Duveen Fund for The Tate, Lowry seized upon the fact that this was not strictly accurate and added it to his fund of tales of rejection and disappointment. Four months earlier, reviewing the Duveen Fund's inaugural exhibition at Leeds, *The Times* art critic wrote: 'There are two pictures, both by the same

Right: Another brooding, empty, isolated house–perfect fodder for Lowry's vivid imagination. *Heathcliff's House*, 1950.

Above: A brooding study of isolation, not industrial isolation this time, but what Lowry's friend, the dealer Andras Kalman, calls a lonely landscape. Again painted during his mother's final years. *A Landmark*, 1936.

artist, Mr Lawrence [sic] S Lowry, which, without any such intention, might serve very well to indicate the advantages of the scheme. They are called *A Lancashire Village* and *Something Wrong*, the latter representing the emotional effect of what may be an accident and what may be a crime upon the population of a typical industrial town. If the scheme should succeed in bringing contemporary works of art of good average quality into the knowledge and reach of the inhabitants of such places it will do something that has never been done before.' This was praise indeed, to be singled

out in an exhibition of 1,400 works – and of which only 345 were bought.

This particular purchase, however, was not all that it was represented to be. It would seem that the *Eccles Journal* had been somewhat over-enthusiastic in assuming that the painting would go automatically to The Tate, simply because the scheme was operated from Millbank. In other words, they had jumped the gun. The fund, created by the newly ennobled Lord Duveen who, as plain Joe Duveen, dealer, had made a fortune demonstrating the validity of his own premise that a priceless work of art at any price was a bargain, was, in fact, set up for the purpose of buying works by contemporary British artists for presentation to museums and furnishing touring exhibitions; only a very few got to the Tate. *Coming Out of School* was not hung there until 1949, long after Lowry had been specifically bought by The Tate, for The Tate, and the thrill of its arrival on such hallowed walls tempered by the prolonged delay.

Lowry, being Lowry, took the twenty-two-year gap between misconception and fact, personally; he took it as an indication that the great gallery did not want the thing, no matter what Duveen's advisers might have thought. Thus, he was now faced with the embarrassment of explaining the misunderstanding both to his parents and to friends who rushed to congratulate him. 'I hope it is the beginning of all the recognition and success that you deserve...' wrote Harold Timperley. Lowry was quick to disabuse him of his illusions; it was, he said, not triumph but rejection in another guise.

But there were shows enough to keep hope alive and, soon, a modest number of sales; drawings at three guineas a go, four if framed, and the occasional larger commission from a reputable gallery. In 1928 he had several pictures accepted by Goupil, the gallery where years before the young Vincent van Gogh had worked during his year in London; they showed them in their window 'but unfortunately without result'. He exhibited with the New English Art Club, a club which remained stubbornly non-academic and non-establishment, despite early controversy and complaints in such papers as the *Pall Mall Gazette*, which called the New Critics 'peevish' and the New Artists 'defiant' because they were making so little headway. Lowry could not help but admire a club that, at the turn of the century, had held out against urgings to 'choose popular subjects to make their pictures popular';[14] it had been suggested that they should give the British public what it wanted, pictures

of dogs and babies, instead of pursuing 'a wanton search for the squalid and the ugly.'[15] It might have been Manchester talking about Lowry.

Ironically, when he submitted work to the Salon des Indépendants in Paris, where only twenty years before they had scoffed at Henri Rousseau, his pictures were both accepted and highly praised. And when he was shown at the French Salon d'Automne, a French magazine named him first among *le groupe anglais*. 'Lorence Lowry expose deux toiles qui sont d'un observateur amusé et d'un peintre délicat.'[16] By 1931 he was included in the *Who's Who of European Painters* and described as a specialist in industrial scenes. And in that same year when *Election Time*, an archetypal, lyrical Lowry oil full of busy businessmen in dark suits and large shoes, was shown in Manchester not twelve months after it had been praised in Paris, it was priced at just five guineas and, according to records, remained unsold and unsung.

Over the years Harold Timperley was to prove a steadfast friend to Lowry. Their first book and, as it turned out, their last together had not been hugely successful; it sold not well at all. Despite their mutual disappointment, when time came to plan his next, *The Shropshire Book*, Timperley again commissioned Lowry to do the illustrations. When they were done, the publishers did not want them; they wanted photographs. (Ironically, a secret they both guarded assiduously during their respective lifetimes was that Lowry's drawings were all done from photographs.) Harold was embarrassed. Tactfully, he broke the news to Lowry: 'And now about the Shropshire drawings. Dents didn't like them well enough after all. They still want photographs. I was rather surprised, but of course there's always the chance that what one considers to be certainty is not. Anyway, I'm going to send the m.s. and drawings out to other publishers now and see what happens. I want the book to have the drawings, not photographs. Do you feel like drawing the remaining two subjects? Or do you prefer to wait until a publisher decides to accept? I think it would be better if you did them soon, as a publisher likes to have the complete thing in front of him. But you say if you would rather leave them.'[17]

In the event, it was photographs that were used. 'Gammers and gaffers,' commented Edith, 'which was the very image we were trying to get away from.'

Apparently the rebuff did not greatly disturb Lowry; he had, by this time, become sufficiently inured to failure to make scant display of his concern, even to the perceptive Edith. But soon afterwards his relationship with Harold – by then living in Surrey, where he was working as a schoolmaster – and Edith began to wane; his later recollections of the collaboration were not as warm as they might have been, considering the Timperleys' loyalty.

In the spring of 1930, Lowry was given a one-man exhibition in Manchester which would seem, at first reading, to have been extremely successful in that all the pictures were sold. 'A Collection of 25 Pencil Drawings of Ancoats made by Mr L S Lowry at the special request of the Manchester University Settlement' was presented at the Round House, Every Street. The price of each drawing was 3 guineas unframed, 4 guineas framed.

The show opened on Tuesday 25th March and by the Wednesday every picture had been sold. Lawrence Haward, Curator of Manchester City Art Gallery, complacent in his experience of Lowry's unsaleability, had not bothered to go until the second day. He hurried to explain the situation to Lowry: 'I found that most of the drawings which I wanted to submit to my committee had already been purchased when I came up the next day, but I have persuaded Miss Pilkington to offer to the Rutherston Collection your drawing of *Stony Brow* which she had earmarked.' Margaret Pilk-

ington was, at that time, Director of the Whitworth Gallery, Manchester, and had a particular eye for a Lowry; *Stony Brow* had been singled out by the Manchester Guardian critic – not Bernard Taylor who had died in 1928 – as a 'strange *tour de force*'.

This was to be the first acquisition of a Lowry by the City Art Gallery; it was followed in September with a second. In that same letter Haward tried to make up for his tardiness. 'I wonder if you will consider my suggestion that you should at your leisure make one or two studies of Piccadilly as it is today with the sunk garden, the loafers, the ruins, and all the rest of the mess and muddle.' After writing to confirm that he would be free to draw what he wanted to draw – 'Have you any special views in mind or any particular size of drawing or will you leave these matters to me?'[18] – Lowry produced exactly what Haward had asked for. When they were done he left the drawings at the Gallery with an eager note to the effect that he would be interested to hear Haward's comments. The curator's remarks when they came were not couched in the most diplomatic terms: 'I think they are very interesting in so far as they do give a glimpse of the kind of people who are found at that site today, but I wonder whether you could not have a shot at a drawing of the site and the public using it that you would get from a first floor window of Lyons' Popular Café.'[19]

Lowry did not 'feel inclined' to make any further drawings. He wrote: 'Had you told me, when I asked you had you any special view in mind, I would have acted upon it, but under all the circumstances I am afraid that I cannot spend any more time on this subject.'[20] In a draft he made but did not send he had added, and crossed out, the words 'and after you had left the choice of subjects to me.'

That was Lowry retiring hurt from the fray, a hurt that was only minimally assuaged by the purchase, two months later, of *An Accident,* an evocative, atmospheric oil made in 1926. Manchester bought it for £21 having knocked Lowry down from the £30 asking price. 'I didn't want a pound or two to stand in the way of a sale,'[21] Lowry remarked later and lived to see the insurance value rise to five figures.

The Ancoats Exhibition made a gross total of £60, an achievement which apparently gave Lowry little pleasure. He felt the price of the pictures to have been set too low. As usual, Manchester had failed to value him. It was not, he told Maitland in 1970, 'the price of a bricklayer or a navvy...But I was pleased to do them. I suppose it was something that someone was noticing them. I sold one to Manchester. I was very pleased to [have] work there. I've never seen it since. I suppose they are all in the cellar because they don't like me in Manchester.'[22]

Years later Hugh Maitland wrote: 'He does not look back with any satisfaction on the fact that Manchester was to buy a picture for a public art gallery, and later bought others, but thinks he has been neglected on the whole by Manchester as compared with some other places, a point which he seems to feel keenly.'[23]

This supposed inability to attract either attention or a market for his work was, in those years, less than is generally believed; but it is a belief Lowry propagated himself, not in a deliberate attempt to distort the truth, nor as an exercise in self-pity, but because it was what he believed to be true. If, in retrospect, Edith Timperley could call it his 'old song', at the time when she knew him best she instinctively recognised it for what it was—a cry from the heart. He felt himself to be a failure. He felt neglected, misunderstood and under-rated; and nowhere more so than at home in Pendlebury. He had come, painfully and slowly, to accept the rejection of the outside world; he never did learn to accept the rejection of his mother. He fought it constantly, yearning to hear her praise. 'I'm a perfect fool to keep on. I'm a lunatic, don't you think?' he

would say, fishing for rebuttal. 'Well, you never can tell,'[24] she would reply and he would seize upon her tepid words and repeat them to other as examples of maternal encouragement. Maybe he believed, or at least suspected, that her judgement of him was justified; after all, she was the family arbiter of taste.

In 1939 he received a letter from the *Manchester Guardian*[25] asking if he would be interested in writing an occasional art criticism for the paper. Bernard D Taylor, one of their former critics and Lowry's one time teacher, had died long before and they were, as the writer Gordon Phillips put it, at that time without a critic. Lowry showed the letter to his mother who 'laughed and laughed and laughed.' When she had recovered herself sufficiently, she told him: 'You could never do it, Laurie. The show would be over before you could get it properly phrased.' He repeated the story frequently, and without obvious rancour, as an example of her understanding of him.[26]

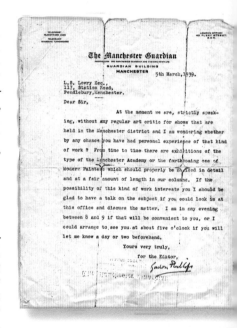

Above: In 1939 Lowry received a letter from the *Manchester Guardian* asking him if he would be interested in writing an occasional art criticism. His mother scoffed at the very idea. "You could never do it, Laurie,' she told him. Lowry never took up the offer but carried the letter round in his suit pocket until it all but fell to pieces.

For nearly fifty years Geoffrey Bennett saw himself and Lowry as kindred spirits: they were both, as he said, of a generation whose parents had 'a scathingly poor view of their own progeny'. And they both, he added, spent their lives 'struggling to escape down this long dark tunnel to find our self-respect.'

Bennett found his by making a happy marriage and taking Holy Orders; whether Lowry ever achieved his is another matter entirely.

Chapter 8

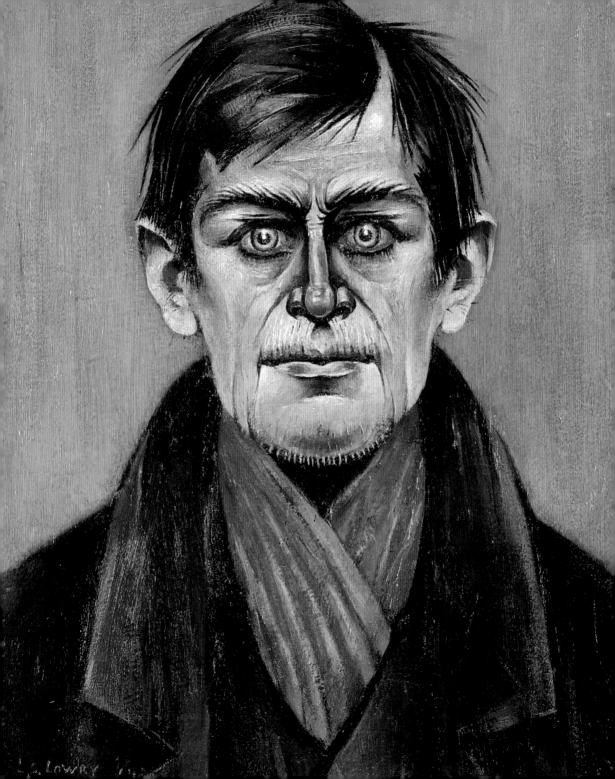

Man with red eyes

If Laurence Stephen Lowry was a man for secrets, it was a trait he no doubt inherited from his father. Both were successful in maintaining the mysteries they sought to preserve until after death, when they were past caring, but the undisclosed fact in Robert Lowry's life was to lead indirectly to his passing.

Robert Lowry, who it transpired had a need both financial and emotional to continue working well past retirement age, quite literally caught his death of cold.

'He would not be told,' said his son bluntly[1]. Robert had been suffering from a head cold since Christmas but, again, much like his son, he was not a complainer. By February the sniffles had turned to pneumonia, despite which 'he got up and went out and that was the end of him. He came back and he went to bed and he never got up again.'[2]

Robert Lowry, at the age of seventy-four, was still collecting rents. He had never been made a partner in the firm where he had been nearly all his working life. He had fulfilled neither his wife's nor his own expectations of himself. He died, as he had lived, a disappointed man. His tragedy was that, had he found the courage to confide his difficulties in his son, Laurie might well have collected the necessary rents for his father. He had not felt close to his father for many years, if indeed he had ever felt close to him. He called him 'Dad' and maintained a kind of distant joviality with him in public, almost as if he were a mere acquaintance; he displayed no evident grief at his loss, only concern at its effect upon his mother. 'He died very suddenly though he had been unwell for some time. Mother is very ill just now.'

What Lowry did not know, and was not to know until certain papers came to light, is that his father was deeply in debt. The parlous state of Robert's finances, no doubt exacerbated by the demands of care for a sick wife, was the secret he kept from his family until the day he died. His sister in London wrote in astonishment to hear of it, his friends from Bennett Street were shocked by it, his son ignorant of it until the creditors rushed to claim repayment of their loans. Lowry attended to them all with courtesy and speed; within less than a year all obligations had been met. But from that time on everything changed; life at 117 Station Road had never been easy; now it was to be nigh on impossible – or 'difficult' as Lowry put it with an uncharacteristic lack of hyperbole.

The death, announced the next day in the *Manchester Guardian*, transformed Lowry's life, and not for the better. Elizabeth Lowry, now seventy-three years old and ailing still, took to her bed. She became what Lancastrians called 'bedfast' and there she remained for the next seven and a half years, totally dependent physically and emotionally, upon her only son. From this time on, until her death, she expected his presence each evening to read to her before she slept. She would allow no one else to tend her, not even the local woman who came in to clean and cook a midday meal each day, nor would she let anyone else bathe her sores or brush her hair.

Far left: Lowry once said that this savage portrait was, in fact, a self-portrait made when he was exhausted by the stress of caring for his ailing mother. He had risen from bed one morning, looked in his shaving mirror and this, he declared, was the image he saw. *Head of a Man (with Red Eyes)*, 1938.

Over page: Bought by the Tate Gallery on Milbank in the '60s, this oil is a more detailed version of the pencil drawing entitled *Dwellings*. Originally thought to be a building on Ordsall Lane, Salford, art historians have recently decided that the tenements stood near to Salford Royal Hospital. *Dwellings, Oldfield Road, Salford* 1927.

At one point in this time, Lowry became so overwrought or over-tired that the doctor, while visiting Elizabeth, advised her son to take a few days away. He complied, under protest, travelling to the Fylde coast and writing daily, sometimes twice a day, postcards of greetings and concern to his mother at home in the bedroom in Pendlebury. She, for her part, complained petulantly about the quality of care administered by those who tended her in her son's absence, in much the same way as she had complained about the ministrations of her niece May, daughter of her sister Mary, who being widowed came briefly to live in 117 Station Road until she could bear it no longer.

Despite his concerns and preoccupations, Lowry did not abandon his art. He might have stopped going to art school but he worked doggedly on at home, painting long into the night, derelict landscapes mired in dark waters and strange heads of men with staring eyes and untamed hair.

One, later called *Head of a Man with Red Eyes,* he said was a self portrait painted when 'I was out of my head'. He had risen one morning, looked in the shaving mirror and this was the reflection he saw. 'I don't like that, it scares me,' remarked one young woman who came upon it years later. 'It scares me too,' replied Lowry.

(That particular picture, the strangest of them all, is in a public collection – in The Lowry, the brilliant art complex built in his name on the banks of the Irwell. Here viewers may pass on by should they find the red-eyed man too disturbing; but those of the strange heads in private hands have a more peripatetic life: *Boy in a Yellow Jacket* was quickly sold by its owner after he was diagnosed with a terminal disease and decided that the picture had bought him ill fortune; *Head of a Man* was sold after a mere three weeks ownership by a Manchester man who found it too disturbing to live with.)

Later, in the '50, he said: 'I think I reflect-ed myself in those pictures. That was the most difficult period of my life. It was alright when he was alive, but after that it was very difficult because she was very exacting. I was tied to my mother. She was bedfast. In 1932 to 1939 I was just letting off steam.'[3]

Two months after Robert's death, Lowry had two pictures accepted by the Royal Academy in London. Although this was what might be described as a milestone in his artistic career – a first acceptance by the Royal Academy – Lowry was so taken up with the effects of his father's untidy departure that the event seems to have passed him by with undue comment. Such recognition, however, did not go totally unremarked, no matter how uninterested in his art he might have believed his family to be. Robert's sister in London, Laurie's Aunt Lowry, wrote: 'This is a very great honour, my dear. Two pictures in the Royal Academy. Your father would indeed have been proud. Uncle is going down on Saty [sic] to see what time the RA is open and the best way for me to get there...I am thankful you have your Painting, Laurie, for you will not care to go far away from Mother...it will take you out of yourself a little.'[4]

Almost of their own volition, Lowry's work was attracting the beginnings of attention. In 1932 he exhibited again, finally, with the Manchester Academy, and in 1934 he accepted an invitation to join their ranks. In the same year he was elected a member of the Royal Society of British Artists, after showing with them in 1933.

A Hawker's Cart had been to Rochdale (1931), *Going Home from the Mill* by invitation to Southport (1932), *A Football Match* to Bradford (1933); others went to Huddersfield, to Preston, and a total of six to the Arlington Gallery in London for the 1936 annual show of the RBA. Despite all this, his prices had not greatly increased. At Preston Lowrys were listed at 30 guineas each,

119

whereas a Sickert was up for £400.*

The fact that Lowry's pictures were now travelling the length and breadth of England, had less to do with Lowry's own efforts at promotion, which were negligible, more to do with a contact he had made at the Mosley Street exhibition a decade before. The connection with W H Berry, at that time the Director of Oldham Art Gallery, had turned out to be one of the most important in his artistic life. Berry had made it his business to keep up to date with the artist and his work[5] and by 1923 the relationship had become such that Lowry was invited to lunch at Berry's home in Cheadle Hulme, Manchester. It was here that he met Berry's wife, a striking woman deeply involved with the art world of London, who commuted each week between Manchester and London; her name was Daisy Jewell and she was head of the framing department of James Bourlet and Sons, Fine Art Agents extraordinary. The effect of their ensuing friendship and of Miss Jewell's unswerving faith in him was to be greater than either of them could have hoped; the results of her active encouragement and her systematic efforts on his behalf were not to be fully realised for nearly twenty years – and then only fully understood by the members of her staff.

Lowry and Daisy Jewell made an immediate connection and from this time on a trip to London was not complete without a visit by Lowry to the sumptuous showrooms in Nassau Street where she presided, a figure of some awe and certain influence, behind an impressive mahogany desk. Miss Jewell was quick to introduce Lowry to Armand Blackley, a director of the company, who having absolute faith in his charismatic head of department supported her enthusiasm. When Lowry was elected an Associate of the Royal Academy in 1955, Blackley wrote congratulating him: 'I wonder, in those far off days, when we had the pleasure of see-

ing you at Nassau Street, if you ever thought this would happen. Both Miss Jewell and I did, and it is very nice to see honour being given where honour is due.[6] Lowry replied: 'Yes, I not only never for a moment thought this would happen, but I often wondered whether I would sell the pictures, except the odd one every few months or so. In fact I frequently wondered why I kept on painting these mill scenes…You and Miss Jewell seem to have been right.[7]

Salford City Art Gallery, under their Director A J M Maltby, had for quite some time been displaying interest in the local artist who seemed to be attracting interest further afield. In years following the 1921 exhibition Maltby would travel to London at regular intervals to talk with Miss Jewell and view Lowry's latest work. At an exhibition in the Peel Park gallery of the work of indigenous artists in 1931, Maltby showed Lowry's paintings beside the sculptures of Sam Rabin, his former companion in Valette's life class. The local press, reviewing 'A Summer Exhibition of Recent Paintings by Eminent British Artists' described them as 'a talented pair already on the road to fame.' Lowry's opinion of Rabin, a young Jew whose parents escaped the Russian pogroms to arrive in England on the day Mafeking was relieved, is not on record. Rabin, however, was a staunch admirer of Lowry's work, the single figures of his later years in particular; in this he was one of the few, along with Fitton and Valette, from the Manchester school, to appreciate Lowry the artist. It is interesting to note that those who did both understand and admire Lowry were successful in their own right.

Lowry's work was exhibited again in Salford in 1934 when it hung alongside the paintings of Lucien Pissarro, Stanley Spencer and Richard Sickert; and again, in 1935 in London, when the *Daily Telegraph* critic singled him out for praise: '…the chief interest lies in the indication of a younger**

*At auction at Christie's in London in November, 2005, both Sickert and Lowry were offered for sale. Sickert's painting of Eugene Goossens conducting went for £40,000; a Lowry industrial landscape, *The Footbridge,* went for £370,000.

**Lowry was then 47.

generations' aims...British painting does not naturally run to schools, and the best canvases are the most individual, like L S Lowry's industrial towns.'[8]

Lowry remained discouraged; not that he gave up nor was ever, in truth, in serious danger of so doing. Early in 1937 he complained to the Timperleys: 'Art, so far as I am concerned, is devilish dull. No money in it. Plenty of bills in it. That's where you writers have the pull, a bit of paper and a pen and you're all right. I'm getting old and will come and see you as soon as I can crawl... Matters still about the same here, though my mother is much weaker, I aren't so bad. I feel rather better than I did–there was room for that...'[9]

In London, Daisy Jewell, as careful as ever of Lowry's interests, was pressing him for more paintings, not because the work they had in stock had already been sold, but because no matter how often they were sent to shows or how far they travelled, 'they always came back.'[10] Finding fresh work to exhibit was becoming a worry. 'Could you arrange in the circumstances,' Miss Jewell wrote to Lowry, 'to send us one or two new ones down by passenger train?'[11] She knew from experience that Lowry rarely left Manchester and his mother. Long gone were the days when he would breeze cheerfully into the Bourlet showrooms in his voluminous old mackintosh, his pockets stuffed with paste sandwiches and bits of paper bearing sketches of the strange people he observed on the way; he would sit chatting with uncharacteristic ease with the formidable Daisy Jewell, she smoking black Turkish cigarettes while he drank tea from fine bone china cups so delicate they made his hands look even bigger than they were. They were a curious couple, Miss Jewell and Mr Lowry, but they had a good rapport and a rare understanding. It was she who had contrived to send Lowry's work to the prestigious French salons, not to

Above: *A seat in a Park,* 1952.

mention the length and breadth of Britain. But, in 1938, she excelled herself; she virtually manipulated Lowry's arrival in the upper echelons the English art world which, even to this day, exist in fine exclusivity in the square mile that runs from the Royal Academy of Art, down New Bond Street and into its equally exclusive tributaries.

The story is told by Bert Jones who had been at Bourlet's, man and boy, all his working life; he knew the ways of his employers as well, if not better, than most. Daisy Jewell's efforts on Lowry's behalf had not lessened over the years of neglect and when, early in 1938, she heard that A J McNeill Reid, a director of the prestigious Lefevre Gallery off St James's, was to call at Nassau Street, she prepared for the visit in what seemed to her staff to be a quite extraordinary manner. Some time before the dealer's expected visit, Bert Jones came through from the workshop to check, as he always did, that everything was in the state of meticulous order that his

Right: When an artist names a painting *Front Gardens*, the imagination conjures up an image of suburban flowers in suburban flower beds. But this is a painting by Lowry so, of course, it is no such thing. *Front Gardens*, 1944.

superior demanded. He saw that there were a few pictures propped against her desk including two Lowrys which had that morning been returned from an exhibition. As he began gathering them together Miss Jewell put out a hand – 'Leave the Lowrys', she said. 'I'll attend to those.' Bert Jones was astonished; it was unthinkable that Miss Jewell should put pictures away herself, climbing ladders in the dusty warehouse, or that

they should be left untidily lying around. 'Nothing was ever allowed to remain in the showroom when it was not actually being viewed,' recalled Bert, years later. 'Miss Jewell was punctilious about such things. They must have been left there for a reason. It couldn't have been a mistake. Miss Jewell didn't make mistakes.'[12]

McNeill Reid, unwittingly, made sense of the story when he came to describe his

personal discovery of Lowry on a television documentary in 1968, some thirty years later. 'I had been persuaded to go to Bourlet's to see the work of an artist who did not sound very promising. My attention began to wander and I spotted through an open door a small picture sitting on the chair in the adjoining room. I went through and saw a very lovely little street scene with masses of figures in it–signed L S Lowry. I asked Miss Jewell...who L S Lowry was and she said: "Oh, he's a Manchester artist." "Well," I said, "could you send down half a dozen, say, to the gallery tomorrow morning, and if my partner MacDonald likes them as much as I do we will have a show." MacDonald did like them. I wrote to Lowry and, naturally, he was delighted because he was in despair feeling that nobody would ever want his pictures at all.'[13]

Above: This is a man Lowry said he saw. But it could equally well have been the artist himself, observing the world through a hole in an imaginary fence. *Man looking through a Hole in a Fence,* 1963.

and British art and were credited with a keen eye for fresh talent. Reid Senior had himself trained briefly as an artist in Paris where he struck up a friendship with Vincent van Gogh who was himself struggling for recognition; at one time the pair made a joint suicide pact on which, fortunately for the art world, they both reneged.

In May McNeill Reid wrote direct to Lowry, announcing his intention to give him a one-man show in their London showroom in January the following year. 'We hope that between now and the time of delivery of your pictures...you will be able to paint some very good canvases which will please the critics and the public,' he wrote. Lowry could hardly believe it. It would be his first in London and certainly the first to carry such clout. But, none the less, despite the understandable elation there was a certain apprehension. It was the assumption of new works that worried him. What with his duties at home, the demands of the ailing Elizabeth, and the need both to collect rents and to fulfil his office commitments, he knew that such a request would be impossible to meet. Besides, he had never been a quick worker; his output was limited by the demands of his perfectionism; he was known to take months, even years, over one picture, leaving them long periods of time before examining them again and, quite frequently re-working a picture or adding to a scene. He was a hard man to please when it came to his own work and incapable of releasing a picture until he, personally, was totally satisfied that it was 'as good as could be.' It would have been impossible for him to have produced twenty or thirty new works in seven months.

He wrote immediately to Reid: 'I am not quite clear. As I understood you would want all fresh things. My idea is to show eight or ten fresh ones (they are pretty much on the same lines as the ones you have seen) with the remainder chosen from what are with Messrs. Bourlet. A small show; twenty-four

Lowry's recollection of the event stressed Miss Jewell's surprise as much as his own; he was obviously unaware of her manipulation of the viewing–or maybe it just made a better story. 'Mrs Berry [Daisy Jewell], who was in charge, smiled, perhaps a little sadly. "He's a Manchester painter called Lowry. We've been sending his pictures to the shows for years. They're always hung–and they always come back."'[14]

This time they did not come back. Miss Jewell could not have picked a more persuasive champion for Lowry. Both McNeill Reid and his father, Alexander Reid, had a fine reputation in the trade; they were widely consulted by collectors of both French

or twenty-five in all. We had better be clear on this point. Do you agree to a show on these lines?'

McNeill Reid did agree, but in the intervening months Lowry fretted and fussed, dashing to London on day trips and consulting Daisy Jewell every step of the way. According to Bert Jones, she spent more time conferring with Lowry than she ever did advising Winston Churchill on his selection of pictures to be submitted to the Royal Academy. She wrote frequently to reassure him, advising him on the time and manner of his attendance at the forthcoming private view and sending him a list of the critics whom, like fairies at a christening, she recommended should receive personal invitations at home and direct from the artist; long before the concept of the word had been coined, she was a master of spin. Either past experience or a touch of paranoia in his psyche convinced Lowry, in his darker moments, that something untoward would happen to prevent the show taking place; in fact his concern was not that far wide of the mark. The show did indeed take place but before the end of the year the country was at war.

For the first time a Lowry exhibition attracted a large number of reviews in the national press; and a large number of sales. Included in the sixteen special invitees was Eric Newton of the *Sunday Times,* a critic who, with Jan Gordon of *The Observer* (and later Maurice Collis who missed the 1939 show) was to become one of Lowry's most constant and committed advocates. He wrote: 'Mr Lowry has formulated his own creed and consequently he will fit into no pigeon-hole. His vision is personal to himself... and owes nothing to any other artist. Like Cézanne he has gone straight to life... and his only concern as an artist is to translate his attitude to it into paint. He belongs to no school, but he may ultimately be the founder of one.'[15]

At the other end of the critical spectrum, *Time and Tide* found Lowry crude, awkward and primitive. As Collis was to point out when he wrote the first monograph of Lowry: 'In reading what was said...one has to bear in mind how exceedingly difficult it is to judge a new style, because an original work looks odd at first sight. Even if you like it and think it is good, it is hard to be sure how good it is, because it upsets current theories. In 1939 it was particularly difficult for English critics to say how good Lowry was because there was no common denominator between his style and that of Paris. They were quite unused to such a phenomenon.'[16]

Collis failed to remark that when Lowry had exhibited in Paris, the French critics had no such problems, despite the fact that they were steeped in the work of the Post Impressionists. If he found his colleagues in confusion and judged them to be obtuse or lacking the courage of their own convictions, no such accusations could be levelled at Newton who, by 1945, was calling Lowry a master, a mystic, a poet.

But for every critic that enthused, there was one who sneered. Some found him naïve, some found him childish and, of course, some found him primitive; some decided he was all three. None, however, went quite so far as the *Spectator*'s Michael Ayrton who wrote: 'I resent the Lowry automaton so fiercely that I must concede part of his actuality by the very degree of my revulsion, but I am inclined to think that some part of Lowry's convention rises out of his inability to draw the human figure.'[17] It would seem that Lowry's work was to inspire passion: passionate admiration or passionate loathing. Just as the good burgers of Manchester had mocked and laughed not so many years before, half a century later, the *Evening Standard* critic Brian Sewell was to echo their scorn in ringing tones: 'I don't care about his profound provincialism – many a backwater has produced great artists. I don't even care that his work is inept, tedious, repeti-

Over page: One of Lowry's most exuberant paintings, done to commemorate the end of the Second World War, a picture in which not only the children enjoy the rare treat of a special tea, but two bowler-hatted businessmen cavort in joyful abandon on the roof of one of the flag-decked terrace houses. *V E Day*, 1945.

tive, lacklustre and stuck in a rut. I care only that the English, who for centuries were the best collectors in Europe, should have so far lost their connoisseurship that they take to their bosoms this half-baked amateur and turn him into a folk hero.'[18]

Lowry was dead and past caring by the time Brian Sewell wrote those words; Ayrton's comments, however, rankled well into old age. The collector Monty Bloom, who being a perceptive man knew Lowry as well as anyone, was in the habit of following prices achieved at auction. Lowry relished discussions with him on such matters and would ask in seeming innocence: 'How much did Mr Ayrton's picture fetch, can you tell me Mr Bloom?' 'Oh, about two hundred pounds,' Bloom would reply. Here would follow a short pause—Lowry's timing was well practiced and highly skilled. Then: 'And can you tell me, Mr Bloom, how much that picture of mine fetched?' 'Something over two thousand, Mr Lowry.' Another pause, rather longer. Then: 'Isn't that interesting, sir,' Lowry would say, his blue eyes glinting with mischief. 'I wonder how that can be, don't you, Mr Bloom—because I can't draw, you know, I can't draw.' Lowry would no doubt have been amused to know that the same disparity in his prices compared with Ayrton's continued well into the twenty first century.

Sales from the 1939 show were less than McNeill Reid had hoped, more than Lowry had imagined. Miss Jewell kept the absent artist up to date on developments by means of almost daily letters—'Quite a number have been bought by collectors' or 'Lord Bearstead bought the one from the window.' The best news was that The Tate had acquired *Dwellings, Ordsall Lane, Salford*, 1927. Miss Jewell announced: 'Mr Reid felt that if the Tate Gallery buy they would probably only do so at a reduced price. I have therefore suggested that it would be better to allow them to have it for £15 rather than loose the chance...'[19] Lowry was so delighted with the sale that he present his preliminary drawing for the picture to the Gallery as a gift.

The man behind the purchase was Sir John Rothenstein, newly come to the Tate and highly involved in some enthusiastic reorganisation in his new domain. He records in his memoirs: 'I was convinced that a number of British painters then active or recently deceased were of greater significance than either critical opinion or that of the general public allowed.'[20] Accordingly he emptied three rooms at the Tate of 'all that was flashy or drab' and hung a collection of works by, among others, Sickert, Steer, Augustus and Gwen John, Stanley Spencer, Paul Nash—and L S Lowry. He commented: 'Today when a number of these artist have long figured respectfully in public collections and histories of art this may seem an unadventurous assembly of pictures, but I derived the liveliest satisfaction from the sense of doing some justice to the most serious British painters of the time, most of whom had hitherto received a very meagre measure of public recognition.'[21] He confessed himself to have been 'simply riveted' by his first sight of Lowry's work in Reid and Lefevre and 'very much moved by the exhibition'.[22]

It was not to be many months before all Lowry's worst fears were to be realised. Fate did indeed intervene in the progress of his artistic career. The Second World War broke out and McNeill Reid wrote personally to Lowry to tell him that the gallery was to close 'for an indefinite period...I feel I would be much better employed making munitions than standing about in a picture gallery...We will therefore, I am sorry to say, have to cancel your show which was fixed for next spring.'[23]

By this time, however, Lowry was in no fit state to care. Far worse had befallen him.

He was now well into middle age and, lacking both the confidence and the self-

esteem, he could not know that this was, in fact, no more than a postponement. Reid knew it; Daisy Jewell knew it; only Elizabeth Lowry, isolated in her sick-bed, looking with uncomprehending eyes upon the paintings of her son, refused to recognise so much as the possibility of it.

Publicly Lowry said: 'I had some very good notices of that show and it made me feel that I had justified myself to my mother...She was the only one left.'[24] But privately he admitted: 'And then Alex Reid gave me a show and my mother couldn't understand it.' At home the show had changed nothing. His mother's assessment of him was his assessment. Having been raised in the belief that she had an instinctive and unfailing eye for beauty, he acknowledged her judgment to be true and valid. If she saw no worth in what he did, then there could be no worth, despite what others said. Only her conversion to his vision could bring him fulfilment.

At last, on 12 October 1939, in the most momentous year of his life, she died, uncomprehending and complaining to the end. She had lived to her eighty-third year, her hold upon life as obstinate as her hold upon her son. She died as she had lived, a spoilt, selfish, petulant woman who, even in death, refused to recognise what others now freely acknowledged: that her son had brought, had she had the will to see it, much honour to their name. By her death without recognition, she had robbed him of joy in that honour, deprived him of motive for ambition and denied him the pleasure he most sought: her pleasure in him. Where now was glory in success if she was not to know of it? What now the pleasure in sales if she were not to marvel at them? What now the purpose in anything, even life itself, if she were not to share it?

'It all came too late,' he would say, spurning honours and rejecting acclaim. 'It all came too late for my mother to know of it.' And yet it had come in time, in good time, for her to know of it, had she wished to know. Or perhaps she did know in her heart, but had neither the generosity nor the love to acknowledge it.

When the funeral was over and the few surviving relatives had departed, Lowry returned to the office, a sad, solitary figure whom none could comfort. 'What is there left? What is there left?' he would ask young Openshaw, who, sensing that no reply was required, gave none.

A week later, on a bleak October day when the wind lashed the leaves off the sparse trees on Princess Street, Harold Timperley found the grieving man hunched on a seat before the Pre-Raphaelites in Manchester City Art Gallery, his eyes dimmed with unshed tears. Fearing for his friend, Harold took him gently by the arm and led him, unresisting, home to Cheadle Hulme and Edith. For three weeks Edith cared for him, feeding him and playing the piano for him and watching gratefully as the lines of tension eased from his face if only so long as the music lasted. She rose early, noting that he barely slept, and sat with him through the morning drinking cup after cup of tea. She walked with him in silence for hours across the golf links adjoining their home, her short legs striving to keep pace with his long ones. He did not go to work, nor paint, nor even talk of art or ambition or any of the things that once obsessed him. He had only one cry: 'What is there left? What is there left for me now?'

Now that she was dead and he had all the time in the world for painting, he did not want to paint. 'I had no need to paint after she died,' he said years later, as if surprised by the strength of his need to prove himself to her. 'There was no longer any need.' He cannot have meant that the legacy his mother left him, a net sum of £1,028.16s.4d., had relieved him of the need to make money from his pictures. Had he considered the money an incentive to idleness, he would have given up his office job, and this he did

128

not do. Three decades later he was still saying; 'I had no interest in life after my mother died...her death made all the difference to my life.'

Slowly he recovered, or made semblance of recovery, leaving the Timperleys' home with embarrassed thanks and promises to take care. He returned alone to the bleak house on Station Road; he moved his paints and palettes from the attic to the parlour where he hung his parents' portraits with his painting of himself as a young man in a flat cap–looking, according to art critic John Read 'like the hero of a working class play'. He put them there, he told visitors lest they should think him vain or sentimental, to keep the wallpaper from falling from the walls. He locked his mother's room and, a full year later, made a painting of it from memory: a sterile, empty room with an empty bed and a counterpane of the purest white; there is, in the picture, no hint of the woman who lived out the last seven years of her there in unhappy seclusion, no personal effects, no humanity.

It was many months before the desire to paint returned and, even then, it was not so much something he actually wanted to do, more of a way of filling the empty hours. When he did begin to work again it was without enthusiasm until, of a sudden, the compulsion returned and art became a therapy to ease his grief.

'It was the only thing I had to do. I worked to get rid of the time, even now I work for something to do. If things had been natural as were years ago I wouldn't have done the paintings. My mother's death did it. I feel it still...I miss her yet.' He was eighty when he spoke those words. He went on, 'I've not cared much about anything since she died. I've nothing left and I just don't care. Painting is a wonderful way of getting rid of the days.'

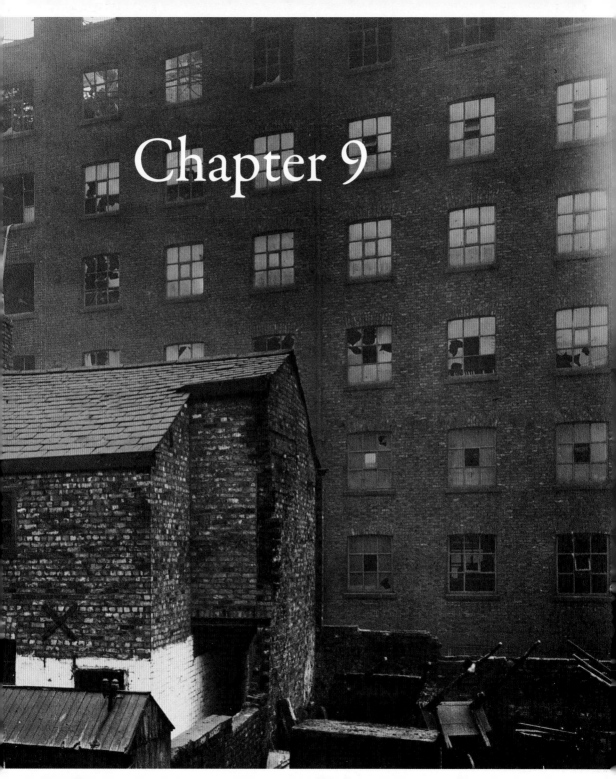

Chapter 9

After she'd gone

Lowry was fifty-two years old when his mother died, fifty-two when artistic recognition seemed finally within his grasp, fifty-two when the Second World war broke out.

Time for a change of life, it would seem; time for a break with the past; time to move on – or so his friends and colleagues thought, and confidently waited for him to marry or move house – or both.

Lowry changed nothing, moved nowhere, married no-one.

He stayed on, alone, in the old house while the dust gathered on the silent piano and the cobwebs frayed on the tall ceilings. He seemed almost to merge into the gloom of the cluttered interior, the darkened windows in the weathered façade echoing the shuttered eyes in his sorrowful face, much as his later paintings of solitary, empty houses in derelict landscapes echoed the artist himself. 'These are symbols of my mood, they are myself,' he said.

He was too old for active service – and anyway he had flat feet, a condition which apparently had kept him out of the trenches in the First World War – but not too old to volunteer for fire-watching duties on the roofs of the larger department stores in Manchester. Here he found a kind of camaraderie, a superficial bonhomie with the other men who watched with him; nothing, however, that outlasted the time and place. He was, he said, always first down in the morning to capture the destruction while the smoke and grime still hung in the air.

He was also, it seemed, too old to marry,

though this was what most of his friends assumed he would do now that he was no longer tied to his mother.

'Her dominance successfully prevented any thought of marriage,' said James Fitton, looking back on that time with the benefit of hindsight. 'While she lived he had no need for another woman,' said Edith Timperley. 'His mother absorbed all his thoughts and all his time,' said Lucy Snarr. Elizabeth herself had told her sister Mary, 'Laurie will never marry.'

She knew, perhaps, that Lowry was a loner. He was not, as later commentators came to think, a lonely man in the popular sense of the word – more a man who was alone in a crowd; an observer rather than a participator in life, one who was ease with himself, and comfortable in his own company.

And so, instead of a wife who would have been a constant presence, he did something very different, something which only came to light some years after his death. He chose as companions a series of young women whom he befriended and patronised, not in a condescending way, but by way of encouragement in their artistic ambitions. Some he financed, some he tutored, some he simply guided; all he influenced and one or two he changed their lives for ever. Each of them he could take or leave at will – his will.

His friendship with each one, save the last who by virtue of her position in the chain of friendships was undoubtedly special to him, endured roughly a decade; each one, save the last, was gently dropped when a new protégé came into his life. He described them as his

Left: Because this young woman bears such a strong resemblance to the Ann of the '50s portraits, the two women were at one time assumed to be one and the same. This picture, however, was painted in 1923 so is more likely to have been the girl called Ann who lived on Swinton Moss and helped Lowry care for his mother. Close inspection shows that, some time later, Lowry has updated the painting and given her '50s eye make-up and a plait. *Head of a Girl Wearing a Cloche Hat*, 1923.

young friends, his niece, his goddaughter.

Some, such as the Rev Geoffrey Bennett, disapproved. 'Has he got a girl with him this time?' he once asked the Marshalls, dealers of Newcastle. 'Only his niece,' replied Mrs Marshall disingenuously, who knew full well the implication of Bennett's question. 'Ah,' remarked the Reverend Gentleman, 'that's what he is calling them now, is it? The last one was his goddaughter.'[1]

What is most intriguing about this series of relationships–which, he insisted and they insisted and everyone who truly knew him insisted, were not sexual relationships and never consummated–is that all the women had the same look about them; they were all dark haired, full lipped, wide eyed and young. This fact, which only came to light after his death, fosters the speculation that Lowry had taken for his muse a woman in a specific image–the memory of a lost, early love, a young girl perhaps glimpsed from afar but fixed in the mind's eye for life; a pupil of his mother's who came to the house with her ribbons and bows and wide, inno-

cent eyes; a parlour maid with her whalebone stays and voluptuous form; a model in the style of Dante Gabriel Rossetti, the artist he collected with what in anyone else might be described as a passion; or, perhaps, Elizabeth herself, who in her young days had something of the look of the mystery woman; or even himself in the guise of the daughter he never was.

The first of whom he spoke was the

Top left: According to the critic Mervyn Levy, Ann was one of the Lowry dream women... who occupied a similar role in his personal mythology as that of women of Rossetti. *Portrait of Ann*, 1956.

daughter of a farmer on Swinton Moss, a swathe of agricultural land within sight of Station Road. Walking across there one day years later with a young artist called Harold Riley he began reminiscing about her. 'Did you court her?' asked Riley, intrigued to hear of a woman in the life of the painter whom he had considered to be a confirmed bachelor, in the literal rather than the idiomatic sense of the phrase.

'Oh, no. I enjoyed her company. I liked her. But I never spoke to her of feelings.'

'Did you tell your mother about her?'

'My mother knew her. She came to help me with my mother sometimes...she was an invalid, you know.'

'And did you tell your mother how you felt about her?'

'Oh no. My mother was not the sort of woman you could discuss feelings with. I

Above: Painted as a commission following Lowry's first London show in 1939. *Royal Exchange*, 1939.

135

it all up'. She played tennis 'not very well' and the piano rather better. It is interesting that many of Lowry's drawings around this time feature young women with tennis racquets and their hair in a single plait tied with a bow. Just as he had posed for Riley to take his photograph outside the farm which he said was Ann's home, in the '60s he posed for a later protégé to capture him on film outside another house – the one in Lytham St. Anne's where Maud, whom he later referred to as Ann, was supposed to have lived with her parents.* She, he told a would-be biographer, Tony Ellis, a Salford Curator who suffered a tragic, early death in a car crash, 'came to my father's funeral, caught a cold and died. She was twenty-six.'[2] Years later Lowry, who said he believed in re-incarnation, maintained that part of his attachment to a later Ann, the one he called his goddaughter, was because she was born at this time.

Then, of course, there were the three girl cousins, all pretty young women with long dark hair and much given in their youth to the wearing of full, frilly skirts with ribbons and bows; and in particular Grace, the eldest, who was a pupil of Elizabeth's and bore a striking resemblance to a 1923 painting by Lowry of a girl wearing a cloche hat

Of Lowry's days in the life class at Manchester School of Art, Fitton recalled: 'The School of Art was full of good looking girls and I was always falling in love. But Lowry might have been in a room with a bunch of retired policemen for all the effect it had upon him...the others would tease me about my amours, but not Lowry. He would listen when I spoke of them...but it didn't seem to impinge upon his mind simply because the sexual urge was not there. I formed the impression – and it is one I retain to this day – that Lowry was an asexual being, a kind of neuter. He was interested in, and affected by, women but only in the way that

would not have spoken to her of that. She would not have liked it.'

When Riley pressed him further, he became embarrassed and added quickly: 'She died when still a young girl. Of the 'flu. Her name was Ann.'

She was the first he named specifically as Ann – the name that has become a kind of shorthand to describe Lowry's muse: The Image of Ann.

The first, too, to have suffered an early, tragic death.

He told the same story to the art critic Mervyn Levy, giving the date of the farmer's daughter's death as 1913.

Clifford Openshaw, who came into Lowry's life in 1928, heard of another girl. She was called Maud and she was 'the daughter of some friends of my mother'. She lived with her parents in Lytham St. Anne's and he visited them frequently in the time that Openshaw knew Lowry. She was a dancer who, on the verge of fame had become disillusioned with that world and had 'given

*The people who did live in that house, questioned in the '70s, insisted that they never knew L S Lowry.

Top left: Pat Cooke took this picture of Lowry during a visit to Lytham St. Anne's. He told her it was the house in which Ann lived. 'I believed him implicitly' she said.

he was interested in, and affected by, people. He persistently avoided any area that might demand involvement.'[3]

In retrospect Fitton professed surprise that Lowry did not marry. 'There must have been women in the same physical condition as he, women who wanted not a lover, but a companion. Lowry would have been a very caring companion. He was an eminently gentle man. But possibly his mother's dominance prevented marriage.'[4]

Fitton seems to have forgotten his own earlier assertion that Lowry was a loner, that he was well content with his own company and the last thing he would have wanted was a constant companion: 'He avoided any friendships that would have impinged upon his personal solitude.' Or, as Lowry

Above: A year after his mother's death, he painted a picture of her empty room and told a friend: 'I had no interest in life after she died...her death made all the difference to my life.' *The Bedroom, Pendlebury,* 1940.

137

Right: It was, Lowry said, the first portrait he had painted for thirty years and he had done it because 'she insisted I did.' After due and proper deliberation the painting was accepted for the Royal Academy's Spring Exhibition where it caused the predictable stir, both in the press and with a public more accustomed to works of industrial desolation from L S Lowry. No-one seemed to realise that he had been painting pictures of a girl called Ann, in one guise or another, for nearly forty years. *Portrait of Ann*, 1957.

Far right: In the '20s, Lowry and his family spent what holidays they took at his mother's favourite boarding house not far from the beach where tennis was played. *The Tennis Player*, 1927.

himself said: 'I was obsessed with painting. I couldn't have gone on as I did and been fair to a wife. When I painted seriously I painted not from ten 'till four, you know. But from ten 'till about twelve [midnight] or two in the morning. You couldn't do that and be fair to the wife.'[5]

This last statement was one which a later commentator, an eminent psychiatrist, called an 'excuse', rather than a genuine reason and typical of the kind of rationalisation offered by true loners such as Lowry.

When he moved to Salford Art College where quite a few of the female students, not to mention the models, were again possessed of striking good looks, there was one called Ada Jones, whom he is said to have

met out of school–for weekend outings with their sketch books. There is no record of Lowry himself ever having spoken of her but local rumour has it that he was rather taken with her; one of her friends firmly believes the couple were once engaged to be married but there is no mention of this in any of Lowry's papers, nor any other person who claims this as fact.

There was one other fellow student of whom he spoke frequently. 'I have never married, never had a girl in fact. There was *one* girl at art school. Then one October she wasn't there and that was the end of that. I think I must have been what they call a "cold fish". Even now I prefer to be by myself'.[6] When he spoke those words–to the critic Edwin Mullins–he was nearly eighty.

Once, in the '20s, while on a visit to Manchester City Art Gallery with her husband, Edith Timplerley came across Lowry in the company of a young girl. 'She was very small. Smaller than me and I am barely five foot. And she was younger than me. I was twenty-one. She was very pale and very sad; her features were fine, her face intelligent and sensitive. She had about her an air of faded gentility. She appeared nicely dressed until you looked closely at her; she had on a blue serge coat which the wind went right through–it was no wonder she looked half starved with the cold. It was obviously her only respectable coat but quite unsuitable for the weather. I found her pitiful. This slim child haunted me for days. I have never forgotten her. Some time later, when the boys were taking me to the Christmas pantomime, I suggested to Lowry that he brought this girl with him. He said he could not. If he went out she would stay at home with his mother; Elizabeth could not be left and it was this girl, apparently, who stayed with her when both Lowry and his father were away.

'I was surprised, initially, to find Lowry in the company of a young woman. He had never mentioned her to us and yet there was an obvious bond between them. He treated her with immaculate concern.'[7]

Years later, when Lowry came in great distress to stay in the Timperleys' home after the death of his mother, Edith tried to think of someone who might care for him, as she had cared for him. She enquired about the frail young woman who had so impressed her on that one meeting. 'Oh,' said Lowry abruptly, 'she's dead. She came to my mother's funeral, caught a cold and died.'[8] His discomfort was so great that Edith asked no more. But she formed the impression that 'it was the double shock, the double blow of the death not only of his mother but of this girl as well, that nearly sent him over the edge.'[9]

Chapter 10

'Her name is Ann.'

Once Lowry had returned home after his brief respite at the Timperleys', friends and neighbours rushed to invite him for lunch or dinner or walks across the Moss, anxious that he should not feel too alone in the old house. They little realised that his was exactly what he needed to feel – alone.

He pondered endlessly as to why people were 'so kind'. It puzzled him. 'What do they want of me?' he would ask Edith. 'What can I offer them – why are they so good?' This rallying of good neighbours was something foreign to Lowry; so long as his mother had lived they knew he would not leave her and had not bothered to ask. Now they were anxious to help, if help were needed.

One such was Enoch Leatherbarrow, a local shopkeeper and Methodist lay preacher. They had met on a bus soon after Elizabeth's death when Lowry was in a state of visible confusion, and had quickly struck up a friendship; soon afterwards they had started taking long walks across the Irwell Valley together, during which they enjoyed a companionable silence. Now, Enoch Leatherbarrow began inviting Lowry for supper or Sunday lunch where he entertained the children with games of push-halfpenny and silly jokes. Embarrassed by so much taking and so little giving – as he saw it – Lowry asked Leatherbarrow if he might invite their 13-year-old daughter, Kathleen, and a friend to the pantomime. They worried that he might be bored by the company of a girl forty years his junior but, observing his delight in childish pleasures, worried no further. It was, nonetheless, an undertaking Lowry viewed with some trepidation and when the great day arrived he acted, according to Kathleen, 'like a cat on hot bricks'.

The outing was the beginning of a friendship that lasted until Kathleen married and moved away in 1948, when their correspondence continued spasmodically before drifting to an amicable silence. But when he died a photograph of Kathleen in Wren's uniform, which she had sent him not long after she had enlisted some months before the end of the war, still stood on his mother's piano. She had signed it 'With much love from Kathleen'. The portrait of her which Lowry had painted from it remained, thirty years later, in his studio; he had given her parents a signed copy but refused to part with the original. It now forms part of the Lowry Estate collection.

Kathleen was surprised by the sentiment implicit in the discovery. She had observed no particular emotion in their relationship, simply a mutual pleasure in each other's company. 'I felt almost as if he were enjoying my childhood vicariously, as if, perhaps, he had had none of his own. There was a sadness within him that I could not define...

'He was a vastly unconventional man fettered by the conventions of his nature and of his upbringing, and, as an unconventional child myself, this appealed to me. There always seemed to be, in him, a little boy struggling to get out.

'Looking back, I wasn't aware of him being any particular age, simply an adult and, in that, unusual in having time for me. He

Left: Lowry took several holidays in Ireland with Pat and Brian Cooke. Much against his usual practice, he bought several notebooks while there in order to capture the scenes that attracted him. Once again the horse is half hidden – Lowry became skilled at finding ways of disguising the fact that he was not adept at drawing horses. *The Cart,* 1953.

never treated me as a child, but as an equal. Even though I was young he took notice of my opinion and, in fact, seemed to value it. He was so genuine himself that it seemed that only in young people, who had as yet not discovered the need for pretension or guile, could he find the same honesty.

'If I saw a picture he had done that I didn't like I would say so, if he asked, and that fascinated him. "What's wrong with it?" he would pester, "What don't you like about it?" If it was one of those horrible heads, I would answer: "Well, it frightens me," and he would nod gravely as if I had made a statement of great profundity. He often said that those heads "just happened"–that he didn't set out to paint them but that they appeared on the canvas almost as if he had nothing to do with their creation. And they frightened him too.'

Kathleen's father accepted the relationship between the artist and his daughter as

an innocent means of bringing light into the life of a man in deep depression. Her mother, Lillian, initially had certain reservations. 'You should not call upon him alone,' she cautioned, but her daughter was a rebel and continued to visit Lowry whenever she wished. 'He behaved immaculately at all times. Young though I was I would have soon noticed if there had been anything fishy about him, and I'd have run a mile. I can't remember him ever putting a

foot wrong. Whenever he actually invited me to the house, a friend was invariably included. He made an enormous fuss of us when we went to tea; there would be cream cakes, masses of them, and chocolates, all laid out on a trolley in the front room. He would make the tea himself, whistling as he did so. He had a marvellous way of making one feel very special.'[1]

Even when she arrived on roller skates, he displayed no surprise, in much the same

Above: Lowry once told Monty Bloom that he had been tempted to put a mill chimney in the middle of a lake landscape. 'But then they'd only call me Salvadore Lowry,' he added savouring the conjunction of the two names. *The Lake,* 1951.

way that he treated the appearance of any of his unconventional friends as quite unworthy of comment. 'If he met me in the street,' remarked Margo Ingham, part owner with her husband Ned Owens of the Mid-day Studios in Manchester, 'and I was all in purple, hair included, with a skirt half way up my thighs, he never betrayed by so much as a flicker that he thought my appearance in any way remarkable.'[32]

The 14-year-old friend, Margery Thompson, who was a frequent companion with Kathleen on outings to the pantomime or to tea with Lowry, was to develop a relationship of her own with the artist. 'I have never forgotten that first outing. He seemed to enjoy it as much as we did, except that he was enormously worried by the responsibility of taking out two young girls.'

In time Margery came to call him 'Pop', though very much later and after she had married. He called her 'The Infant', as much, she said, as a reflection upon the difference in their ages as to establish that 'he had no designs upon my person.' In her teens she would tease him gently about his chances of 'getting off with' her widowed mother. 'He didn't like that one bit and would mumble about it all being nonsense because he was far too old for her; she was, in fact, just three years younger than him. But I soon realised he didn't like such jokes, that he was uncomfortable in the face of expectations of role playing that he was unable to fulfil. I soon stopped.'

Margery saw the house in Station Road, with its soft gas light and blazing fires, as a place of infinite mystery and fascination, where they spent afternoons filled with laughter. She remembers particularly the way he escorted her to the bus stop when she left with 'a kind of old world courtesy that came naturally to him.'

He took her to concerts to expand her appreciation of music and afterwards would ask her intently: 'What did you think of that?' She rarely knew what to say. 'Most times I would wait for him to express his opinion then, after a suitable pause, bring it out as one of my own. I am sure he knew what was going on. There was always an air of amusement about him. He wasn't laughing at me, but at life. He was always surprised by life; he never lost his sense of wonder. At times he would almost parody himself. "Child", he would say in doleful tones, "there's nothing, nothing left. Now get on with your tea."

'He was always quoting de la Rochefoucauld at me, things like "Friendship is just a business arrangement", which hurt. I took such maxims personally. I thought he meant him and me...

'When I knew him he used to wear a battered raincoat and, when we went to concerts, it would get rolled up in a bundle and shoved under the seat. Once he took me to tea in the Midland Hotel...Suddenly, without warning, he took the lid off the tea pot and stirred the tea noisily. Everyone turned round with raised eyebrows. I was young and must have shown my embarrassment. "These people,' he said, "don't know me and I don't know them. It doesn't matter, does it?"

Lowry encouraged Margery's interest in painting, giving her occasional lessons. Once she did a painting of a house which he liked and wanted her to finish. 'But...I did not realise how eager he was. I thought he was humouring me and so I never bothered. I did not understand, then, how important it was to him to have someone who took art seriously.'

In 1954 Margery married and moved to Southampton, after which Lowry visited occasionally and wrote spasmodically until, eventually, the friendship faded. 'He used to write copious, copious letters while I was in the Forces, about all sorts of things, concerts that he went to and how he couldn't concentrate there, that he would rather listen to it on the radio, because "the shape

of the gentleman's nose" would be too distracting, and about pictures, about my work, about my family which he used to visit. So, later, when he didn't reply to my letters I didn't mind because he had been so good about writing to me all those years before. One time I said to him, did he like getting letters? Yes, he did, but he didn't like writing them. Well, I said, would he like to get letters and not answer them? Oh, he couldn't do that. You see how Victorian he was really? Well, I said, if you don't mind not answering them, I am very pleased to write to you. Oh, all right then. Well, I didn't mean he hadn't to answer anything, which is rather what he did. I went up several times to see him only to find the bird was missing.'[3]

At about the same time as Lowry was entertaining Kathleen and Margery to tea and cakes, a new arrival in the offices of the Pall Mall Property Company had also caught his attention. Her name was Doreen Crouch. She was 15 years old and she came to work as a temporary replacement for the young clerk, Clifford Openshaw, who had gone off to war. But she was 'a blonde, plump, buxom teenager, reserved and terribly shy...'[4] and as such never became what others described as an 'Ann figure' in his life.

None the less, he was to have a strong influence on the development of her artistic appreciation although she was hardly aware of it at the time. 'I didn't know much about music,' she recalled, 'but my mother and I were both fond of it and I had picked up some knowledge from her. Mr. Lowry quickly realised this from the odd snatches I would whistle around the office. "That's from so-and-so," he would say, almost as if he was trying to educate me. Sometimes he would ask: "Have you read so-and-so?" and if I said: "No," a few day later he would turn up in the office with a copy of whatever it was for me to read.' She was grateful for his interest and reciprocated when she could by doing Lowry's household shopping for him.

Three years later, in October 1948, Doreen married and Lowry was a witness at her wedding. 'It was,' she said, 'the only time in my life I ever kissed him. I remember him looking quite astonished when, in the emotion of the day, I went up to him and gave him a warm peck on the cheek. He was not displeased, I could see that in his eyes. He was always very careful to keep his shell around him but, on occasion, I could see beneath it. There was a look there that I could recognise and if I ever tried to probe, immediately the barriers would come up again. I often felt there were times when he would have appreciated a good big hug–but I never dared. I was undemonstrative too; as an only child I too had a shell and so appreciated, and respected his.' After her marriage he became more of a family friend, helping with the washing up after supper or dandling their daughter, Christine, on his knee. But in 1956 Doreen and her Polish husband John Sieja emigrated to Canada, mainly for the sake of Christine's health. They wrote for several years, chatty letters from her with news of the family, from him with news of the office and the doings of the now not so young Clifford Openshaw. Inevitably the

Above: An informal snapshot of Lowry sketching in Ireland, taken by either Pat or Brian Cooke–neither of them could remember which one took it. Lowry often said that he avoided work whenever possible; this lake landscape was obviously more than he could resist.

Over page: The incongruity of people apparently going nowhere was exactly the sort of scene that Lowry most enjoyed. Eccentricity and absurdity were grist to his mill. *People walking towards the Sea,* 1965.

letters became fewer and fewer until 1970 when they stopped altogether.

Lowry's eventual move from the family home in Pendlebury, with its locked room in which his mother died, was prompted more by circumstance than desire. Had the landlord of 117 Station Road, one Louis Duffy, not required the house for his own use, it is more than possible that Lowry would have remained cocooned in comfortable familiarity for the rest of his life. He had no particular urge to leave Salford, and professed to hate the house in Mottram-in-Longdendale, on the windy fringes of the Derbyshire peaks, where he went in 1948. He always said he had bought The Elms because some friends, Frank and Constance Bradley, lived near-by but, after only a few months they moved away leaving him in his new home, miles from the city centre and even further from Salford with its inspirational landscape and poignant memories.

He came to The Elms in the August and in the following September there arrived on his doorstep 'a scruffy village kid' clutching a roll of her drawings. She had been brought by her father, Frank Gerrard, a local builder who had been working on alterations to the artist's new home. That first meeting, while friendly enough, gave no hint of the importance and influence their subsequent relationship was to have upon the future of this 'gauche and gawky child.'[5] Her name was Pat Gerrard, later to become known as the artist Pat Cooke.

'He was very kind,' she recalled, 'but I was young and drawing the usual rubbish you draw then, too influenced by others, too pretty-pretty. I knew the work was hopeless, not from anything he said, but by the things he advised me to do: to go out and draw from life. "Only draw what you know," he told me. He said nothing hurtful; he never did, never about anything. He would always try and lead you; this was his way.'

Pat went out and drew as Lowry had ad-

vised and, when it was done, took it back to show him. From that time on she visited him each week, straight from school.

'I learned so much from him. He made me draw from the thing, made me observe the real thing first and then adapt it to my own style, but never, never to get my ideas from art books or other paintings...'

After leaving school and spending two years at Manchester School of Art, Pat decided to try for a place at one of Britain's premier art colleges, the Slade. She collected together the work she had done and went once more to Lowry for advice. 'He looked at my work carefully, and without speaking. And then, quite out of the blue, he said: "I'll write you a note to the Slade and put it in with the one from your Art School." I'm sure that had more to do than anything with me getting in there.'

Over the next three years the relationship developed into a real friendship. He visited her in London, taking her to concerts, to the theatre or to Brighton by steam train for the day to marvel at the Georgian façades or explore the wonders of the pier. Pat was no longer 'a scruffy village kid' but a beautiful young woman with an almost childlike delight in life and a smile that lit up her face. She had a keen sense of humour and a ready, infectious laugh. Lowry expanded visibly in her presence, but was particularly protective of their privacy, rarely introducing her to other acquaintances. In a man as firmly wedded to compartmentalisation in his life and the isolation of his friendships, this was not in itself surprising; but with Pat he was even more possessive than usual; as if he wanted nothing or no-one to impinge upon their friendship. He was to repeat this pattern, usually for no more than a year, with each of his subsequent protégés. 'It was quite a difficult thing to please him in the end because he wanted a hundred per cent of your attention a hundred per cent of the time. He was very demanding and a very powerful personality.

'He was enormously interested in everything and everyone...he didn't sit and stare at people, he just soaked it all in. Because he was so much alone he could observe that much easier. He was always telling me: "Be by yourself and observe; you can only do it if you walk alone."'

When she left the Slade at the age of 21, Pat became an art teacher in Altrincham, Cheshire. Two years later, in 1957, she married Brian Cooke, a young scientist and moved to Knutsford, some ten miles away. 'He [Lowry] was not so much upset that I had married, more that I had moved away and could no long just pop in to see him. On the other hand, he did tire of people; he tired of everyone sooner or later. Each friend had his or her allotted span in Mr Lowry's life and when it was done, he moved on. I don't think anyone was important to him after his Mummy died. I did at one time flatter myself that I might have been; but although he enjoyed my company and the fun we had, I don't think any of it really mattered to him...Subtly he always let one know that there was another Ann around the corner.'

After her marriage, Pat felt instinctively that her relationship with the artist had changed yet again. Lowry had established an easy rapport with Pat's husband Brian and the three would travel together for holidays in Sunderland or Ireland or where ever took their fancy.

'I was no longer the scruffy village kid, nor even the student; I was his jester, his clown. I suppose in a way we did look incongruous together, me with my back combed hair and elaborate eye make-up. In Ireland I often used to see people eyeing me curiously, and I would nudge him and together we would speculate about them speculating about us. Mr Lowry was fascinated by my make-up, particularly my eyes. He would watch me intently putting it on in the car, asking: "Why do you do that?" or saying: "Put on some more black stuff." He was

disappointed I didn't wear nail varnish; he
loved long red nails.'

It is interesting that in most of the portraits he did at this time of unnamed
women, or one called Ann, they invariably
wore the heavy eye make-up that Pat used
throughout the '60s and beyond. In only a
few of his later drawings, discovered after
his death, did Lowry give his women fear-
some long nails.

'There was nothing sexual in his interest.
He had no real understanding of sexuality,
because, I believe, he had no experience of it.
I remember him being obsessed with a play
called *The Devils*, starring Dorothy Tutin;
he went to see it at least half a dozen times

and was always talking about it. But the
sexuality baffled him. I think he kept going
to see it in the hope that one day it would
all become magically clear to him. I don't
think it ever did.'

In much the same way he later became
fascinated by the London production of
Pirandello's *Six Characters in Search of an
Author* which he returned to see three, if
not four or more times. The play, according to one critic, was '...the tragedy of a
man tormented by the enigma of personality...[...]...he achieves intelligence only to
recognise that he can communicate with no
one, not even with himself, and that no one
can communicate with him – that he is, in

151

L.S.Lowry 1959

the fullest sense alone.'[6]

Pat was one of the few people to whom he showed the stress which each exhibition caused him. 'They really made him awfully poorly. Sometimes, if it had been a big show, he would get an attack of the shingles. Each exhibition took so much out of him, but he never showed it to those outside. He never let on how much he cared.' He became irritated by the fact that Pat needed to exhibit her work regularly and was constantly advising her to slow down. If they were sitting quietly together, on the sea-front or in the window of a Sunderland hotel, he would shout suddenly: 'Stop it', and knock the sketch book from her hand. His behaviour puzzled her but she accepted it because she loved him and he had given her so much. She dedicated one show to him and, although she had first asked his permission, when the time came he was embarrassed and didn't turn up.

'He hated anything that smacked of pretension or pomposity. But when I dedicated my Salford show to my father, his reaction was quite different. He came to the opening, even though he had been ill...And just as he was leaving, he came over to me in the middle of the gallery and kissed me on the cheek. I was so astonished and touched; he was not a man who liked personal contact and that was the only time in my life he ever volunteered a kiss. Latterly, in old age, he enjoyed a goodbye peck but he never returned it.'

After he died she said; 'He left me a wonderful legacy: the memory of so much happiness, the sheer pleasure of his company and the privilege of sharing the thoughts of such an incredible mind.'

It was Lowry, himself, who initiated a meeting with the landscape artist Sheila Fell. He had been taken, unwillingly, to her first exhibition at the Beaux Arts Gallery in London after which he specifically asked to meet the artist–a request which cannot

Left: A rare medium for Lowry; watercolour. He once said that he was no good at painting with watercolours because he was inclined to use them like oils. On occasions, visiting friends with children of school age he would borrow their paints – 'for a bit of fun'. *Yachts*, 1959.

Over page: A bird's eye view from the perpetual observer. The industrial north at play. *The Bandstand, Peel Park, Salford*, 1931.

153

have been totally unrelated to the stunning photograph of Sheila Fell at work, displayed in the catalogue: she was small and slight, with large almond-shaped eyes, long dark hair and full red lips. An archetypal Ann figure if ever there was one – all of which is not to diminish the impact upon him of her work which he genuinely admired. Perhaps it was the happy combination of the two that attracted him.

He had already bought two of her pictures when they met by arrangement early in 1956 and went for lunch in a small Greek restaurant in Bloomsbury that Lowry knew from outings with Pat. He had lamb chops, she had octopus – a fact that intrigued him almost as much as the amount that this tiny woman could eat at a sitting. She was somewhat on her guard, not knowing what to expect of him or indeed what was expected of her; she thought he looked rather like Jacques Tati, with the same almost zany sense of humour. (She was not the only one to note the similarity: a waiter in a Welsh hotel he visited with the collector Monty Bloom, insisted that he looked like Jacques Tati playing General de Gaulle and took delight in addressing him each morning at breakfast as *Mon Général*.)

Suddenly, without preamble or warning, he leaned across the table and said: 'Look here, Miss Fell, how are you off for money?' She said she was all right although, of course, she was not. 'Well,' he went on, 'I would like to meet your parents. I like your work and I would like to help you. Would £3 a week be agreeable?'

Sheila took some persuading. 'I wanted to struggle as I knew he had struggled.' Finally, however, she gave in and took him home to Aspatria, the Cumberland village in which her parents lived. 'Somehow it was all arranged between them, almost as if I had nothing to do with it. I got the feeling that he could have, would have, given me more, but he didn't want to make things too easy for me. He knew me very well. Right up un-

Right: The artist in the image of Ann. Her name, in fact, was Sheila. Sheila Fell. And she was a landscape artist. After his death, she said of Lowry: 'I miss his wit, I miss his humour, I miss him...As a companion he was marvellously humorous, inquisitive, mischievous as a child and gentle, but he was more than that: he had great shrewdness and understanding. In short, he was unique.'

til the time he died, he knew me very well.'[7]

That summer and for many summers afterwards, Lowry 'hung his hat and walking stick on the railings' at the bottom of their garden. Most times he came by arrangement but 'sometimes he would arrive unexpectedly for the odd weekend–once in his carpet slippers by taxi, all the way from Manchester'.

It was, according to Sheila, 'the beginning of a long, and for me, a very enriching friendship. Knowing him changed my life because, had it not been for him, I think I would have just gone down. Nobody liked my work. If he hadn't come into that first exhibition and bought, it would have been a total flop. He was the one person I could rely upon to buy and to keep on buying. We never did drift apart,' she said. 'Ours was the sort of relationship that renewed itself every time we met.

'When he was in Cumberland with me we would go out together while I was doing seascapes, really big ones out in the open air

and the wind...mostly he would just sit and watch or go for a walk; sometimes he too would draw and once, when we had worked all day, sitting facing Skiddaw, I looked to see what he had done; it was an industrial landscape.'

Much the same thing happened to the artist Harold Riley. He and Lowry had gone to the Lake District together and, after a day sketching beside Wasswater, the deepest and darkest of the lakes, Riley glanced at Lowry's sketch to find that he had put a tall, black chimney emerging from the water. 'I must have shown my surprise,' recalled Riley, 'because Mr Lowry looked at me and said: "You can't see it, can you?" I shook my head. "No," I said. "I can," he announced, with a grin. And I do believe he could.'

After Lowry died Sheila, by then herself a Royal Academician, was asked to contribute a few words to the R A catalogue for the 1976 Lowry exhibition. She wrote: 'My admiration of his work was and is enormous; but also of him as a man. As a companion he was marvellously humorous, inquisitive, mischievous as a child, and gentle; but he was more than that: he had great shrewdness and understanding. In short, he was unique.'

Later she said: 'I miss his wit; I miss his humour; I miss him. He was a great humanist and no one ever seems to mention that. To be a humanist one has first to love human beings, and to be a great humanist one has to be slightly detached from human beings after having had great love for them; which is exactly what he was.'[8]

The portrait that Lowry offered to the Royal Academy for their Spring Exhibition in 1958 caused something of a stir. And not in artistic circles alone. The press, too, were quick to take notice. Not only was the painting unusual in that it was a portrait–and this from a man now better known for harsh scenes of industrial desolation–it was also the portrait of a woman: a

young woman with a stern regard and dark hair drawn back from her face to allow full appreciation of her hard black eyes and rich red mouth.

In early 1958 the *News Chronicle* published, to coincide with the opening of the Exhibition, a photograph of Lowry with his surprising portrait. The artist was captured, in paint-bespattered suit, brandishing his brush as if he were a conductor with his baton, and with an expression of such mischief and delight on his face that, were it not for all the other paintings in the image of Ann, one would be tempted to declare the whole thing a huge joke.

The reporters, of course, wanted to know the identity of the sitter. It was called, Lowry announced, still grinning hugely, *Portrait of Ann*. This titbit of information only served to whet the reporters' interest as, no doubt,

it was intended to do. After further probing the artist confided that she was his godchild, the daughter of some friends of his, a girl of distinct opinions and strong will. 'She is a modernist who did not want her picture to be realistic—it had to be stylised.' The sitter herself, he said, 'could paint very nicely—when she likes.' He added: 'She is the only person who can tell me what to do.'

For the first time Lowry was experiencing the curiosity of those who look at a portrait and wonder more about the sitter than the artist, in much the same way that art lovers have for centuries speculated on the identity of Leonardo's *Mona Lisa*.

In 1959, when the portrait was included in Manchester City Art Gallery's Retrospective Exhibition of Lowry's work, it was listed in the catalogue as 'lent by the sitter'. Although there is considerable correspond-

Above: Artist Pat Cooke with her mentor L S Lowry. In the background, on the wall of Lowry's sitting room, directly behind his head is a portrait that Pat painted of him. It was, he said, the best that had been done of him. The one he liked best. *Picture Denis Thorpe.*

157

ence relating to the borrowing of the other exhibits, there are no letters to or from the Goddaughter. So far as anyone at the Gallery could remember, the picture was brought to the exhibition by the artist who gave her name, for the index of lenders, as Miss Ann Helder. In his letters of the time, however, mainly to Doreen in Canada, he referred to her as Ann *Hilder.*

Above: Lowry at home in Mottram in Longdendale.

This simple fact was an early indication of the web of mystery and obfuscation that was to surround the identity of Lowry's Dark Lady. From that time on there was much talk of Ann from the artist himself, many anecdotes, stories of outings, of small adventures, of trips to the Edinburgh Festival, to the Midland Hotel for Christmas lunch, to Devon on holiday in the 'white two-seater Rolls Royce' she had received from her father for her 21st birthday. Many, many tales, but not a single sighting; not a single solitary one on record.

'Ann came in here the other day,' Lowry once announced to the Marshalls of the Stone Gallery, Newcastle upon Tyne. 'Why ever didn't she make herself known?' enquired Mrs Marshall, irritated that she had missed the chance of a face to face meeting with Lowry's elusive muse. 'She wouldn't do that,' he replied, 'she's a very private person.' This missed encounter was typical of the many such missed encounters that littered Lowry's conversation throughout the '50s and '60s. *Ann and I came to call but though we knocked loudly we couldn't make you hear.*[9]

One of many anomalies in these stories was the fact that the earlier paintings of a girl with tied-back hair and kohl-lined eyes – pictures as far back as the '20s and '30s – looked strangely like the '50s Ann. One profile portrait, *Girl Wearing a Cloche Hat,* done in 1923, bears a great resemblance but also shows signs of later additions by the artist – exaggerated eye make-up and a long, dark plait – which begs the question: was he attracted to Ann Hilder because of her resemblance to the early girl, or were the later portraits a true reflection of the later woman? Or was she a complete fiction?

Goddaughter Ann, he had said several times, was born shortly after the death of one of the young Anns, who went to his father's funeral, caught a cold and died. This was in February, 1932 so Ann Hilder or Helder or even Hilda would have been twenty-five, exactly as he told the press, when the Royal Academy Ann was painted.

There was rarely any indication in Lowry's conversation that the relationship amounted to any thing more than a fond goddaughter-godfather friendship. On one occasion, though, in response to Prof. Maitland's eager enquiries on the subject, he responded: 'I wish I had tried to marry her but I'm eighty-three and she's thirty-seven…' 'Well,' replied Maitland, 'it's been known to occur before now.' 'Yes' Lowry replied firmly, 'and it is very foolish.'

To others, on other occasions, he had her variously working with the poor in Naples, running a business in New York, painting at home in Pontefract, doing social work in Reading, and training as a classical dancer in Italy.[10] While still a child, she had lived with her three maiden aunts in Musselburgh, near Edinburgh, after her parents had mysteriously disappeared for the duration of the Second World War. 'They were involved in very secret work that they could never talk about.'

There is not a single one of these particular stories that bears closer investigation. Her portraits, he said, would go to her in his will, but when he died there was no mention of her. And the Lowry family solicitor, Alfred Hulme, whose father had been Lowry's father's solicitor and had helped his mother to make her will, said he was not aware of anyone of any such name in any of Lowry's previous testaments nor had he any recollection of the artist making mention of her.

Those who knew Lowry well and heard him talk of her, who saw his eyes sparkle and his face light up at the mention of her name, are mostly sure that she existed, or even exists, both as the Goddaughter and a flesh and blood person in her own right. 'I could not bear to think he had to make her up,' said one.

As to her place as Lowry's sole inspiration for his Image of Ann, they are less sure. The critic Mervyn Levy accepted the portraits as fantasy while believing in the existence of Ann Hilder. 'They are composite archetypal portraits partly of his goddaughter and partly evocations of his mother and the daughter of a farmer in Swinton Moss near Lytham St Anne's whom Lowry had met and grown close to on childhood holidays.'

In placing Swinton Moss near Lytham St Anne's (which it is not), Mr Levy has confused the earlier Ann with the later Maud, so that they become one person. And who can blame him? The legend of Lowry and his Muse is littered with false leads and dead ends.

Levy continued: 'Ann was therefore one of the dream women and played a role in his personal mythology similar to that occupied by the women of Rossetti, an artist for whose sultry, goitred stunners Lowry possessed a consuming passion.'[11]

Many would dispute that Lowry's 'passion' was for the women themselves, believing more that it was for the artists' conception of them, for the 'workmanship' of the drawings and the 'painterliness' of the Pre-Raphaelites; he collected Ford Maddox Brown and Lord Leighton as well as Dante Gabriel Rossetti. 'I don't like his women

at all, but they fascinate me, like a snake. That's why I always buy Rossetti whenever I can. His women are really rather horrible. It's like a friend of mine, you know, who says he hates my work, although it fascinates him. He's got seven pictures of mine.'[12]

More revealing, perhaps, are Lowry's words spoken to Monty Bloom, who in the '60s became a good friend and an addicted collector of Lowry: 'The Rossetti women are not real women. They are dreams. He used them for something in his mind caused, in my opinion, by the death of his wife.'[13]

Was Lowry, in fact, like the Pre-Raphaelite poet, using his image of a woman called Ann for 'something in his mind caused by the death' of someone dear? And, if so, who was it? Which one of the many had somehow impinged herself upon his mind to the exclusion of all others. Or, again, was it all of them, living and dead, each one of them in possession of the dark regard of the masterwork?

159

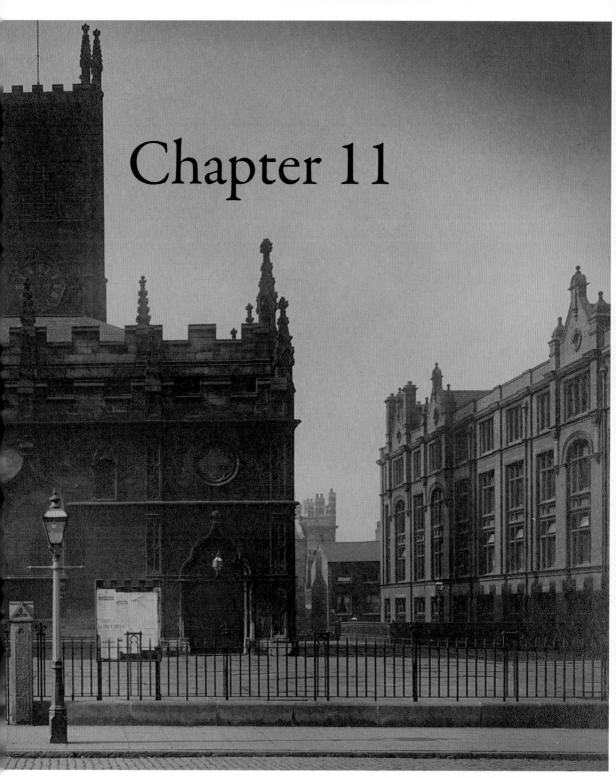

Chapter 11

'They are not real women, but dreams.'

The arrival of the last in the line of Ann figures in Lowry's life is as much the subject of misinformation as he would have wished. One story he told was of the arrival of a woman called Mrs Martha Lowry on his doorstep with her 13-year-old daughter Carol Ann. She wanted to know if they were perhaps related–or so this particular story goes. He invited them in and that was the start of it all.[1]

The girl in question, however, remembers it very differently. How could she forget the arrival on her doorstep of a famous artist, an imposing figure, six foot and over, with a face like carved granite and clear, clear blue eyes? She had with her that day a young friend, Jenny, who equally remembers quite clearly, even so many years later, the occasion of Lowry's arrival one bleak afternoon in 1957 at the small flat in Heywood, near Rochdale, where Carol Ann lived with her mother.

Lowry, never one to miss an opening for a good yarn, also told an alternative version. Earlier that year he had received a letter from Carol Ann Lowry. Could they be related? she asked. The letter intrigued him but, as with so much of his correspondence, he did not reply. He put it in his bulging wallet, along with the invitations, the old envelopes and the assorted letters he used for incidental sketching.

Months passed. Pat married, Doreen emigrated, Sheila immersed herself in her work.

One day in late autumn of that year he was sitting in Piccadilly Gardens, Manchester, wondering what to do with himself. 'I often did that. I didn't want to go home to an empty house.' An early dusk was gathering when of a sudden, through the mist, appeared a bus with the destination clearly marked: Heywood.

As if it were fate.

Lowry took out his wallet and, finding the letter from Carol Ann checked the address: Heywood Road, Heywood. On an impulse he boarded the bus.

The conductor put him off in Heywood Road. He began to search for the house. At a dry cleaner's shop he stopped. It was Tuesday, half-day closing. He knocked and waited while the street lamp at his back projected his silhouette grotesquely against the glass panels of the shop door. Slowly, tentatively, the door opened and in the half-light stood a child.

She was thirteen years old, serious, slender and dark eyed; her long brown hair hung in a single plait over her shoulder.

Lowry stood and stared. It was some moments before he spoke. Long moments, which to Carol Ann seemed longer.

Abruptly, he said: 'Does Miss Carol Ann Lowry live here?' The girl was astonished. No one had ever addressed her so correctly before. She remembers to this day the sound of her own voice: 'I'm Miss Carol Ann Lowry,' she replied with all the confidence she could muster.

'I'm L S Lowry,' he replied. 'Who?' queried the child. Then she remembered. 'Ooh,' she said, her eyes wide, and opened the door fully, stepping aside to let him pass through the shop into the living room beyond. 'As

Left: One of Lowry's fantasy women–shades of Coppelia and the puppet master. unsigned and undated.

163

soon as he was in, he summed up the situation – two small children (I had a little
friend with me), frightened out of their wits.
He asked when my mother would be home.
I told him seven o'clock and he quickly left,
promising to return later.'[2]

He did return later that evening, although
Carol Ann barely remembers the second
visit. Arrangements were made of which the
child was not aware until very much later.
He paid her fees at the convent where she
was currently at school, helped with the rent
on the flat above the dry cleaners, and arranged for her to attend Saturday morning
classes at Rochdale College of Art, where
his friend Leo Solomon was then Principal.

If Carol was surprised at the precipitous
way in which this elderly man entered, influenced and later preoccupied her young
life, she did not remember it that way. Years

later, in her forties, she explained: 'I accepted thing as they came along. Without
question. A fourteen or fifteen-year-old
now is very, very aware and questioning in
a worldly sense; I never was. Even now, I'm
still not. I still accept things. But then I was
even more like that. I was not even aware
that he was a great artist. Not for years.'

From the time of that first meeting in
1957, some months before he revealed his
image of Ann to the Royal Academy, Lowry became to Carol 'more than my mother,
or my father or anyone. He made me. He
moulded me. He fashioned me in his image of Ann and in so doing made me to
a great extent like him. I was sufficiently
young for him to be able to do it; and sufficiently malleable. I think he recognised
that, right from the beginning. Had I been
a different sort of person he would not

have been able to change me, to make of me what he wished.

'Looking back, though I was not aware of it at the time, I think I was filling a gap in his life, supplying perhaps his need for a family. Yet ours was never a father and a daughter relationship; he was more of a grandfather, a fairy godfather who came along with gifts, not merely material gifts, but gifts of character and education. He taught me so much and displayed, by example, the virtues of perception, of humility and of humour. When he found me, I was at an impressionable age and of an impressionable nature: I cannot help but feel it was fate that brought us together, that enabled each of us to fulfil a need in the other.'

It had been her mother's idea to write to the artist whose name they bore. Mrs Lowry, usually known as Mattie, was a weaver by trade and had recently separated from her husband, William, a cotton-spinner. Carol grew up in Rochdale, a quiet, thoughtful girl in whom all Mattie Lowry's ambitions and aspirations lay. Life was not easy. She sent her only child to private school and worked twice as hard to meet the cost of the fees and the uniform. In the daytime, after she had left the weaving sheds, she cooked chips in a Bury tripe shop and in the evenings helped out in the bar of a nearby hotel. It was here that she heard talk of L S Lowry and determined that Carol should write to him. One evening, Mrs Lowry arrived home, found pen and paper, sat Carol down at the kitchen table and dictated a letter. 'I remember thinking what a silly idea it was,' Carol recalled, 'writing to someone we didn't know. But mother was like that – very ambitious for me. She had a bee in her bonnet that it would help me. But nothing happened and we just went on with the routine. We never got a reply.'

Only a visit six months later.

'He seemed to be my friend right away, rather than my mother's. He treated me as a child, but in an adult way. He never talked

down to me. Gradually, as I got older, our relationship changed though, again, I was not aware of it. He became someone whose company I enjoyed, whom I loved and who was important to me, without me realising it. I accepted him and his presence in my life without question. He was simply "Uncle Laurie"; the name seemed come naturally after I had called him "Uncle" inadvertently a few times. It's funny but in all those years of calling him "Uncle Laurie" and him introducing me, on occasion, as his niece no-one ever said, in my presence, "Well, come on then. How are you related, exactly?" I'm sure some must have checked.'

As with the other girls he befriended, with Carol he behaved immaculately. According to her: 'He was always, invariably, extremely circumspect in his behaviour towards me. Very much later, when I was grown up, people put it into my head that he might have felt differently towards me, but I absolutely cannot believe it to have been so. I don't think there was ever a physical thing for him, with any woman. He was a passionate man, but not in the way that we understand passion with all its sexual undertones: he was passionately involved with the mills,

Top: A critic once called Lowry an entomologist 'stalking human insects with his butterfly net...Lowry has become a collector of people.' *Girl in a Red Hat on a Promenade*, undated.

passionate about music, passionate about his mother...I never saw any of the possessiveness or jealousies that others talk of. We would discuss together subjects like love and marriage, in relation to me and my future and he never displayed any resentment, any fears for me in that respect.'

It was in this spirit of confidence in Lowry's understanding of her and her emotions, that Carol Ann married a property dealer and former pilot, John Spiers, without warning and without a single member of her family present. She knew her mother would disapprove–no man was good enough for her daughter–and so opted to exclude everyone rather than hurt her mother further by telling others while neglecting to tell her. Her mother was predictably irate; Lowry appeared to be both understanding and accepting.

'He never said anything to me that indicated, even obliquely, that he might have been upset; I sensed no change in his attitudes or his affection towards me. But many people have told me since that he was indeed very upset. Perhaps I misjudged the situation, or the strength of his possessiveness of me. I hope I did not. I hope he was not hurt. I would never have intentionally hurt him, not for anything.'

She was confident that had she confided in him, he would not have tried to influence her. 'He would have said, as he always did: "You must do what you think best, Carol." He only led and guided you, never made your decisions for you; he would never presume to try to sway you, but would simply indicate, perhaps by a gesture or a look whether he approved of your actions or not.'

He gave them, as a wedding present, a painting of three cows by James Lloyd, an artist they both admired; forty years later it still hung in pride of place in her home.

Throughout her years at college–first at Hornsey, and later at Swansea, where she qualified as an art teacher–Lowry wrote regularly to Carol Ann and visited her and

took her away on holiday, to London or Sunderland or Scotland. He gave her a more than generous allowance and, when she began teaching, settled a five-figure sum upon her. He did not tell her that, in 1970, he had made his will in her favour. 'He had given me so much, I didn't expect any more.'

But now, with her marriage, friends and acquaintances, observing that he had not been present at the wedding, assumed a rift. They decided that he would now change his will. He did no such thing. He left everything just as it was, just as he had decreed in 1970.

Despite repeated prompting, Carol Ann has never assumed her part in Lowry's life to be more important to him than any other. 'I think' she said, 'that I was simply the tag-end of what I, for want of a better

description, call the Ann thing. I filled a gap
when he needed it and, perhaps, had he lived
longer or had he been younger when we met,
he would have passed from me to another,
younger, Ann. I was fortunate, enormously
fortunate, that I was the last.'

After Lowry's death the discovery of a
stash of hidden drawings, beautiful, disturbing, dark drawings that some critics
have dubbed Lowry's erotic work, gave her
cause to wonder about the true nature of his
regard for her. For a brief moment she feared
that she was the model.

The feeling did not last–there are
similarities in these drawings to so many of
the Ann figures that there is no reason for
Carol Ann to assume that it was she alone
who inspired them.

None the less it came as something of a
shock to her when they were first laid before her.

In the cold, grey days after Lowry's death,
when his will was still the subject of ill-in-
formed speculation, Carol Ann received a
call from one of the artist's executors. There
were some private things that had been
found in his house and now rested, officially
sealed, in the vaults of the National Westminster in Manchester. It was felt that she
should see them. Carol Ann went, as summoned, to the bank and there, in the vaults
was shown a collection of unseeen, unknown
Lowry works.

There were drawings and paintings, some
meticulously worked, some barely begun, of a young, slender girl, her dark hair
drawn into a single plait. She is dressed as a
ballet dancer, a doll, a puppet, her costume
cut low to reveal the sensuous curve of her
breasts or the dark shadow of her nipples.
Some are delicate, tender, innocent; others
violent and bloody; in one her head is sev-
ered from her body with a mighty sweep of
an axe, in another with a sword, in yet another with a knife. In one she is prostrate
beneath a guillotine, her head half separated from her body. In some the collar of her

grotesque costume is monstrously huge, like an instrument of medieval torture; in another it is a metal belt that confines her. She is alone, the presence of a man only occasionally indicated by the hand that wields the weapon. In only one, an oil, is another presence suggested, a shadowy, ghostly shape who stand behind, less an observer than a puppet-master, a man who pulls the strings. The manipulator. The controller.

Some were revealed only years later, hidden or over-painted beneath a few of his more traditional works–an elongated, penile shaped figure converted into a wall behind which lurked Lowry's people, a bridge between two mills, or a rock in the sea where the dangerous looking stiletto heels of the woman's shoes have become a spike of stone.

At first, looking at the array of women there, in a dingy bank vault, in the presence of two elderly men, Lowry's executors, Carol Ann felt herself blushing. She was embarrassed, more by the surprise of the discovery than by the content. After a moment, though, she felt herself go cold. In one of the drawings the girl had a distinctly retrousé nose, very like her own.

'My God, it's me.'

It was only later, when she was able to look privately at these strangely beautiful, yet–to her–enormously disturbing works, that she was able to think clearly about them. 'They are not me explicitly,' she said, 'And they are not Ann the Godchild. They are the dream figure–the image of an Ann that haunted him...

'They are the essence of his real, his secret, his private image of Ann, whoever or whatever she was; the one who somewhere, sometime in his life, hurt him dreadfully. Or perhaps it was all of us, each in our own way who hurt him.'[3]

As the critic Richard Dorment, wrote in the *Daily Telegraph* after visiting the Arts Council Centenary Exhibition at the Barbican in 1988: 'The section of the exhibition I found most revealing of Lowry's troubled inner life was that devoted to the late pencil drawing of the 1970s. A grotesque young girl with clawlike fingernails encased in a mini-skirt that looks like an instrument of torture...[...]...seemed to me to reveal a sexual anxiety which is never so much as hinted at in the work of the previous 60 years.'

Viewing these works thirty years after the artist's death, an eminent Irish psychiatrist, saw in them no eroticism, only a dreadful fear of female sexuality. He saw the restricting collars and belts the women wore, less as a form of punishment, more as a kind of strait-jacket.

'A safe adult woman is a woman that's in a strait-jacket,' is what Professor Michael Fitzgerald of Trinity College, Dublin, believes these pictures signify. 'Lowry must have been terrified of sexuality. Completely terrified.

'He was a child. Himself and his mother, that was a mother and child relationship. At home, even though he looked after her, he was still the child. He had to compartmentalise himself, to keep himself away from these women, and it's almost phallic–I know these were the fashion at the time, these high shoes, but they are slightly phallic. It's just the phallic woman is the most dangerous woman. She's the real dominatrix.'[4]

To many of the critics the discovery of Lowry's hidden works came as much of a surprise as they had to Dorment. None, however, was able to offer a solution to the intriguing question: who or what was the muse?

To his young protégés they had come as more of a shock than a surprise: Pat Gerrard refused to acknowledge them as his work: 'He could not have done them,' she said vehemently, 'unless it was for a joke.'[5] She had not seen them, only heard the rumours–inevitably exaggerated. 'I don't believe they could be his work',[6] announced Sheila Fell, deeply distressed by one draw-

Right: The teenage Carol Ann with her mentor and friend, L S Lowry – or Uncle Laurie as she later came to call him. 'He taught me so much,' she said after his death, 'and displayed, by example, the virtues of perception, of humility and of humour.'

Far Right: One of Lowry's haunted faces in an imaginary portrait that he entitled. *Boy in a Yellow Jacket*, 1935

ing she had seen reproduced in a newspaper. 'I think they must have been designs for a ballet or a dance,' said the dealer Tilly Marshall who had dealt with a wide range of Lowry works.

None of them had seen the originals.

Only Carol Ann accepted them, unquestioningly, as his. She had no choice: she knew where they had been found and there was no denying his immaculate workmanship. Later she was to discover similar, violent sketches on the backs of Christmas cards or bills, and bits of tortured figures painted on both sides of heavy cardboard and then torn into little pieces which she painstakingly tried to fit together, much as one would a jigsaw puzzle, in an attempt to discover the secret of Ann. It was an impossible task.

And so despite much research and many questions, the truth of the origins of Lowry's image of Ann remains, as he would have wished, as much of an enigma as her creator. Was the true muse the first Ann, the girl who in dying young retained her innocence and her mystery? Or did she insinuate herself into his life even earlier, perhaps without a meeting or a word – a child when he was a child, seen playing in her frilled skirts and satin bows on the sands at Lytham? Or a pupil of his mother's, sitting obediently at the piano playing her scales? Or perhaps a servant girl, her voluptuous youth encased in whalebone stays, like the tortured girl in the hidden works?

Was she perhaps the slight dark girl who opened the door of 117 Station Road to visitors when Elizabeth was still alive? Or the pale, fragile creature whom Edith Tim-

Right and Far right:
A late drawing of
Lowry's titled *Grotesque
Figure* 1970. Lowry in his
studio viewing one of his
many portraits of Ann
H. His formal painting
attire of a three-piece
suit and tie covered
by the paint-flecked
protective overcoat

tery who kept herself to herself?

Is Ann then a composite figures as his industrial scenes were so often composite scenes? Was she a fantasy of love he never knew but always feared to find? Was the pain she inflicted upon him real or imagined – the composite pain of a man shackled by the repression of his childhood?

The influence of Rossetti and the Pre-Raphaelites on his image of Ann cannot be denied and it was Lowry himself who said of the Pre-Raphaelite women: 'They are not real women, they are dreams.'

Was Ann too a dream? An untouchable image from his childhood, a gentle girl who abandoned him in death, a later protégé who deserted him in marriage, or his mother whom he saw forever in her own image, and who, in the end, rejected him more than any other?

A final theory, one among so many advanced as to the reason and origin of the hidden works: Lowry was greatly attracted by the ballet and went many times with Carol Ann or Pat or Sheila. Among his favourites, if not his very favourite, of the many ballets he saw was *Coppelia,* which tells the story of an old puppet master who falls in love with a beautiful young village maiden. Frustrated in his desire for her, he sets out to create a clockwork doll in her image and succeeds in making a puppet woman so beautiful that he promptly falls in love with her. Driven by desire, he then contrives to bring her to life by means of magic – all of which, of course, goes horribly wrong and ends in tragedy.

And the name of the doll with whom the puppet master is obsessed? Not Margery nor Kathleen; not Sheila nor Pat; not Carol Ann; nor even, at least not exactly, Ann Hilder.

The name of the doll is Swanhilda. 'And that,' remarked one psychiatrist who saw the pictures and heard the name of the puppet master's doll, 'is deeply, deeply significant.'[8]

perley met in the Pre-Raphaelite room in Manchester City Art Gallery? Or Maud or Kathleen or Margery or Pat or Sheila or Carol Ann? Or even someone on the periphery of his life, such as the tall, dark, dramatic gallery owner, Margo Ingham? Or the darkly handsome Alice Crompton who did charitable works and was his mother's friend? Or a quiet, reserved girl at art college? A model, a sitter, an actress on stage in an incomprehensible play? Or perhaps it was the real Ann Hilder, if there was such a reality, a woman of mys-

Chapter 12

L.S.LOWRY

'Giving myself up to it.'

It was not until 1951, one year before Lowry's retirement from Pall Mall, that the critic Maurice Collis made the journey to Manchester to meet the artist on his home ground. Lowry was now more clerk than rent collector, the daily rounds of the rented properties managed by the Company being undertaken by Clifford Openshaw, who had returned from the war unscathed.

Despite the fact that he was still working, Lowry contrived to conceal his occupation from such an important visitor – and succeeded so well that Collis went on to produced a poetic, even affectionate, monograph of a man whose life was totally dedicated to his art.

'I get up, not so early, perhaps, but not too late, and work at my painting until half-past twelve. Then I take the bus into Manchester. I do that everyday. After lunch I walk about, often down the Oldham Road or to other corners I never grow tired of. I get back to Mottram in time for a late tea, which is my last meal of the day. After tea I start painting again and continue far into the night...I work in the night so as not to feel my loneliness...

'Sometimes I listen to music at night. There was a time when I often went to concerts. But in these last years I grew disturbed by having people beside me when I wanted to be close to my music. Now I never go. I turn on my wireless and sit in the dark, listening, listening, giving myself up to it."

It had not been easy for Collis to find a publisher for his project; Lowry was not a popular subject, not in the art world and not among book publishers who had, as yet, to discover that the general public, given the opportunity, were fascinated by this paradoxical man. Eventually, Collis persuaded Lowry's dealers, Reid and Lefevre, to finance the publication. It was to be the first, but by no means the last, of its kind; it sold only modestly.

The critic had first met Lowry in February 1943. The war was still raging in the skies over the capital when Alex Reid had decided it was time to give Lowry another London show. This exhibition, the second in Bruton Street and shared with the Polish born artist Joseph Herman, was again a success, despite the foul conditions and the artist's misgivings. And, almost more significantly, it attracted the attention of several important collectors and critics – Collis among them.

'If the public has not had all its native sense knocked out of it,' he wrote, referring to what he called *the intolerable pressure exerted by Paris*, 'it will strongly support Mr Lowry, for he is essentially an English artist, one of our very few. Yet he has been made less fuss of than men with half his talent and none of his claim to our attention as an Englishman.'

Collis was hooked and was to remain so for as long as he lived. His current irritation was with those colleagues and buyers who failed to see in Lowry what he saw in Lowry.

'While critics and patrons have been fuddling away their time with fancy gentlemen,

Left: Lowry always maintained that he saw this man in this contraption. 'I came across that thing on one of my perambulations. There was this man travelling slowly along in an extraordinary upright box on wheels. I followed it. I couldn't help it. And the man had the face of a poet. Suddenly he stopped and turned on me: "What the bloody hell are you following me about for?"– and plenty more of like language. I felt a fool.' *The Contraption*,1949.

177

smart at serving up the latest receipt from abroad, he has been quietly working in urban Lancashire, perfecting his own style and transforming, in the way only a genuine artist can transform, a reality of back streets, ragamuffins, courtyards, football, tow-paths and tenements, into feeling and beauty...

'The construction of his street scenes is instinctive and subtle; their multitudinous figures, thrown on apparently haphazard, form a pattern actually quite balanced, a balance not only of design but of colour...

'In short, what you have got is a little English master, though the fact may pass unnoticed if the pubic is so debauched by concoctions from overseas that it cannot taste honest home-brew.'[2]

These words, first written in a critique of the 1943 show, illustrate how Lowry was slowly, almost imperceptibly, making his mark, in his own way, on the London art scene. As Collis put it: 'This retiring, unassertive, nervous man was in fact challenging the world of art.' The art world, of course, did not take kindly to being challenged, particularly by one whom they saw as a *peintre de dimanche*, as Michael Ayrton put it. But Lowry now had a Mayfair gallery who had taken him up wholeheartedly, a prestigious framing company who backed him industriously, and several important critics who wrote of him enthusiastically. And it was, as Daisy Jewell remarked, 'good to get a show at all in these times.'

It was typical of Lowry who, contrary to his self-propagated reputation for miserliness, was generous to a fault when it came to the support of other artists. When he discovered that his fellow exhibitor was having little success in the show, Lowry, who had himself struggled so long in an uncaring market, made a point of buying one of Herman's pictures on his next visit to London. Again in 1955 when the two artists once more shared a show, Lowry bought another Herman picture and presented it to Salford City Art Gallery.

This was something new for Lowry; a touch of confidence, a touch of pride, a touch – albeit small – of self esteem.

It was as if, as Lowry's would-be biographer, Hugh Maitland, remarked, his life had begun when his mother died. Lowry, of course, would have vigorously denied such a presumption; for him it seemed as if his life had ended; purposeful life that is, life with meaning and reason: *What is there left?*.

Art now was simply a way of filling the hours until his own death might be achieved. Or, if all his later assertions are to be believed, that is the way he saw it...unless, of course, this was simply the way he wanted the world to *think* he saw it. Wheels within wheels, layers upon layers, mask upon mask: the consummate actor playing a role so long and so well that the part became the player and the player the man?

He told Maitland: 'My life altered utterly and completely after she died...[...]...In the first part of the war you couldn't do anything...but after 1945 my life altered utterly and completely.'[3] From his tone of voice it could not be assumed that he felt his life had changed for the better; simply that it had changed.

Years later, when he had refined the role – the artist *malgré lui* – he announced on television: 'I've tried three times to stop. After my mother died...for three months. And I said I'd have to get something. I'd go mad. And twice since. I can't say what kept me on, but something did. Isn't there, at the beginning of *The Pickwick Papers*, a cab driver who had a cab with enormous wheels and when he once starts off, he can't stop? Well, I'm like that. I can't stop. It's a pitiable story.'[4]

It was, of course, a bit of Lowry self-parody. The tale was told with a deadpan expression – as was his wont – the mockery revealed only by the twinkle in his still bright blue eyes. He was in his element – a young audience of unsophisticated film makers, hanging on his every word, the interviews

Left: During the Second World War Lowry, who was too old to fight, was a night-time fire watcher on some of the larger department stores in the centre of Manchester. He was, he said, always first down after a raid to see the destruction before the dust had settled and the smoke had cleared. *Blitzed Site*, 1942.

sympathetically done either by the director Leslie Woodhead or Harold Riley, an admiring young art student from Salford who already knew him as well as could be.

In retrospect Leslie Woodhead was to remember Lowry as the consumate performer. 'He had a marvellous ability to ham it up for the cameras–he gave the impression of enjoying himself immensly. And what was particularly nice for us was the warmth which which he greeted us when we arrived each morning–and when we finished he said how much he would miss us all and sounded as if he really meant it. Such warmth was surprising but deeply moving.'

One morning when the crew arrived, Lowry performed his customary inquisition:–'What do you make of that, Sir?'–on the sound engineer, a man not renowned

for his artistic perception. 'Well', said the technician, while the rest of the crew busily disassociated themselves from the encounter, 'I think there's something missing from that picture. I think it could do with a cat!' Lowry grinned and patted the man on the shoulder as if he had uttered a great truth. 'You're absolutely right, Sir. I must put one in immediately.' And he did.

In fact, by this time, the paradox was made, the persona fixed, like a mask an actor wears and cannot shed; nothing that was to happen to him from the time of his mother's death to his own was to change him basically from the man he then was. Fame and fortune were to come, honour and understanding and all that he had once most desired. Films were to be made of him, much was to be written about him and more said;

Right: When Monty Bloom first went to Lowry's house in Mottram in Longdendale, he mentioned that there were parts of Wales, particularly his birthplace in the Rhondda Valley, that he thought were grim enough for Lowry's taste. 'I'll take you if you like,' he said. 'How much notice would you require?' Lowry took his pocket watch from his waistcoat and examined it. 'Give me ten minutes. I've only got one suit – and I'm wearing that. I can throw the rest together in no time.' *Bargoed*, 1965.

Over page: Lowry's Victorian heritage is no-where better illustrated than in his beach and seaside pictures. No-one is ever undressed. There is not a bathing costume in sight. Men wear their bowlers and their boots, women wear their coats and shoes. Only the children look ready for a paddle. *Lytham St. Anne's*, 1943.

but the effect upon him was as of rain upon granite. He changed a few ways, adjusted a few attitudes, bought a few things, but his life-style remained the same – the frugality and abstention from indulgence as seen in the non-smoking, non-drinking, non-womanising habits of a lifetime. His modesty and humility remained, and his determination to go his own way as an artist. The enjoyment he derived from his observation of what he liked to call the great Battle of Life was enough to bring him contentment, if not actual or lasting joy.

By the end of the '40s it had become apparent even to the most casual acquaintance that the artist was far from well. He suffered from colds and coughs, from rheumatism and a touch of lumbago, none of which he suspected were the true cause of his persistent melancholia. 'I feel very depressed,'[5] he wrote to a friend on his 62nd birthday, 'and I don't feel too well either.' Six months later he wrote again: 'The winter has had a queer effect on me. I can't quite describe it – a feeling of desolation.'

Then, in the summer of 1951 there arrived by post an extract from a paper due to be published by the *Journal of Mental Science*. The authors, Norman Colquhoun and Harold Palmer, were looking for the artist's comments and observations upon their work, which was entitled 'Pictorial art viewed from the standpoint of mental organisation as revealed by the excitatory abreaction techniques of psychiatry.'[6]

'We venture to suggest,' wrote Palmer and Colquhoun, 'that [Lowry] reveals himself as a spectator of a world in miniature and moreover that the position he assumes is that of looking down on this world from a height. He is not making a social comment on man or on his environment, but revealing a type of mental organisation which sees the world from the heightened standpoint of a watcher or spectator. Moreover, the spectator himself becomes identified with the scene he is watching; he is not only spec-

180

tator, but is himself aware of being under observation.'

Palmer was a pioneer in the development of ether abreaction, a technique which encourages disturbed patients by exposing them to a light dose of ether, to recall their memories. Such patients, Palmer had found, tended to describe what they saw in their mind's eye in one of four very distinct ways; stage three was a stage of disassociation – and what particularly fascinated the psychiatrist was the resemblance between such disassociation in the patients' recollections and Lowry's paintings. His art, Palmer noted, was 'an example of visual imagery corresponding to the third stage of my ether work.'[7]

To Palmer, a doctor who had worked with the Eighth Army in Cairo during the last war, this disassociation stage was not new; he had heard it described many times by soldiers suffering from shell-shock. But he had never seen it illustrated so graphically, and by a man who was neither being treated with ether, nor suffering the trauma of battle.

Lowry was immensely taken both with the paper and the accompanying letter from Palmer. He wanted to know more. Was he 'going off his head'? Was he shell-shocked by the Battle of Life?

He wrote to the doctor, proposing that he should visit Palmer and his wife in St. Albans. 'To say I was astonished is possibly to put it too strongly,' the psychiatrist recalled. 'But I was certainly flattered that he should travel all that way to spend the weekend with us.'[8]

Nothing Lowry said or did on that occasion, nor on any subsequent occasion – and there were to be several more visits – was to change Palmer's impression of him as 'an observer, a spectator' of life – an impression that was to be re-enforced, years later by another psychiatrist in another place. But then he – Dr Michael Fitzgerald[9] – believes that Lowry suffered from a high function-

ing form of autism known as Asperger's Syndrome: 'Asperger's [sufferers] are massive observers,' he said. And the detachment Lowry demonstrated to Palmer and Colquhoun was 'an autistic detachment.'

Fitzgerald added: 'He was born with that. He came genetically by it – it's 93 per cent inherited. It is largely a genetic condition – you would find other members of the family with these traits ... But what they have is the capacity to see detail.'

As far back as 1928 a critic writing in *The Studio* observed exactly this capacity for detail, and as if from a great height, in his work. 'It is penetrative, incisive, stinging and may even be sarcastic. There is something almost Olympian about the observation...where fly-like congregations of busy humans are seen from above, legs half bent in the effort to get on, little heads full of little personal concerns.'[10]

According to Palmer,* however, 'Most of us experience this feeling of both viewing and taking part in a scene, but usually at some critical point in our lives. But Lowry experienced it many, many times, seated before an empty canvas on which the images would develop beneath his brush as if of their own volition. He was a severely depressed man; sometimes he would wake in the morning, engulfed in a feeling of awful desolation, and, not knowing how he was going to get through the day, would find himself, somehow, before his easel with perhaps a brush in each hand and no recollection of having painted what he now saw before him.'[11]

Or as Prof Fitzgerald put it: 'I see the autistic world as a one person world, the art as a one-person art, it comes from within; it is not influenced by people outside...[...]...True creativity of this nature comes utterly from inside, so the normal world is a social world where people chat and they have coffee and

*It should be emphasised that although Asperger's Syndrome was identified in Vienna in 1944, because of the time and place of Dr. Asperger's work during the Nazi occupation it was, quite wrongly, associated with Nazi thinking or collaboration and was not written about in England until 1981, long after Palmer had published his paper.

they do this and they do that and they do the other...Now in the autistic world it all happens inside the head, everything happens inside the head.'[12] He goes on to quote W B Yeats's statement that a 'poem, just like a picture or a piece of music, assumes an autonomous existence, representing its own self-contained truths.'

Earlier, he had written: 'The style of his paintings was wholly original...There is absolutely no doubt that [Lowry] was an original painter and a genius.'

For his part, Lowry was constantly trying to find a reason for his depression; something to blame. One time it was because his housekeeper at Mottram had moved away and he was struggling to find another that suited as well. Another time it was his feet: 'I have developed bad feet,'[13] he wrote to one friend. 'I now have great sympathy for those poor souls I see tottering about gingerly as if they were walking on hot bricks – I am fast qualifying, I fear, to become one of those unfortunates. Please don't laugh.'

Such incidental irritations, however, disrupted the good humour Lowry usually showed to the world. His moods varied from exuberant, almost hysterical, joviality in public, to terrible despair in private, so that only the closest and most intimate members of his shifting circle of acquaintances were aware of the extent of his depression. Over the long years of exposure to each other's company, Maitland with his scientific mind came to realise that the effect of maternal bereavement was deeper and more crippling that even he had first suspected. Lowry was, in Maitland's view, suffering the depressive effect, in a clinical sense, of a prolonged period of mourning which, when combined with the deep-seated complexities of his personality, produced bouts of severe melancholia.

When Maitland came to realise the extent of the problem, he regretted strongly his earlier light-hearted ragging, particularly over the painting Lowry had done of the

Left: In November, 2006, a thundering industrial panorama, similar to this one, sold at Christie's in London for £1.4 million. (Not quite a record – that belongs to Going to the Match which went for nearly two million.) This painting was sold by Bury Council to help provide extra funds for Council expenses, much to the dismay of many local residents. *Industrial scene*, 1950

Over page: The artist David Carr was once rash enough to tell Lowry that he could not possibly have really seen all the odd people who appear in his painting *The Cripples.* 'Right,' said Lowry, 'I'll show you...We started about three in the afternoon in Piccadilly Gardens. Up Oldham Street we saw a man on a trestle...A while on we saw an old gentleman being helped on to a bus, then a man with one leg, then a man with one arm and, I am ashamed to say, I was quite pleased.' Between them that day they counted 101 memorable figures. *The Cripples*, 1949.

185

bedroom in which his mother had lived and died. 'Taking after Sickert,' he had teased. 'painting bedsteads and bedroom scenes?' Lowry showed no irritation. 'I just wanted to do that,' he replied without emotion, refusing to display any sentiment in the decision to paint such a picture.[14]

There was, of course, no cure, no solution, no panacea for Lowry's state of mind. But he had courage and he had the will to survive. Despite himself, he had his dedication to his art and he had his friends, each neatly compartmentalised and enjoyed in their turn with an intensity that lasted so long as his need for them.

One of the men most attuned to Lowry's quirky sense of humour was an artist by the name of David Carr who was struggling for recognition much as Lowry had struggled for recognition. For Carr it never came; he died on the eve of a first one-man exhibition in New York. He came from a well-known family of biscuit makers but having no wish to make biscuits, nor indeed anything else save pictures, contrived to get himself cut off from his family with the meagre sum of £300 a year. His introduction to Lowry came about by letter: 'I have been given your address by the CEMA having written to ask whether your picture entitled "On the Sands, Lytham" was still for sale. I saw it in their summer exhibition at Bristol where it was priced at £35. Last June I purchased your painting "The Mill Chimney" from the Lefevre Gallery and would like to say what tremendous pleasure it gives me. At about the same time they showed me your Whit-week painting which I should have certainly bought as well if I'd had the money, for like all people who sometimes buy a painting, my desire for pictures far exceeds my purse! Not long afterwards I saw "On the Sands" and that started a pretty conflict indeed. Whitweek or Lytham? Well, Lytham has won, that is if you will sell it to me now and perhaps Whitweek will follow later. For the last few years I have been working on the

same style of landscape as yourself and being the holder of an MOI* permit (painters as permits, my God!) have had good opportunity for exploring the so-called hideous parts of London, Ipswich and Bristol, concentrating almost entirely on the dock areas of those towns. But, unlike you, I try to express my feelings through the buildings alone; the boats, the cranes, the railway trucks are the monsters who live in my world and people it.

'Your painting is much more to me than just a decoration on the wall, and has given a new vision of town life, and often when not working I wander about trying to see the landscape through your eyes; through the people to the buildings and feel vaguely ashamed of myself for refusing to recognise them in my own work. But it does seem to me that when men build they give their work a character so different from their own souls that I can't begin to fit the two together in a picture. The very problem that you have solved. Please excuse me for talking about my own feelings but I couldn't resist the temptation of doing so to someone who understands the soul, the character or what you will, of those slums and town fringes, as you do in their queer and often ghastly beauty.'[15]

For Lowry the letter was a delight. It is doubtful if he had ever before received anything quite so attractive to him; it would seem that, at last, he had succeeded in communicating something of his vision – and that to another artist. He was quick to reply: 'There must be innumerable ways of looking at the same aspects of life. A silent street, a building, for instance can be as effective as a street full of people to me. It is the outlook or message that matters. I see lots of people everywhere, myself, one lot going one way and the other lot going the opposite way as a rule. I sometimes wish I didn't see folk everywhere.

'True what you say about your own work –

* Ministry of Information permits allowed artists to buy petrol for travel. Lowry was an official War Artist which gave him much the same facilities as well as access to canvas and paints.

Above: A rare medium for Lowry–watercolour. But he enjoyed experimenting with the paint boxes of the children of his friends. *Going to Work*, 1959.

you are seeing buildings and so on rather than folk. But, as you say yourself, it is how the subject matter affects you that counts. In my view, I should say that should you ever instinctively feel that folk are necessary to what you are seeking in your pictures, you will start putting them in, you won't be able to help yourself. Simply nature telling you to. I have been that way often myself.'[16]

From those two letters sprang a relationship that was to sustain Lowry through many times of doubt, to inspire him to yet more quirky paintings and to introduce him to a man with a view of life as bizarre as his own. As Carr's wife, Barbara, put it:

'They saw the odd side of life together.' Already the painting that Carr had picked out to buy with his meagre savings was just a trifle on the odd side. *The Beach,*ˊ 1941 was a far from ordinary beach, crowded as it was with big booted business men, their bowler hats stuck firmly on their head or resting lightly on their prone stomachs, and with one figure who looks rather like a policeman in a helmet climbing out of the sea. Once he had met Carr face to face, Lowry was no longer surprised that this painting had been Carr's first choice; it was as if he had instinctively recognised a kindred spirit.

ˊ Alternatively known as *On the Sands,* 1941.

188

it. Early in 1944 they met in blacked-out, blitzed, sandbagged London where Carr, infecting Lowry with his enthusiasm and energy, rushed the older man up and down New Bond Street, admiring the Old Masters in the gallery windows and venturing inside to inspect the new. They found much in common, not only in their attitudes to their art but in their highly individual concept of humanity. Neither was disappointed in the other.

To Carr, Lowry confessed an affection for the Surrealists–'Because they all look so ordinary.' And he related with delight the saga of *Laying the Foundation Stone*. This satirical painting came about as the result of a visit Lowry made to a ceremony at a Salford School. 'Well, when I got there and saw those four rows of kids looking a picture of misery, singing oh so piteously, and the clergymen looking at the sky as if they wished themselves elsewhere and the Mayor weighed down by his chain of office–well, I had to leave. I couldn't stand it. I couldn't help myself laughing...I had to keep excusing myself to have a good laugh.' When the painting of the great day was done, Lowry sent it to the Mayor and 'he who should have been most annoyed by it, liked it very much. He took it in triumph to show the City Fathers and they were very, very angry.'[17] Canon Fletcher, the Vicar, was particularly irate. 'You are no gentleman, Sir,' he told Lowry. 'You are no gentleman to make fun of us like that.' Lowry replied: 'I don't pretend to be a gentleman, but I am entitled to paint what I see.'

That he painted what he saw was one of Lowry's most persistent claims in the face of criticism. When a Manchester Academician accused him of exaggerating the size of people's feet, he retorted: 'All the people I see have got big feet.' And when, years later, he managed unwittingly to give a dog five legs, his reaction was much the same. 'Four legs would have unbalanced the painting,' he insisted. 'You couldn't have taken one

away. And anyway, why shouldn't a dog have five legs?'

Nothing that Carr and Lowry hatched together, however, was to be quite so odd as Lowry's painting called *The Cripples*. It was a picture at which some took offence or found distasteful. But, as Lowry–seeing nothing unacceptable in the work–said time and again: 'There but for the grace of God go I.' He did not find the characters, the grotesques, offensive because, in his mind, he was painting images of himself. More and more he seemed to identify with the misfits, the down-and-outs, the unfortunate souls who congregated in market places and street corners to beg or simply to gaze uncomprehendingly at passing humanity. It was as if he felt himself to be disabled in some way, either by past denigration of his peers or the humiliations inflicted by his mother. Whatever the cause, there was no criticism implied in his characterisations of the sadder examples of life's homunculi only sympathy and a kind of implicit understanding. On a visit to Mottram, Carr was shown the picture, as yet unfinished. He examined the work with visible fascination, suggesting a refinement of deformity here, an adjustment of maladjustment there. Then, standing back for a final assessment of the half-finished canvas he declared that he did not believe that his friend who insisted that he only painted what he saw, had actually *seen* all in one place and all at one time, such a grotesque number of grotesque forms.

This was, as Carr well knew, an undeniable challenge to Lowry. 'Right', he said, grabbing his battered old hat and shrugging on his equally battered old raincoat. 'I'll show you.'

While Carr drove, Lowry kept count. Lowry later described the trip: 'We started about three in the afternoon in Piccadilly Gardens. Up Oldham Street we saw a man on a trestle. "That's only one," he said. Then a while on we saw an old gentleman being

Above: Lowry's preliminary sketch for his curious painting Woman with a Beard, whom the artist insisted he had met a Paddington train. Monty Bloom, who bought the painting and the sketch, called her 'Lowry's Mona Lisa'.

helped on to a bus, then a man with one leg, then a man with one arm and, I am ashamed to say, I was quite pleased.'[18]

Between Manchester and Rochdale that day they counted 101 memorable figures. A few weeks later, travelling by himself to Bury, Lowry failed to match that total, observing a mere ninety-three; but, as he excused himself to Carr, 'I can't easily look on both sides, you must admit. On that first journey you took one side and I the other which is an advantage.'[19] The picture, he reported, was coming along quite well: 'I have operated on one of the gentlemen in the far distance and given him a wooden leg – I think you would approve. I still laugh heartily at the hook on the arm of the gentleman; that suggestion of yours was a master stroke.' Only to David Carr would he have spoken in this way; they had always enjoyed mutual observations of 'the odd side of life' which others with a more congruous turn of mind might have found unacceptable. He knew Carr well enough to believe that he, Carr, would understand that Lowry was not laughing *at* the unfortunate characters in his picture, only at his image of himself. I feel like them.

When Lowry proposed to McNeill Reid that he should do a painting of the particularly macabre Glasgow ceremony, the Necropolis, Reid remarked that it might 'make quite a good picture – provided one can see the funny side.' Carr saw more than the funny side: 'I find [*The Cripples*] both amusing and repulsive (Barbara can't bring herself to look at it),' he wrote of the original drawing.

Lowry, the actor, was skilled at adapting to the company he kept. When such company suited his taste or purpose, he would change his attitudes or manners to match those of his companions or their expectations of him; the change, of course, was skin deep; much as a chameleon might adjust his colour to his surroundings Lowry would adjust his performance to his audience. He was, quite literally, different things to dif-

ferent people. He acted the part, whatever it might have been, so convincingly that each thought–and think to this day–they knew the true Lowry. He fulfilled people's preconceptions of him; they saw in him what they most wanted to see; they imposed their mood upon him and he did not like to disappoint. He was the mystic painter to Collis's critic, the cloth-capped Lancastrian to his Bond Street dealers, the Victorian gentleman to the child in Carol Ann. To the pseudo-intellectuals who came in search of the ethos of his art the Lancashire accent would broaden and he would play the simpleton; to the students who sought nothing more than advice and understanding he was a patient guide, a teacher. With Openshaw he was one of the boys, with the collector Laing a connoisseur of music; with the Marshalls of Newcastle upon Tyne, he could be bawdy, cantankerous, perverse–but they were dealers and he delighted in what he called *testing the waters*. He was gregarious with those he liked, a recluse with those he did not. He was the cynic to Riley's romantic, the romantic to Leggat's cynic. With law lecturer Ian Stephenson, a later friend who came to know him through a mutual love of the Pre-Raphaelites, he was the well-read philosopher who liked nothing better than to engage in erudite debate. And with Maitland he was the sensitive, thoughtful artist who hastened to dispel the Professor's growing distaste for what he saw as callousness in his friend's obsession with the grotesque and the deformed.

To Edwin Mullins, whose critic's eye detected in such work 'Lowry at his most humorous,' the artist was less defensive. 'There's a grotesque streak in me and I can't help it...I can't say why I am fascinated by the odd but I know I am.'[20] To friends, he elaborated: 'They are real people, sad people. I'm attracted to sadness. I feel *like* them.'[21]

And so, while some critics and several friends took his abandonment of the industrial scene in favour of the single figures as

an example of perversity, the artist himself saw it simply as a progression of his artistic vision.

'No-body likes them,' he complained, a hint of devilment in his grin. He was comfortable again, back in the familiar role, an easier coat to wear than the ill-fitting acclaim that had lately come for the mill scenes and industrial landscapes. Thus he went on painting the misfits and the down–and-outs, the beggars and the drunken figures tumbled at the bottom of a flight of stairs or sprawled in isolation on a street bench.

'Without knowing what it was, I had an instinctive feeling that the time had come to drop the industrials. Now I feel more strongly than ever that the figures just stand on their own two feet.'[22]

The scene was now set for the arrival in Lowry's life of yet another discerning patron who popped up like the pantomime demon king to declare his liking for the single figures–'just as they were all going to be thrown on the bonfire.' Not that Lowry was ever known to venture into the overgrown garden at the back of The Elms to do anything even vaguely horticultural, far less light a bonfire. Such a phrase–or threat–had become a part of the Lowry legend: Bennett arrived on his doorstep professing an interest in the early drawings 'just as I was going to consign them all to the bin'; Alex Reid gave him a show 'just as I was going to give it all up.' And so on. The Legend of Lowry is littered with such incidents, all of which–he said–combined to keep him going. 'It was if it was destiny,' he declared. The truth, of course, had less to do with destiny, more to do with courage and compulsion.

'I was going to put them on the bonfire, I was you know,' he told Bloom, years later when the two had become firm friends with a good understanding of each other. 'They were sordid. They were what other people call sordid–but I am fond of sordid pictures. You are too. Very fond of them.' Monty

agreed, laughing. 'It's a bad trait,' he said.

'No,' replied Lowry, 'it's a very good trait to have. Getting to the truth in painting is like getting near to life. You can't paint those down-and-outs in a sentimental way.' Monty interrupted. 'But you didn't think anyone wanted them.' 'That didn't matter to me,' said Lowry. 'All my life I have done what I wanted to do. It is very funny, really. Isn't it odd. It's all so true to life.'

When Monty Bloom first met the artist, at an exhibition in a gallery in South King Street, Manchester, he had already com-missioned an industrial scene from Lowry through the then curator at Salford City Art Gallery. He had caught sight of some of Lowry's work in a BBC documentary made by the veteran film maker, John Read, and much to his surprise found himself drawn to them. Bloom was not a collector of art and he would have found it hard to find an explanation as to why he suddenly wanted to buy paintings, particularly works as dark as these. He had made his money building up bankrupt businesses and selling them as going concerns, and so—with the natural

Above: *Children Playing*, 1958.

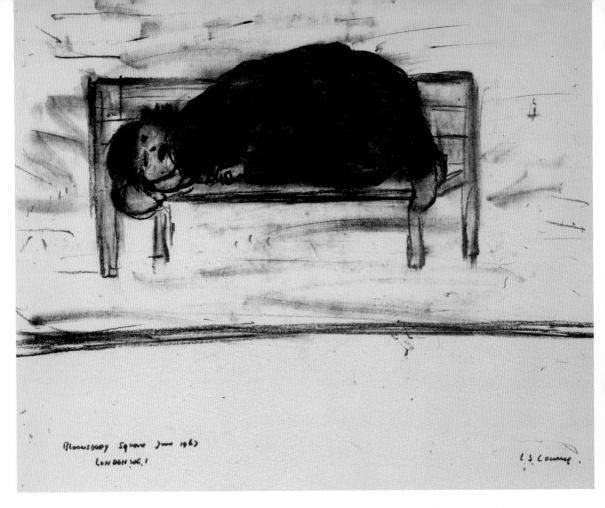

Bloomsbury Square June 1963
London WC.1

L.S. Lowry.

Above: For years Lowry travelled regularly to London, either to see his dealers, or Daisy Jewell at his framers. And, just occasionally, he would spot a character odd enough to be included in his gallery of misfits and down-and-outs. *Bloomsbury Square,* 1967.

impulse of a businessman – he had sought to justify this compulsion to possess a Lowry by first consulting his bank manager; the man confirmed the wisdom of such an investment. Lowry's work, he told Bloom, was increasing in value daily.

It was years before Bloom told Lowry this fact, but it delighted the artist none the less: *Well, I never! Well, what do you make of that, Sir?*

And so, catching sight of the artist at the show, Bloom introduced himself. Lowry was quick to recognise the name of a potential buyer. 'I've a picture for you at home,' he declared, and the upshot of the meeting was

that Bloom drove Lowry home to Mottram to view the work he had commissioned.

When they arrived at The Elms, Lowry ushered Bloom into his workroom – he refused to call it a studio; he thought the name pretentious; he worked in the room, so workroom it was. He produced a large industrial which had, in fact, been done some time before. Bloom liked it very much indeed, but as his gaze wandered round the room he saw a mass of separate paintings of single figures that he liked much more.

Bloom hardly knew how to tell the artist. 'I like the mill scene,' he began tentatively. 'But I think I prefer those...'

'I prefer them myself,' said Lowry, his voice betraying nothing of the emotion, pleasure even, that he must have been feeling. He picked up about a dozen and put them around the easel.

Bloom selected six and asked: 'Do you want to sell these?'

Lowry looked at him sharply. 'Do you *really* want to buy them?'

Bloom nodded. 'How much?' he said.

'Would ninety pounds be all right?' asked Lowry.

'For the six?' queried Bloom, still the businessman despite this incomprehensible urge to buy something without what he would consider to be a commercial value.[23]

'If you want them, you can have them,' said Lowry and took the six pictures and handed them over. Bloom took them away with him that night. They were the first of their kind that Lowry had sold.

Before they parted that first evening, Lowry to return to his nocturnal painting, Bloom to drive home to Southport, the visitor remarked that there were parts of Wales, particularly his birthplace in the Rhondda Valley, that he thought were grim enough for Lowry's taste. This appealed to the artist. 'There's a terrace of cottages at Cwm Ebbw Vale I'd very much like to see,' he said. Monty knew the place; he had been born in Ebbw Vale. 'I'll take you if you like,' he said. 'How much notice would you require?' Lowry took out his twenty-five shilling pocket watch* and examined it. 'Give me ten minutes,' he said to the astonished Bloom. 'I've only got one suit and I'm wearing that. I can throw the rest together in no time.'

It was, in fact, several weeks before the pair set off for South Wales. Lowry might have had only one suit but Bloom had a wife and family to consider. From that time on, for the next six years, they visited Wales every six months. Lowry could not resist a temporary return to the kind of industrial

scene that echoed the foreboding, if not the harshness of Lancashire; he was to make some fine pictures of Wales.

'I have laid in a 60" by 45" canvas,' he was soon reporting to Bloom, '...my general idea as regards design, but I must get over to Ebbw Vale again as it isn't a subject one can dash at right away. It is a wonderful subject if I can get it satisfactorily.'[24] They did, indeed, go to Ebbw Vale again, and to Abergavenny, and to Abertillery to see a fortune teller called Mrs Flook, and to Swansea where Carol Ann was at college, and to Merthyr Tydfil where Lowry found the subject for his largest painting (63" by 50"), the brooding composite *Bargoed*.

What Mrs Flook of Six Bells did not foretell was the extent of Bloom's obsession with Lowry's work. He bought and bought and bought almost to the point of financial distress; he sold two shops in Gorton in order to buy *Woman With a Beard* (which, with a nice touch of irony he called *Lowry's Mona Lisa*) and others; he bought everything that took his fancy from Cousin May's feral cat, Charles, to the artist's impression of his own funeral.

Above: This one he saw pushing a pram in Winchester. 'The moment I saw the good lady I pulled a scrap of paper from my pocket and hurried alongside her scribbling away. Well, my dear sir, her language – Oh! It was quite appalling! Oh, terrible! I wouldn't dare repeat what she called me.' Preliminary sketch for *Woman with a Beard*, 1959.

* When Lowry was a young man wrist watches were only just coming in and were still damned by some as 'effeminate'. Lowry used an inexpensive pocket watch all his life.

Right: Old Road, Failworth was commissioned directly from Lowry by Mrs Ruth Johnson née Heath, who recalls in a letter dated 19ᵗʰ September 1968: 'I did indeed commission it from Mr Lowry who is an old acquaintance. We used to meet regularly in the shop of a Modern Art dealer, and under the poor man's nose we arranged our deal...Lowry knew the road in which we lived as children very well.' Ruth Johnson was born and brought up at 137 Old Road and her recollections of life as the daughter of a mill worker are recorded in, *Old Road: A Lancashire Childhood, 1912-1926* by Alfred Brody. In the present painting the group outside number 137 shows the Heath family, Ruth Heath is seen as a schoolgirl with her satchel, her younger sister, Reenie, is standing on the pavement and her father and mother, Harry and Nelly Heath, are by the door. *Old Road, Failsworth.* 1957

'There'll only be two at my funeral, the Vicar and the undertaker and he'll be looking at his watch to see if it's time to go to the match.'

It got to the point where he hardly dared to take them home. His patient wife, Phyllis, had tolerated her husband's addiction with initial good humour, but finally would say wearily: 'But Monty, where are we going to put them?' He hid them in the boot of his car or smuggled them into the house late at night and stashed them in the wardrobe of the spare bedroom. One, *Father and Two Sons*, a particularly disturbing picture based on his two cousins, Billie and Bertie, and their father, he lent to Salford rather than face Phyllis with it. By the '60s Bloom had sixty Lowrys on his walls and forty more hidden around the house. By the '70s he had by far the largest collection anywhere and by 1972 Bloom's Lowry collection, which had started with six single figures for £90, were valued at a quarter of a million pounds.

Early in 1962 Bloom had been approached by Frank Constantine of the Graves Art Gallery at Sheffield; they were organising a retrospective exhibition of Lowry's work for the autumn and were wondering if they might borrow a few pieces from Bloom. 'Certainly,' said Bloom, 'come and take your pick.' Constantine travelled to Southport in search of the odd one or two; he took away forty-two and showed thirty-nine of them.

It was to be the first time that the grotesques had been exhibited. They were, Maurice Collis decided, 'solitaries, unable to mix with their fellows and deeply afflicted by their isolation. They are the projections of his mood, ghosts of himself.'[25] Thirty years after Lowry's death, Michael Fitzgerald, Professor of Psychiatry at Dublin University, applied much the same description to the artist himself. There was, he stated, a discernible association between creative genius and autism spectrum disorders. The symptoms he sited were virtually

L.S. LOWRY 1957

the same as those Collis applied to the grotesques.

Lowry, despite himself, was inordinately proud of the show. He went to it many times, as often, in fact, as he could persuade someone to run him over from Mottram to

Sheffield. 'I'm going again to Sheffield,' he wrote to Bloom on 5th October that year, 'this time with Mr. Alick Leggat and again at the weekend with Doctor and Mrs Maitland who are off to Malaya at the end of the month. So I shall know this show by heart if I keep going like this.'

Two years later the pattern was to be repeated in an almost identical fashion. Ronald and Phyllis Marshall (known as Micky and Tilly to all but Lowry who invariably referred to them as Mr and Mrs Marshall) of the Stone Gallery, Newcastle upon Tyne, had found the same entrée into the artist's affections. They had met briefly at the Harrogate Festival of Arts in August, 1960, but neither had pursued the acquaintance. It was a year or more before Lowry presented himself at the Gallery. He professed to be passing and had entered on impulse. Now retired, he was much in the north-east, having discovered in nearby Sunderland a small, comfortable hotel called the Seaburn which had sea views that were particularly stark and grim and Lowryesque. He had called there by chance during a tour with Pat Cooke and her husband, and finding the staff happy to serve a full cooked lunch at three o'clock in the afternoon, he was to make the hotel practically a home-from-home. A bolt hole from fame.

Tilly Marshall was somewhat sceptical. 'At that time,' she recalled, 'we had had numerous shows of modern artists and had been extensively reviewed. Anne Redpath had got virtually a page in the *Guardian* which, I should think, was more than Lowry could resist. He always seemed to feel a bit competitive about her–she was with Reid and Lefevre too.'[26]

That day at the Marshall's, she remembered, 'Lowry sat and talked...he went all through the gallery, upstairs and down, and found a little Rowlandson he liked. Then he sat down again. We had tea. Still he sat on. We had sherry, he had orange squash. Still he sat on. We suggested dinner. He agreed. It must have been past midnight when we dropped him back at the Seaburn. Five weeks later he turned up again. And so it went on for years. I always say he came to tea and stayed for fourteen years.'[27]

During the first marathon visit they discussed his work. Mrs Marshall, who did not care for the industrials, remarked that she greatly admired the single figures. She could hardly have said anything to please

him more. It is no wonder he stayed on... and on.

'Do you?' he said, as if no-one had said such a thing before. 'No-body else does. They won't show them, you know.' 'We would,' she replied. And they did.

Much as Constantine had done, Micky and Tilly travelled to Southport to view Bloom's collection. They hoped to select four or five works to include in their show. After about half an hour, as Monty recalled, 'they went into a little huddle and then said; "We would like to base the whole show on these pictures, may we take forty-eight?"'[28]

They showed all forty-eight in October 1964 and no others.

One of the major attributes of the Marshalls of the Stone Gallery was their ability to put on a good show and, in so doing, to attract the right critics and the right sort of publicity. 'Mr Marshall,' remarked Lowry in a letter to Monty, 'is very imaginative and seems to be a very good dealer.' The subsequent success of the show, he decided, was due 'to the cleverness and the personality of the promoters. They are marvellous people, you know. Remarkable.'

The critic Edwin Mullins travelled from London for the week and was given two private views, one in the presence of the artist and one, the first, without. Lowry, at 77, had acquired a powerful sense of presence that was impossible to ignore. He was over six foot tall, well built without being bulky, with a strong face, clear blue eyes and a shock of white hair that showed no signs of thinning with age; he was no longer a figure of fun, nor had he been so for some years past.

If Lowry was in a gallery, everyone knew about it.

The critic was enthralled; and in the *Sunday Telegraph* the following weekend he admitted with some surprise that he too had been infected by the artist's ability to perceive the unusual in the mundane: 'For several days now all railway porters, newspaper vendors, men seated on park benches, not to

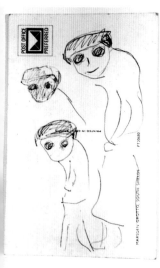

Above: There's a story Lowry told about waking up in the middle of the night in his first floor room at the Seaburn Hotel in Sunderland and seeing someone looking in through his window. The next morning he awoke to realise that what he had seen was the top of a street lamp. Sketch from Lowry's papers.

mention my friends, have been pure Lowry.

'I once heard him described as an ento-mologist stalking human insects with his butterfly net. Lowry has become a collector of people...'

The entomologist himself, temporarily abandoning his dislike of social occasions, attended his show each day that week; he mingled charmingly with the critics, chat-ted with the reporters, posed for the tele-vision cameras. A girl from one of the papers confronted him. 'Tell me, Mr Lowry,' she said, 'why has this man Bloom got all those pictures? And why have we never seen them

in London?' 'That's simple,' replied Lowry. 'Mr Bloom said. "How much?" And he went on saying "How much?" And now there are none left.'

To Mullins, as the walked together on that first day beneath his gallery of grotesques Lowry said: 'At last I feel I'm getting what I've wanted.' Then suddenly: 'I think I'll die, Sir. There's nothing left. I'm old.'

He paused, a typical Lowry pause; for pure effect; a pause that would have done Pinter proud.

Then, with a grin: 'Well, perhaps not till after the private view.'

Above: Monty Bloom once asked Lowry what he did with his old clothes. 'I wear them,' he replied. Here he is photographed in his workroom in his second suit – the one he wore at his easel..

Chapter 13

It All Came too Late

'Like most things in Lowry's life,' observed *The Guardian,* whose writers so often had the knack of putting a finger on the essence of Lowry 'it came too late.'

The event to which they were referring was the great retrospective Lowry exhibition staged by the Royal Academy in the autumn of 1976. It had been planned to take place in his life time but Lowry, foiled the plans of the RA to uniquely honour the living artist by dying nine months previously.

'He was indeed unlucky in terms of timing,'[1] remarked Jonathan Horwich of the auction house Christie's. He was referring, however, to the fact that Lowry's first one-man show in London, which should by rights have brought him to national fame, came just before the outbreak of the Second World War which understandably put such things as paintings and painters on hold for the next five or six years. And, more subtly perhaps, there was a reference here to the fact that Lowry's work when he first began was not only out of tune with the times, but so far ahead of his time as to be virtually unacceptable to current tastes. It took a long time for the art world to catch up with Lowry and his vision.

Then, in May 1968, soon after his eightieth birthday, came the 'final paradox in a life of contradiction. For at a time when his work is at last fetching high prices,' according to the mass circulation *Daily Mirror,* 'he is giving up...

Lowry had indeed announced that he had stopped painting, though like everything else he said, such words should be taken with just a tiny pinch of salt. 'Just like the old mills,' he said, settling himself comfortably into his favourite chair and resting his feet on the mantelpiece above the fire. 'I'm shutting myself down. I'm having a sit-in, a one man strike.'[2] He seemed pleased to have found a modern idiom for his announcement and displayed no regret at consigning his life's work to the past; it should be added that, when he made his statement to the press, there were several examples of his paintings littering various surfaces in the gloomy old sitting room – the music stand on the piano, the top of the bureau, the large dining table which was already covered with letters and bills and pencil sketches – and some – such as *Man Looking at Something* – which looked suspiciously as if the paint were still wet.

'I have done no work at all,' he wrote to Monty Bloom in 1965, 'though whilst I was in Middlesbrough yesterday I saw a queer sort of tower on a dock I felt would be worth doing – but I fought against it! But I expect to go there often so I may fall yet, but I hope not – that would be too dreadful.'

He had already accepted Associate membership of the Royal Academy, ten years previously, thanks largely to the lobbying of a new friend the artist Fleetwood Walker and an old one James Fitton – who was now an established figure in the London art world; Fitton might have been a man of the north just as Lowry was, but, unlike Lowry, he had made the move south in every sense of the phrase. Now, years later, he was determined to get his old friend elected a full member of the RA, and happily embarked upon a course designed to bring Lowry into his world, just as earlier he had trotted Lowry along to the Café Royal where the friend of his youth, who had drunk Vimto with him at a dockside stall, remained aloof and unimpressed.[*]

Once, having received from the then Prime Minister, Harold Wilson, the suggestion that he should bring Lowry to dinner at Number Ten, Fitton wrote to apprise his friend of this honour. He had found it a difficult letter to write, each opening sentence sounding more pretentious than the last: 'Seated next to the Prime Minister last night...' 'As the Prime Minister was saying to me...' 'The Prime Minister has asked me...' He completed the letter, eventually, as modestly as he could contrive and sent it off. He received no reply. When next they met, Lowry made no mention of it until, unable to contain his curiosity any longer, Fitton asked: 'Did you get my letter about dinner with the Prime Minister?'

The question appeared to have fallen upon deaf ears. The pair were, at the time, walking down Piccadilly to Burlington House; finally, without breaking his stride or turning his head, Lowry remarked: 'Aye, I 'ad thought better of you, Jim.'[3] When the invitation from Harold Wilson finally arrived at The Elms, Lowry sent the predicable answer: 'Not only have I a previous engagement for the whole of the previous day, but I must plead that, at my age, I find such engagements over-tiring.'[4]

A secret that he told only a select few, including Hugh Maitland, whom he regarded as his official biographer, and Alick Leggat who helped organise his correspondence–which might otherwise have remained forever in the large fruit bowl on the sitting room table where envelopes

and their contents were invariably chucked on arrival[**]–was that this was not the only letter he had received from Downing Street. The first had come from Harold Macmillan in 1955 offering him an OBE. Then came one from Wilson in 1960 with a proposal to give him a CBE. In 1967 Wilson approached him again, this time with the offer of a knighthood. All of these Lowry, most politely but equally firmly, declined. Four years later it was Edward Heath who wrote, this time suggesting Lowry be made a Companion of Honour. Again he declined: 'I have at all times tried to paint to the best of my ability and I would only hope that any remembrance people may have of me when I am gone may be based on my work rather than on any decoration I might have collected on the journey.'[5]

The Royal Academy, though, was a different matter. When that offer came, Lowry was within five months of 75, the age limit for election; the invitation was accepted without fuss or noise. 'I oughtn't to have been pleased to get in,' he told Maitland, 'but I was.' But, just in case his friend might think he had become grand or proud, he added: 'When I feel uppish, I invariably think of the Italian Renaissance people and Rembrandt–and that keeps me quiet.'[6]

Now, when in London, he would turn up at Burlington House on odd occasions, in his old raincoat and battered trilby, and wander through the galleries, infuriating some of the older members by greeting them, loudly and in a broad Lancashire accent, with the words 'How's trade?'. He was fond of referring to his art as a craft on a par with bricklaying or thatching and, by the same token, called his studio his workroom. Dealers were grocers who sold paintings, artists were men who painted pictures. They were, in short, men who traded: tradesmen. Not the sort of description to go down well with

[*] When his friend Andras Kalman took him to the Ritz ('just for fun') he ordered egg and chips and then, spotting a waiter making a flambé dish at a neighbouring table, remarked loudly 'You think they'd have a kitchen in a place like this.'

[**] One day, while Leggat was helping Lowry go through a large quantity of mail, they found cheques totalling £1500. 'I won't bother with all that,' said Lowry. 'You'd better,' replied Leggat, 'they'll be declared to the tax man.' And, as Leggat told it, 'that did it. Talk of the tax man to Lowry was like a red rag to a bull. He dealt with them instantly.'

the likes of Sir Alfred Munnings who once
told Lowry: 'I dislike your pictures intensely.' To the contrary Sir William Rus-
sell Flint–who loved painting exotic wom-
en–once stopped Lowry in a corridor to tell
him how much he admired Lowry's *Portrait
of Ann*. 'I always liked him after that,' remarked Lowry, with a grin.[7]

Lowry went rarely to Private Views and
attendant cocktail parties, distinguishing
himself on one such occasion by replying
to a waiter who inquired if he would like
a drink: 'That's very kind of you, Sir. I'll
have a tomato soup.'[8] He loved to play the
simple man.

He went to only one Academy dinner. It
was, he remarked, a very curious evening.
He never went again. 'I was a new man
and very shy and nervous so they sat me
between A R Thomson and Vivian Pitchforth. Thomson, you know, is deaf and
dumb. Pitchforth is stone deaf. They spent
the whole time writing notes and passing
them to each other in front of me.'[9] Lowry
retaliated by eating single handedly almost
a full tureen of potatoes which he had persuaded a waiter to leave in front of him, a
fact which Fitton pretended not to notice
and hoped fervently that no-one else would
either. Lowry must have loved that: he had
a fine sense of the surreal–and, in fact, admired the Surrealist because 'because they
all look so *ordinary*'.

It was Fitton's particular friends at the
RA, Harold and Laura Knight, who had
supported Fitton's attempts to get Lowry
nominated. 'They were horrified when they
saw what they had elected,' said Fitton, 'but
afterwards they became acclimatised to
him.'[10] It is interesting to note that it was
the Academicians who adjusted to Lowry
rather than Lowry to the Academy.

It was a sad quirk of fate–and perhaps
another example of bad timing–that when
the exhibitions finally came, grand occasions staged by grand galleries, and followed
inevitably by grand sales to grand collec-

tors, Lowry was no longer a young man and
found the strain of it all rather too much.
From the early '60s the effects of demands
for more work and still more work began
to tell on him. He hid the signs of tension
and worry, just as he had hidden their causes from all but his most perceptive friends,
shutting himself into the bleak stone house
at Mottram, or escaping to the Seaburn Hotel in Sunderland or seeking sanctuary with
the Cookes in Cheshire. There, just as had
Edith in another time and another place, Pat
cooked for him and cosseted him, watching
the stress lines fade from his face and the
trembling of his limbs abate. To Pat's knowledge he had three attacks of shingles, a physical manifestation of the nervous tension
that consumed him and which he endured
without complaint. He came to their house,
moody, inarticulate, withdrawn, grumpy
and difficult to please. He wanted no talk of
art, no visits to galleries, no company save
her and her husband, Brian.

'He was really very sick for a time. Really
poorly. He would hide himself away during
these attacks, but after a time they became
worse and more frequent...[...]...The strain
of hiding them from the outside world
became almost a much as the strain of the
exhibition that had caused them. I first began to notice the effect upon him after the
Graves [Graves Art Gallery, Sheffield, or-
ganised by Constantine] exhibition; then
again after the [Stone Gallery] Newcastle
show; the worst was after the Tate–that really knocked me out.

'He had put everything into that, just as
he had put everything into the work that
made it.'[11]

It was ironic that it should have been the
great Arts Council Lowry Retrospective,
a touring exhibition culminating in a rare
tribute to a living artist, in six weeks at the
Tate Gallery in London, that had finally
and irrevocably put him on the map–and
'nearly finished me off.'[12]

Like everything else, 'it all came too late.'[13]

L.S.LOWRY   1955

The two years it took to plan and organise the show seemed to be almost more than Lowry could endure. 'The Tate Gallery show has been pushed back to Nov-Jan,' he wrote in March 1966 to Maitland who, although still in Kuala Lumpur, had agreed to lend for the exhibition. 'They had been intending to have had a show at Reid's Gallery before it–but, oh dear me, it is terrible, is it not–there won't be enough stuff, so that's that. I have to explain to people that I aren't like Tennyson's Brook–the brook may have done so but I certainly am not going on for ever.' In May he was complaining to Bloom: 'Letters come in from the Arts Council and Edwin Mullins, etc. I feel as if I would like to put them all in the fire. How thankful I shall be when the show is over. I am really tired of it all. More than ever, I think.' He was nearly 78 years old and was to live nearly ten more years.

The work spanned the whole spectrum of Lowry's art, 100 works ranging from a 1906 still life done in the studio of his first teacher, to a 1965 seascape done from his window at the Seaburn. The exhibition opened at the Tate in London with one hundred more works–a grand total of nearly two hundred–in August, 1966, having completed the tour, and closed the following January.

By the time of the opening in Sunderland Lowry had regained his good humour. The following day he wrote from the Seaburn to Bloom: 'I went in one Saturday afternoon and a good many people were there and a gentleman who wore his hat all the time and who I thought was the man who comes in to see about the electricity lights but who proved to be the Lord Mayor–was very interesting and did say they never had had a show like this one before and my expressive face flushed with pleasure at that and we parted great friends.

'There are 50 to 60 pictures not here that will be in the London show...'

The exhibition arrived in London as scheduled; Lowry, despite prophesies to the contrary (mainly his own), attended the opening where he was composed with the critics, respectful of the eminent, and so attentive to the ladies that three spinster sisters who had travelled Wales for the occasion observed that he 'seemed to be in his element. He made such a fuss of us that we felt almost as if we were the most important people there.' This was Lowry playing the celebrity. For a brief moment, or so it had appeared to them, he seemed almost at home in the role.

From that time on there was no denying Lowry's place in the history of British art–except of course with the die-hard traditionalists for whom true art had to come from struggle and obscurity and who seemed to forget that Lowry had served his time in both.

The critics, for the most part, were complimentary; their newspapers gave him ample space in their columns. *The Guardian*, which until this point had been a great support to him, declared he had become a national '*maître populaire de la réalité*'[14] and deplored the cult of personality that had become associated with his art.

This was the first hint of establishment pique that all to often greets success, a peculiarly British attitude that equates popularity with trash, as if the common man who 'knows what he likes' has neither taste, nor judgement.

He was given no more than a year or two in which to enjoy his new status before the more self-consciously serious art commentators began to refer to his work as hackneyed, over-exposed, too familiar–an artistic cliché. After his death, one university lecturer in art history who contemplated writing a monograph on Lowry was warned, in all seriousness, that such a foolhardy venture would have a detrimental effect on his career prospects.

Where Reid's had failed to acquire enough pictures for a pre-Tate exhibition, a small gallery in the Brompton Road, owned by

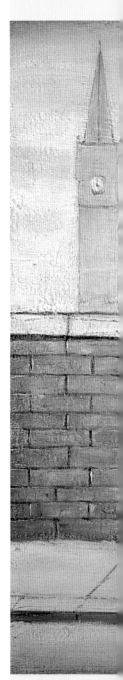

Andras Kalman, a long-time aficionado and advocate of Lowry's work, had succeeded in collecting a total of fifty-four paintings for a complementary 'tribute' to run concurrently with The Tate show.

Kalman, a Hungarian who had come to England in the winter of 1949, opened a gallery in a basement air-raid shelter in South King Street, Manchester, where the weekly £2 rent was paid by the regular pawning of his typewriter. By dint of a lot of persuasion and not a little charm, both of which he displayed in abundance, he managed to obtain for his first exhibition works by Epstein, Matthew Smith, Lucien Freud, Craxton and Gerald Kelly. Invitations to a private view were sent to every influential name he could discover, from the members of the Art Gallery Committee to the town councillors. On the appointed day Kalman waited in vain for his guests, while the canapés curled at the edges and the neighbouring shops put up their shutters. No one came. Not one single dignitary, critic, collector or councillor either replied or responded to the invitation. The second exhibition, in which the works were inevitably less auspicious, threatened to be as great a disaster as the first. On the third day Lowry appeared; down the steps he came, buzzing like a bluebottle round the Gallery until, summing up the situation, he bought a picture. It was, Kalman recalled, only his third or fourth sale. 'It cost him about £20 and I think he bought it only to give my morale a boost. It was the exact opposite of his kind of work, a French picture, Monet style, of a little girl in a white dress.'[15]

Kalman already knew of Lowry by repute as a 'controversial painter, regarded with great suspicion locally' and almost immediately recognised a kindred spirit with kindred views of the art establishment. Visits to the gallery were followed by trips across the road for tea at Fuller's, where they ate walnut cake and discussed for hours their own highly individual views on the dealers and artists of their acquaintance. 'London dealers', said Kalman, 'consider themselves more important than the artist, sitting in their galleries like the brothel keepers of Amsterdam.' Kalman had yet to become a London dealer himself.

He became, and remained, fiercely resentful of the establishment treatment of his friend and attacked such philistinism – the very thing of which they accused Lowry – in his own colourful idiom. 'Art in Manchester was still confused with Bohemian charlatanism; [studios] were full of such people, all basically there to gawp at the nudes. For them art had almost the same connotations as the early porn shops had in the '70s; they came to the art classes from their homes in Alderley Edge with their clipped lawns and their Daimlers in the drive, and in these surroundings Lowry was a complete and utter misfit. His looks, his inclinations, his life-style, was like a parson's compared to theirs.

'You had to see that this was an exceptional man; his whole way of life, speaking, eating, was against the norm. From the beginning there was a strong integrity about him – you had to be an insensitive moron not to see it in the man. From his repression came his strength, from his insularity came the power to concentrate upon his direction – on becoming an artist, on being an artist, on remaining an artist.'

In 1952 Kalman gave Lowry a one-man show. It was not a notable success. In those days Kalman supplemented his income by giving tennis lessons – he played for Lancashire and at Wimbledon – to rich clients to whom, between sets, he sold romantic pictures. 'If you offered them a Lowry they would say: "I can get on a number eight bus and see that bloody sight for tuppence."'[16]

In this same year Lowry reached his 65th birthday. All this time he had continued to work as a cashier and book-keeper at Pall Mall, and he now retired with a pension of £200 a year. Such financial security was es-

Previous page: Two years after he made this picture, Lowry said: 'People...refuse to believe me when I tell them I saw a man dressed just like that, doing just that, from the top of a bus at Haslingden. It was the umbrella propped against the wall which caught my eye...' He put his own initials on the man's briefcase and told anyone who enquired – 'That's me when I retire.' He meant retire from making pictures, of course, and that was something he never did. *Man Lying on a Wall*, 1957.

Left: A typical Lowry family. And is anyone touching? Or holding hands? Or communicating. Of course not. *A Family of Four*, 1947.

sential to his peace of mind if not to his way of life–which remained frugal even after success had been achieved. It was not until 1969 that Lowry voluntarily relinquished his pension with the words: 'It was very good of the P M P Co Ltd., to do what they did on my leaving.' He had failed to cash his cheque for some years but it had taken him seventeen years before he had felt confident enough in his earnings from his art alone to take the final step to give up this small bit of regular income.

And so, in 1957 Kalman took the plunge and moved to London where his Gallery, the Crane Kalman, has continued to mount Lowry shows with faithful regularity–and some considerable success. From this time on Lowry shows were an integral part of London's cultural life–if not in some of the larger galleries, certainly in the discerning smaller ones.

'It strikes me there are too many shows knocking about just now,' Lowry wrote to the art critic Robert Wraight who was staging a show in Cambridge. 'Mr. Marshall's gallery is holding one...Reid's are having theirs on 10ᵗʰ May...it all seems very ridiculous to me–but there it is.' In 1968 he wrote to Bloom: 'A bitter blow about the York show. The young lady turned up when I was gleefully thinking it was off...[...]...they want me, no us, to be there...It is terrible.' In the same year Kalman put on 'The Loneliness of L S Lowry' and Lefevre managed to get sixty more pictures for their February show. Now he had a new concern. 'He was almost ill again,' related Pat Cooke. 'It was not the strain of actually doing the things that took so much out of him–it was the worry. "Are they good enough? Can I still do it? My perspective is not right–Will they like them as drawings–not investments?"'[17]

In 1970 he was shown at the Tib Lane Gallery, Manchester, and at Norwich Castle Museum; in 1971 in Belfast and at the Haworth Art Gallery in Accrington; and so it went on–in Liverpool, in Nottingham

again, at the Whitworth Gallery, Manchester, at Lefevre's; and always at Salford where the permanent collection was continuing to grow; by the time he died they owned more than 300 works.

Then in 1972, the Bloom Collection was shown at the Hammett Gallery in London–only this time it was for sale. Bloom had moved to the south coast and, finding the insurance premiums there to be prohibitive, had reluctantly decided he had to sell off some of the most expensive pieces. The relationship with Lowry was never the same after that; Bloom preferred to think that Lowry–as he insisted was the case–was not concerned about the sale, more about Bloom no longer being able to drop in. 'He never liked people moving away,' said Bloom.[18]

In the opinion of a later friend, law lecturer Ian Stephenson, Lowry's character softened in his final years. 'He was a well-rounded man who had come to terms with life as he saw it. He was very much of the opinion of the philosopher Hobbes that life is nasty, brutish and short. By this time, in his late seventies and early eighties he had developed an elaborate protection mechanism for dispelling the boobies of this world. I once saw him dismiss a reporter who had in some way offended or irritated him by simply shouting "I bid you good day, sir." It worked. The man fled.

'There's a touch of Doctor Johnson about him–a powerful personality of striking intelligence and a considerable command of language who could, just as easily adopt a convincing pose of the cloth-capped ninny. It took a lot of people in.'[19]

It was about this time, when Lowry was in his early eighties, that people began concerning themselves about the contents of his will. There were many who lobbied for a share in his estate and who bothered him for promises of this or that or the other.

He had made his will in the '70s and had no intention of changing it. 'I remember one day at the Marshall's,' Carol Ann re

Right: Lowry had a life-long fascination with the sea. In later years, on holiday in Sunderland, he would wander along the seashore, kicking the pebbles and pondering aloud: 'What if the tide doesn't turn? What if it just keeps coming in and coming in...What if it never stopped?' *The Sea*, 1963.

called, 'Mr Lowry saying to me with that particular glint in his eye that meant he was up to some mischief or another. "Carol," he said loudly, "tell me, what would you do if you had a lot of money?" "I don't know," I said. "What do you call a lot of money?" "Well, say £100,000." I couldn't think of anything. I mean I was only 19 and that was an enormous amount of money. "You'd buy diamonds and furs, wouldn't you, Carol? Wouldn't you? Wouldn't you? Eh?" I knew then that that was exactly what I was ex-

pected to say. So I said, "Yes, I'd buy diamonds and furs." And you could have cut the atmosphere with a knife, Tilly looking almost triumphant, as if to say "I knew it all along".

'Anyway, when we were going home, as soon as we got in the car he said to me: "Would you really buy diamonds and furs, Carol?" I laughed. "No, of course I wouldn't," I said. "What would I want with diamonds and furs?" And he bounced back in his seat with a big sigh of satisfaction. "That's right,"

Over page: *Coal Barge,* 1938.

213

he said, "That's right." He had achieved the effect he had wanted and had succeeded in winding up poor Tilly once again.

'He was constantly winding her up. I am not sure that she was aware of what was going on, but he used to do it continually and more often than not she rose to the bait. Half the time I wasn't aware of it myself and only realised what he was up to in retrospect.'

It was Sir John Betjeman who all unwittingly brought into the open the covetous scrabbling for a piece of the Lowry estate while he was far from dead and certainly not buried. The poet's letter to *The Guardian* appeared in its columns on 10th November, 1975. He wrote: 'I would like to mention a Manchester subject...and he is well over eighty, unmarried, with no heirs, a Manchester artist of international reputation. I have never met him but have followed his work...At his latest exhibition at a London gallery of 36 of his paintings I could see the wide range of this artist. He is associated in the public mind down here only with simplified Gothic against a wide sky under which hurry crowds of factory workers, children and parents. But, gathered into one room, his painting range much further—onto a grey North Sea with nothing on it at all, down into Cornwall and a remote stone circle, up onto the Brontë haunted moors and out into prosperous Manchester suburbs which are his birth place.

'His work is best appreciated, its colour, its variety, humour and loneliness when assembled in a single gallery. This could be in Manchester, rather as the Van Gogh Museum is in Amsterdam or the Rodin Museum is in Paris, the Peter de Wint is in Lincoln and many others. Could it be in addition to the Whitworth Art Gallery or the City Art Gallery? Manchester, I know, is proud of this great artist. Can it assemble a permanent Lowry exhibition?"

The following morning *The Guardian* declared, in a muted leader, its support for

the basic concept of such a scheme, but with reservations not solely related to cost. Somewhat reprovingly the writer began: 'Most British artists have to wait until they died before being honoured. L S Lowry has been luckier than most.'

Lowry's laughter on reading those words must indeed have had a hollow ring. What about all the years of scorn and derision? What about the guffaws from his local peers and the long, long years of brute incomprehension.

Andras Kalman, who was to prove one of Lowry's most ardent supporters, joined the debate as to whether the city—either city—could afford it? Afford it? he asked—'Can the city afford the roads that run into Manchester? Fifty yards of it would pay for a Lowry Museum.'

So began a correspondence that ranged from the sarcastic to the tongue in cheek, the denigrating to the supportive, the violently anti to the violently pro. It was not until nearly a week later when Fred Marple wrote from Rawtenstall to point out that the subject of debate was still very much alive, that the correspondence ground to a halt.

It did not, however, stop the debate nor prevent acquisitive representatives from various galleries and museums, turning up at The Elms, metaphorically cap in hand. Manchester and Salford squabbled endlessly over their prerogatives to him, claiming both the man and his estate as if he were some sort of public monument which could be hoisted from one location to another according to the whim of contemporary opinion. They talked of him wanting to live on enshrined in their belated esteem and, preoccupied with their own interests, saw no irony in their endeavours to involve him in

*It took a long time but it did happen eventually, just as the poet would have wished – except that it was not in Manchester but in Salford. In 1996 The Lowry Millennium Trust was set up with Lottery money to build a massive arts complex, on a spur of land on the banks of the Irwell in Salford Docks where Lowry used to wander in student days with his friend Jim Fitton. It was to house, on permanent loan from the City of Salford, their collection of about 340 Lowry works – in addition to two theatres, an education centre, restaurants and several galleries for visiting exhibitions from all over the world. All this from the purchase of one Lowry pastel by a far-sighted curator in 1936.

their fine plans.

Lowry hated every minute of their machinations. Now well into his eighties he wanted nothing more than to be left in peace. Each new approach he received with initial courtesy and subsequent suspicion. 'What do they really *want* of me?' he asked one intermediary and on being told the extent of their expectations: 'Why do they come to me *now*?' It was, he felt, neither his place nor his privilege to organise the means of his own honouring; it was as if he had had the temerity to propose his own canonisation. It all embarrassed him deeply and although no one said so publicly, there were some who felt the unseemly wrangling hastened the inevitable end; no one, neither single individual nor single organisation could be blamed for the distress to which he was exposed, but together they brought him much pain.

'What should I do with all this?' he would ask Carol Ann each time she visited. 'Oh, give it to the Salvation Army and be done with it,' she would say. And he would smile a small, secret smile which she thought to be a sign that she had divined his intent. She had no idea that the early will leaving everything to her still stood; in truth she had no knowledge of its existence.

Death held no fears for him; only the manner of his passing. 'A married man,' he would say, 'lives like a dog and dies like a king; a bachelor lives like a king and dies like a dog.' He did not want to die like a dog.

He had seen so many friends go. Maitland, heartbroken at the death of his brilliant wife, had died in 1972; and David Carr, slowly and painfully, after eight years living with the knowledge of the cancer that was to kill him; and James Brooke, the restorer in Huddersfield whom Lowry called The Great Man; and—as he reported—Ann Hilder's father; and Harold Timperley; and Daisy Jewell; and McNeill Reid in retirement; and Ted Frape, the Salford curator who had demonstrated so much faith in

Lowry and went quickly and suddenly in the night.

'I think in the end you get tired of it,' he said in 1965, wandering obligingly for the television cameras among the graves of Southern Cemetery where one day he would lie alongside his mother and his father. 'My mother was quite tired of it. My mother was house-fast for fourteen years and bedfast for eight before she died. Never got out of bed for eight years.

'I wouldn't like to do that. But you can't be sorry for a man like Frape, can you? He went off nicely. He went off a bit soon, but he went off very well. When you see people go, inch by inch, that's when you worry about it. Then you wonder who'll look after you. You don't want to be a burden to anybody.'[20]

Thursday 12th February, 1976, in Mottram-in-Longdendale, was a cold, dank day; the mist gathered low in the valleys so that the peaks hung as if suspended from angry skies. Lowry awoke early. His sleep had been plagued by dreams that left him with a feeling of unease that lingered into consciousness. He had a full day before him. He was to lunch with Stan Shaw, the current Director of Salford City Art Gallery. In the evening he was expecting his friend, Philip Robertson, a retired hatter from Glossop, for an hour or two of friendly chat. The lunch went off without problems but when Robertson arrived after nine that evening, he could get no reply. He opened the letter box and peered through, only to see Lowry lying, fully conscious, at the foot of the stairs.

Robertson managed to raise Lowry's housekeeper, Mrs Swindles, obtain her keys and get into the house. He had fallen, Lowry told them, but now he was fine; it was simply that he couldn't get up; now he was back in his favourite chair he was right as rain, thank you, Sir, and good night.

But no, a doctor was summoned and

when he arrived Lowry performed all the exercises and tests willingly enough – and to prove he needed no further care. But when Mrs Swindles arrived the next morning he was again in a state of collapse beside the bed – surrounded by the six Rossetti paintings he kept on his bedroom walls in defiance of all strictures about insurance and robberies. Robertson and another friend,

Frank Whalley,* stayed the night to keep an eye on him. And it was not until the following day, Saturday, that anyone could persuade him, still protesting, to go to the Woods Hospital at Glossop

Such was the humour of the patient that, though the visitors came in tears, they invariably left in smiles; it was he who cheered

Right: A late painting, made long after Lowry had told the press that he had given up. He had done no such thing, of course. He was doomed to paint on, compulsively, virtually until the day he died. *The Notice Board,* 1971.

*Ironically it was journalist Frank Whalley, who then worked for the *Manchester Evening News*, who after Lowry's death finally broke the story of Lowry's rent collecting days.

hand as if to hold him in this world.

One young man, grateful for his friendship, arrived late to find Lowry with his eyes half closed. All he wanted to talk about was his mother. 'I miss her still,' he said. 'Sometimes in the morning I'll wake up and it's very quiet and–I don't know–sometimes my mother is there. With me. And I know that if I get my legs out of bed it will be alright. And that's what I do, Sir, and it is all right. I get dressed and as soon as I've got my collar* and tie on, I'm ready to face the world–as long as they leave me in peace to have my egg for breakfast.

'It's the same when I come into the house in the evening. Sometimes she's there, waiting for me.

'I miss her...I've never ceased to miss her... but she's with me here...I've not long to go.'

The young man left the bedside that night believing that Lowry was on the point of peaceful death. It was, he believed, what he wanted. 'When he was talking about his mother, it was almost as if he had forgotten I was there.'

In the early hours of the morning, February 23rd, 1976, nine days after his admittance to hospital, Laurence Stephen Lowry died in his sleep of pneumonia following a stroke. He had achieved his last ambition. He had become a burden to no one. He had died as he had lived, alone, with dignity, with humour and with courage.

The day of the funeral, Friday 27th, was as dark and as dank as he had said it would be; but there were not two people but two hundred present: journalists by the score, some with cameras, some without; artists and friends, gate crashers and unknown admirers, dealers and collectors, the curious and the concerned, acquaintances from the past of a long, long life.

The Rev. Geoffrey Bennett read the 23rd Psalm and thanked God for 'his life and his work'. 'His friends,' he said, ' are the better

Above: A totally impossible situation–just the sort of thing to make him smile.. *People on a Rock,* undated.

Far right: *Gentleman Looking at Something,* early '70s.

them, not them him. He needed rest and quiet, they told him, but he laughed at their fears and asked them to turn the gaudy flower picture that hung on the facing wall side-ways or upside down, so that it might look more interesting. They did as they were asked and he watched closely to see how long it took each caller to notice the fact: few did. As always, he wanted no sentiment, though for the first time ever he asked Carol Ann for a kiss, which she gave him, holding his

---

* All his life Lowry wore a starched collar, which was fixed to his shirt by a collar stud. Even when painting.

for having known him and the world better for having their eyes opened by his penetrating insight into what lies around them.'

All his life Lowry had been an original, unique in his vision, in his approach to his art, in his attitudes to the Battle of Life. He had resisted all blandishments designed to bring him to a conventional and conformist old age and remained steadfastly, obstinately, his own man. 'I don't care tuppence for what they do in London in the art world,' he had said, 'it doesn't matter to me. I don't think of it. I don't know it. All I am concerned with is doing my own things in my own way – as well as I can.'

Later when the press became aware of his refusal of a knighthood, he softened his attitude just a bit and explained: 'I've just done in my lifetime what I had to do, as everyone else has to do, and did it as well as I could. So I see no call for honours...' He paused a moment, as if in thought. 'It might have been different if I were fifty and had an ambitious wife.'[21]

Or an ambitious mother? Elizabeth Lowry had now been dead some thirty-five years and Lowry was speaking just a couple of days before his eighty-seventh birthday.

All of which goes a long way to defining and understanding his determined refusal to accept honours. Except the Royal Academy, of course; but then, as he said, 'That was good for business.'

For the rest, refusing Edward Heath's offer to make him a Companion of Honour, his words might well be as good an epitaph as any: 'I have been thanked enough. People have bought my paintings.'

And when, nine months after his death the Royal Academy paid their ultimate tribute to an artist they had intended uniquely to honour with a full exhibition in his lifetime, the public came in their thousands to break attendance records, rivalled only by the great Turner exhibition two years previously. They queued through the courtyard of Burlington House and beyond to marvel

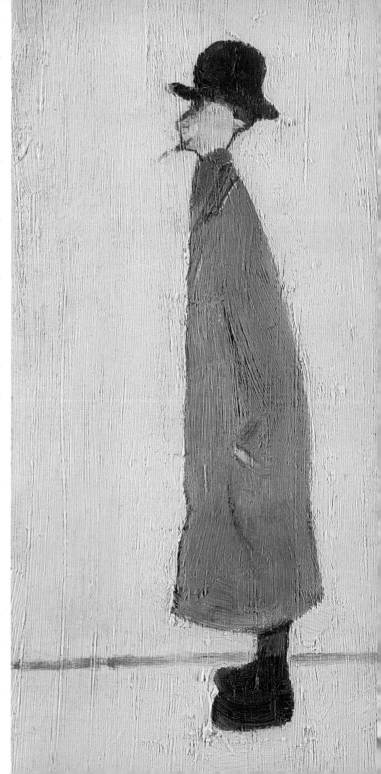

at the range and mastery of this ordinary yet extraordinary man.

Thus it could be said, and said with confidence, that Lowry's continued refusal to recognise the belated courtship of the establishment with what they declared to be a suicidal disregard for the posthumous life of his work, had made not a scrap of difference to his regard in the eyes of the ordinary man.

If artistic immortality could be bought only by the surrender of his principles or the adoption of the very pretensions he most ardently disliked, then for Lowry the price was too high.

'The longer the beard, the shorter the art,' he declared and shaved with a cut-throat razor until the day he died.

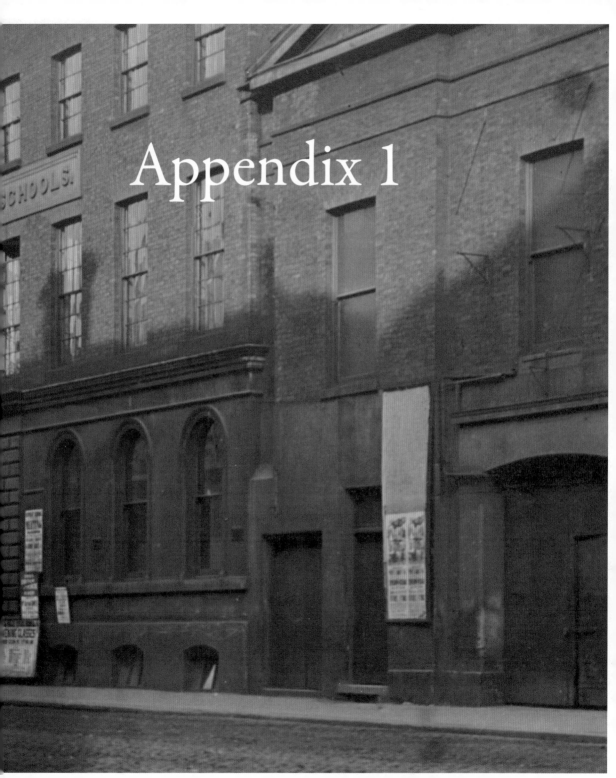

Appendix 1

'Art is an incurable disease.'

This is a transcript of an interview with L S Lowry done by a group of students from Stafford College of Art, together with an (unnamed) teacher, in 1964. It was found among Lowry's papers after he died.

The introduction to the interview, presumably written by the tutor, Peter Burnhill–although he has no recollection of it - reads: 'Before going to Lowry's home in Mottram-in-Longdendale on the hills east of Manchester, the students had prepared a number of questions–as all good interviewers do–but in fact they were hardly necessary. Lowry naturally lead from one aspect of his work to another and the honesty and perception of his answers give a wonderful insight into the joys and sorrows of a painter's mind.

'Most famous painters have won scholarships, belonged to groups or in some way made an impact whilst still young. But Lowry had no easy success–he didn't have a London exhibition till he was 51! He built up his work, not on fashionable styles but on what he saw and, because of this, his reputation is probably the most secure of any British Painter of the twentieth century. At 78 he is still working and finding new subjects and in this interview the humour, the strength and the humility of this man shines forth.'

One of the students, David Hunt, himself now an artist work-ing in Leek, Staffordshire, remembers vividly, even at a distance of forty years, the awkward circumstances of their arrival on Lowry's doorstep:

'We arrived (there were four or five of us, all about 20 years old) and rang the bell. There was a long pause... Then Lowry opened the door, his face half covered with lather and his braces hanging around his knees. "Who are you?" he said, obviously irritated. I told him. "No, that's tomorrow," he replied and shut the door. We didn't know what to do. We just stood there. We looked at the correspondence again, checked the date, which was correct–we had come by arrangement all the way from Stafford. None of us knew what to do so we just stood there. I don't know how for how long–quarter of an hour–half an hour–I don't know. I mean, I was a great admirer of Lowry as an artist. To me he was some sort of a God. I couldn't bear the thought of just going meekly away.

'Eventually, he opened the door again. He must have checked the papers arranging the visit. He just said: "Well, you'd better come in." And so we did go in–and it was mind-blowing. Pictures all around on the walls–I love the quality of the paint–the white impasto background–and the Rossettis and the clocks, all chiming different times. We stayed until the early afternoon–he was extremely pleasant, charming, absolutely charming–and so interesting. He answered everything we asked without hesitation; in fact he seemed to enjoy it. I hope he did.'

Q In your paintings people some-how seem to be solitary...

LSL Well, that's because that's my disposition coming out, you see–in creative work you let all the cats out of the bag, you know, what your disposition is like (and I live entirely by myself, used to live with my parents). It all comes out. I have never been away–not really. I'm not married–I live by myself and I keep myself to myself. I have one or two friends, but not really. Your art is bound to come out in the work, you can't keep it in.

Q How long is it since you've been famous?

LSL I don't know if I'm famous now. Past ten years. 1945 was the first time I made profit on my work, when I was 58. In 1951 (I could have barely kept myself in 1948) could have kept a wife–barely–in 1951-53. I could have made a lot of money, if I'd tried.

Q Has this increase in money altered you?

LSL Not a scrap–I don't care tuppence about it. I'm working for myself now.

Q Commercialism hasn't influenced you?

LSL I'm not interested. I'm too old to be interested in outside things now. I liked to once, to justify myself with my parents who were sympathetic but not interested. But now I don't care at all and if I could stop I would have stopped ten years ago, but I can't stop. I'm unfortunately a creature who cannot be passive. There are people like that.

Q What do you think of the modern English painters?

LSL I don't know anything about them. I'm an old man and they are young people and it's impossible for me to say. Well, I don't understand it. I don't bother about it. I just paint my own way as well as I can, and I go and see my friends. None of my close friends paint. Acquaintances paint, but my close friends I visit every weekend, they don't paint at all.

Q Have you never been influenced?

LSL To be perfectly frank, I have never been sufficiently interested to be influenced. That's putting it a bit strong, isn't it? (*Is that what you wanted? Ask me anything you can and I'll answer as well as I possibly can.*)

Q You have no interest in books on reproductions?

LSL I don't bother. In fact, some of my friends say: 'You're not really an artist, because you seem to spend more time when you work reading *The Financial Times* than anything else.'

Q I can agree with you there. It's no good looking at what everybody else is doing.

LSL Yes, I don't want to be bothered. I want to go to my friends and forget about it.

Q Did any paintings impress you in your early days?

LSL There are four Rossettis in this room. The only man I have ever wanted to possess. I've got about ten or twelve altogether. I'm not a bit like Rossetti and I don't know why I like Rossetti's paintings. Potential poetry. I like his poetry just as much as his paintings—why? I don't know.

Q That is what we come up against. Everybody asks, 'Why do you like a painting?' You can't tell them.

LSL No, you can't tell them. It's impossible to tell them. You either like it or you don't like it. That's the end of it altogether.

Q Then they say if you do like it, you should know why you like it.

LSL I don't agree with that. There is no reason at all why you should like it. I don't know why I like Rossetti.

Q Do you think art education today is inhibiting?

LSL I don't care for it as I used to care for it. Still, that's my age against the youth of today. Because a man of my age can't possibly tell you people what you ought to do, because I'm of my period and you are of your period. It's like these Beatles and things. I don't see any reason why the young people should not like The Beatles if they want to.

Q How do you feel about the upsurge of interest in Northern life?

LSL I think it's a good thing. Nothing seems to be wrong with it. The world changes all the time. It's not for me to judge it, is it? I can't judge your life with my life. I've been asked to go to an exhibition of abstract work up in Sunderland ...well, I can't judge abstract work. It isn't fair to try. I told them that, you see.

Q Do you think television programmes, such as *Coronation Street* and *Z Cars* are a true reflection of

northern life?

LSL No, they are not my idea of northern life. I don't see much of northern life up here you know. I'm away most of the time. I'm very seldom in this house, you know.

Q Do you go out sketching?

LSL I use this place as a place for sleeping and working. My friends don't like me living here by myself, and I don't care for it. But I keep the place on...it's less trouble to keep the place on. If you move you've got to find somebody to look after the place. I'd like a bigger place, but I couldn't get anybody to look after it if I got it.

Q Would you still have painted the same sort of industrial landscape if you had lived, say, in the south?

LSL That is a question I have often

wondered about, but I don't know. What happened up here, you see, was that I lived in the residential side of Manchester up to 1921[*]–a very nice residential side–and then I went to live in Pendlebury, one of the most industrial villages in the countryside midway between Manchester and Bolton. And at first I detested it. And then, after a few years, I got used to it, and then, after quite a few years, I got pretty interested in it and I began to walk about. Vaguely in my mind, I suppose, pictures were forming and then for about thirty odd years after that I did nothing but industrial pictures. That is how it all happened. I wasn't brought up in it.

Q You did other things before it?
LSL Portraits that nobody wanted and landscapes that nobody wanted. Folks say 'Do I look like that?' and I say, 'I'm afraid so.'[**]
Q Portrait painting never appealed to you?
LSL Not as a job. I have painted a friend of mine ten or twelve

Above: Lowry in conversation with Salford born Harold Riley, an artist whom he first came to know when Harold was at the Slade and Lowry was a Visiting Artist. In later years they would walk together across Swinton Moss or sketch together in the grimier back streets of the town.

times,[***] but they have never been shown–shown at the Academy once or twice–but apart from that I would never sell them. She has a lot and she will get the rest if anything happens to me, you see.

[*] This date is not strictly accurate. The move from Victoria Park to Pendlebury was in 1909 but it was in 1921 that he first exhibited pictures of industrial scenes.

[**] In the thirties he did a portrait of a friend as a surprise for his birthday; the man and his family disliked it so much it ended up (according to Lowry) behind the wardrobe in the his spare bedroom.

[***] It would seem that he was referring to the girl he called Ann, his god daughter.

I wouldn't sell them. I could have sold them. I put them in the Royal Academy last year–I didn't much mind whether I sold a picture or not, you know what I mean? I don't do portraits. If anybody came to me and said, 'Would you do my portrait?' I wouldn't do it. I would refer them to some gentleman in London who would do it much better than I would, and be a lot less trouble to myself, wouldn't it?

Q In your career as a painter, when you look back on it, do you see it as a progression along a set theme?

LSL That is a very interesting question. I think so, in a way. I don't say I have progressed. I have gone along a path, I think, that seemed to have been mapped out. But I don't know, of course. One thing seems to have lead to another in a peculiar way. You see, just when I was utterly and completely fed up–because I sold no pictures at all* until 1939 when I was 50–I began to say to my mother when she was alive 'Look, I'm a bloody fool for painting these idiotic pictures, I had better stop', and she said, 'I don't know, you carry on, something might happen,' and later on it did. But I often wondered how I kept on. Because I was not selling a *little* at first. I sold *nothing,* you see. Until about 1938 or 1939. Just before the war.

Q You were still working up here?

LSL I lived in Pendlebury until fifteen years ago and I was working like a galley-slave.

Q You have never become involved in a London art society?

LSL I am a member of several, but I don't show much. I am a member of a London group. I am a member of the National Society and the R. A. I show mostly at Reid and Lefevre,** you see. I'm having a show in June–10ᵗʰ or 11ᵗʰ. I started [with them] in February 1939 and this will be the eleventh or twelfth [show]. I don't know which it is.

Q Do painters have a contract with a gallery?

LSL I have no contract. I wouldn't go on a contract. I wouldn't be tied, you see, because if you do, you are a slave. I wouldn't do that. I would stop painting first. I never would go on a contract. Do you agree with that?

Q If you are on a contract, it isn't what you do, it's what they want you to do? How many painting do you produce in a year?

LSL I couldn't say. Not very many. I take a long time over them. I like to finish things as well as I possibly can and I won't send anything out unless it is to my satisfaction, just for the sake of selling it.

Q Say you saw something, like a crowd coming out of a football match, would you come home and think about it, or would you put it down straightway, or would you form an image in your mind and then put it down?

LSL I should try and just make a very rough note of it so I wouldn't forget it and then work on it sooner or later.

Q Do you work on one painting at a time?

LSL No, sometimes I have as many as twenty going. You take one as far as you possibly can and you can do nothing more to it. And you take it out of the way and bring it back in a month's time and carry on with it.***

Q I suppose one can look at something too long?

LSL You can't take it any further at all. Some have a lot of figures in, you see, and they take balancing. That is in the design, of course. And it isn't easy to balance a lot of figures because a drawing that looks spontaneous has got to be calculated, you see, and very often you get a picture into a position that it is *almost* finished–but not quite. You've got to wait and sooner or later it always comes.

Q When do you feel you can't do anything more?

LSL When I feel I can't, I take it upstairs out of the way...

Q And you bring it down in another month?

LSL Oh, no–you carry on with it. Sometimes.

Q And then you put it away for another month?

LSL Well, yes.

Q When do you know it is finished?

LSL That is very interesting. I had a problem like that last night. Some people–Granada the television people–they asked me that. You just can't tell. You keep it a time and when you find it seems to harmonise, when it seems all right, you leave it.

Q Don't you ever overwork a painting at all then?

LSL Practice, you know. I've done it for a long time. It's experience that tells. In the old days, at first you know, I used to spoil paintings. In those days you just scrapped things, but now I wouldn't scrap

---

*He did, in fact, sell several pictures, including to the Duveen Fund and quite a few big municipal galleries, as well as to important private collectors, but it would seem that none of these were prestigious enough to earn a place in his public history

**Lowry's London gallery from 1938 until his death.

***Professor Maitland once said that on occasion Lowry used to bring a painting round to tea, to see if it was ready to go out into the world on its own.

any. I wouldn't waste my time on it, you see. But at first I did. You do spoil things. You overwork – it's only practice – constantly doing them you get into a habit, you know. Like anything else.

Q Have you ever considered doing, say, natural landscapes? Somebody was telling me that there was supposed to be a crowd of you going out to do landscape painting and you refused to go?

LSL I've done these things about thirty-odd years ago. That was in the Cotswolds, but people did not encourage me to do landscapes. They said, 'For Heaven's sake, keep off landscapes, old chap; you stick to your factory pictures.'*

Q What do you think impressed you more than anything else?

LSL People every time.

Q Is this even more so nowadays? Before it used to be people in a setting – somehow the setting seems to be less important?

LSL They are all about these people, despite what others might say. You see these people in the street, you know.

Q Are the people all northern people or are they universal people?

LSL No, you see them in London. You see them everywhere. You see them a lot, in fact.

Q Doesn't the environment hold any interest any longer? Or have you exhausted it?

LSL I don't really think that. I have gone past it. It is down-and-outs mostly. People in very poor circumstances. They stand at street corners and they are staring at something

and you wonder what they are thinking when they are staring. Have you ever noticed them?

Q Is it the sympathy in you, do you think?

LSL It might be I'm sorry for them. You can't help them, you know.

Q Do you draw and paint them because you are sympathetic? Or because they are interesting?

LSL Well, I suppose they are interesting, because they make a good picture. I think I'm sympathetic, really. I think so. I wouldn't swear to it.

Q Is it with living in the north that you understand these sorts of people?

LSL The people in the south are just the same. The East End of London – the East End of any city – they're everywhere in certain quarters.

Q But do other people see them as interesting?

LSL Very few people see them. Nobody else is doing them as systematically as I am.

Q Similar to Lautrec, isn't it?

LSL Yes. I think so. Possibly. It is the down-and-outer in the poor quarters of any town, and there are poor quarters in every town, you know. You see these characters in every town if you look for them. It depresses you very much when you see them because you see some terrible things sometimes. I saw a man drinking a cup of water once in a place in Manchester where you could wash yourself and all that. And he crept in – he was one of those characters, you know – and he looked around furtively as he came in and then he went up to a tap – not a wash bowl – up to a tap, looked around again, pulled a bat-

tered tin out of his pocket and took a hasty drink, and then took another drink, and put his tin hastily under his coat and then, when nobody was looking, crept out. Very sad, you know. And then on the steps once of a large hotel, I saw a man eating some sandwiches and I will never forget that – he must not have had anything to eat for about a month or two. It was a terrible sight. One half of the world doesn't know how the other half lives.

Q Are these paintings a social comment?

LSL No, I just do them.

Q You are not trying to say anything?

LSL I'm not trying to say anything. I have no message at all – it's simply my way of looking at things.

Q Do you wish people to see them in the way you see them?

LSL Well, I would be glad if people [were] interested in these people because they are part of society. You can't do anything for them and there will always be people like that.

Q You mean they add to the painting, but are not the point of the painting?

LSL Yes, they're part of the painting and that is why I want to do it. But why I want to I'm not sure, you see. I don't know. You see some queer objects. I saw a man on the main street in Brighton on a Saturday afternoon playing a harp. In the shopping street in Brighton of all places. He was a queer bird, you know. Playing a harp in the street and sat on a little stool, he was playing away and he had the oldest rags and the rest of it. He was a big, strong-looking chap. So I saw a young lady, evidently an art student, making a

*In the early '30s Lowry worked on *The Cotswold Book* with writer Harold Timperley, but it did not sell well. When Lowry offered drawings for Timperley's next book, *The Shropshire Book*, they were rejected by the publisher. Throughout his life he did many landscape pictures of the Fylde countryside and the bleak hills of Northumberland, inevitably dubbed Lowry's lonely landscapes.

drawing, and I thought – if she can, I can. I wouldn't have done it but for her, you know. But in the main street of Brighton on a Saturday afternoon – think of that!

Q At this time of the year, was it?

LSL November, I think.

Q You don't go out looking for these people then?

LSL Oh, they happen in every town.

Q You don't, say, take a sketch book and go looking for them?

LSL No, I bash on, perhaps on an old invitation card, blank on one side. They're very good, you know. They fit in your pocket quite easily and they are all right on the other side, and you can do what you want, a small thing – and do it bigger when you get back.

Q So you haven't got any sketch books?

LSL Well, I've used them once. I did these in Ireland last time I was there. These were done in Ireland, you know. Galway Gaol. These are just notes for if I paint the picture. These are very rough. That is a lot of people watching TV and enjoying themselves.

Q How long ago was this?

LSL Last year.

Q It is interesting, looking at these. You've painted as much environment as you have people. But how long is it since you became interested in these people?

LSL About seven years.

Q What is your method of working?

LSL I prefer to get a canvas and see what happens on it. I sit down in the morning and say, 'Before tonight, I think I'm going to put something on you'...You don't know what you are going to see

Above: A rare photograph of Lowry, caught early morning, before he has put on either his collar and tie or the face he presented to the world. *Photograph by Barry Greenwood.*

when you stop. It's very fascinating. Most of my big pictures I've painted that way.

Q You don't ever use sketches and sketch material to contrive a composition?

LSL Oh, you can do. I just really do them out of my head. It's the most complete thing you know, because if you use one of these sketches it is a 50/50 business with you and your sketch, and you and your imagination. But if you can do it entirely from your head as much as you possibly can, it's better to leave it to your imagination. Based on what you have seen through your life.

Q I was going to ask you a question about that big Matisse painting in the Tate.

LSL I don't understand these things actually.

Q Wouldn't you like to?

LSL No, I'm quite satisfied. I'd sooner forget all about it.

Q You have no objection to them, then?

Three Men And A Cat, 1953.

LSL Who am I to have any objection to anything? Everybody has the right to their own viewpoint. I have no right to object to what anybody does, have I?

Q But a lot of abstract painters say that they are progressive in paint-ing, and people who stick to figura-tive painting aren't.

LSL I don't agree with that for a moment. Anybody becomes a museum piece in time, you know. The question is, are you going to survive the museum piece. I think every sort of art is right and none wrong. I don't like judging art exhibitions at all. I don't do it now because I'm allotted with time all over the place and because I feel I'm not qualified to judge now.

Q Have you ever had any urge to teach?

LSL No. I get a lot of people ask-ing me to teach, but I never get anything for it. I have had seven or eight people in the last fort-night looking at work. One young boy came up about 6 o'clock and went about 9.30 and said 'Thank you very much,' and I said, 'That's all right, I'm very pleased if I was any use.'

Q How do you see your own teach-ers and people who taught you at Manchester?

LSL Well, they're all dead, you know, now.

Q Yes, but in looking back on them. What did you think of them?

LSL Well, I don't think their work is what I thought it was at the time, because I'm older now. But they were very good teachers to me. That's the only way I can put it, isn't it?

Q So it comes back to the Life. Did they instil it in you?

LSL If you were going to take this course to get a Diploma–I'm go-ing back fifty-five years–well, you took the whole course–Design and Lithography–Heaven knows what! But I went there wanting to paint pictures as well as I could, and so I took Life and Antique, and I had to spend three years in a life class–two years in Antique before I could do that–you couldn't just walk into a Life Class in those days, you know. You had to do Prepara-tory Antique and then Antique and then you went into the Life Class.

Q Was that the same everywhere?

LSL Manchester, Salford and one or two others, yes.

Q The Slade and the Academy still do those things.

LSL Do they?

Q Oh yes, they have a fabulous an-tique room at The Slade. There's a painting of the Slade antique room in The Slade.

LSL I didn't know they did it now–I haven't been in The Slade for a long time...

Oh yes, plant drawing–thousands of things were needed for the Diplo-ma–I couldn't pass an examination in my life. I only painted pictures because I wasn't fit to do anything else. I'm perfectly frank with you. I had no brains–that's the trouble.

Q Do you think it's a good idea having examinations in Art to produce a painting over a specific period?

LSL It depends what you want. You have to have examinations, don't you, to get Diplomas. I never passed an examination at all. I was ten years in an Art School. I went in and came out and that was the end of that. I've got noth-ing to show for it, except the practice and experience. I got no certificate –nothing at all. Edu-cation has changed, everything changes, you know. Wireless, television–when I was young there was no wireless or cinema. I saw cinema come in. And then wireless came in, television came in. There was no flying when I was very young, you know. I never dreamt of it at all. I remember the first pictures. And a man opened in Manchester – he did very well; he said, 'I'm going to get out of this before it fails.'

Q Would you rather live in the 1960s than any other time you have lived?

LSL I can't say I have particularly lived at all really. I think I've seen a lot of things happen. I don't see anything very exciting about it all. I'm glad I am where I am. I just couldn't face the thought of going through your age again. I would be terrified. I couldn't do it. But that's because I'm my age, you see, and you are not. You're sorry for me, being my age, being near the grave, as you might put it. I don't mind a bit. I was very fond of walking in the old days, and I can't walk now. I am all right when I completely take my time. I couldn't walk a couple of miles whatever you gave me, and I used to like to do twenty or thirty [miles] a day once, you know. Very active until about five years ago, and then went off suddenly. I couldn't do two miles now. I take a taxi – I can't drive a car.

Q Do you ever use any other media such as water colour?

LSL Pencil and oil paintings. I don't use water colour. I can't use water colour. People implore me not to use water colour. 'Please stick to your oils,' they say. I think they're right.

Q Why? Do you think it is too difficult a medium?

LSL No, I treat water colour like oil. I put it on from the tube and that's no use at all, is it?

Q Have you ever tried sculpture?

LSL I thought of going in for sculpture once, but didn't. And sometimes right through my life it has been in the back of my mind about sculpture. I wonder sometimes whether I made a mistake. It's funny you should ask that because it is a thing that has often been in my mind. Even recently sometimes in my mind, although I am too late now, but I did wonder. When I was at [art] school, it was suggested to me by one master there.

Q Did you ever try to model anything?

LSL No. Free-hand drawing, light and shade – that's new to you, isn't it?

Q No. We come from a master of a similar sort. Royal College of Silversmiths.

LSL Oh, did you? What's his name?

Q Littlewood. What is you opinion of Carel Weight?

LSL I think he's very interesting because he is so original.

Q But his pictures strike me as being like the *Eagle* – you know, the *Eagle* comic. He uses violence in it, doesn't he? Every little brick in the wall – do you think it's quite valid?

LSL Anything is valid if you want to do it. I like Carel Weight. Very original.

Q Did you have anything to do at all with people like Spencer?

LSL No. I kept myself up here.

Q Do you have any other real interests apart from Art?

LSL No. That's the trouble. I can't stop. I have none. It's a terrible

thing. It gets you. You'll remember my words some day.

Q Did paintings have an effect on you when you were a small boy?

LSL No, I did little books on the theme when I was eight. And after that I tried to get into different places and couldn't. And then an Aunt of mine said 'I don't know what you are going to do with him, if he's that fond of drawing you had better send him to the Art School'. Well, I didn't mind going to the Art School. I had nothing against the Art School. I'll try anything once, you see. I got interested. That's how it happened. Because I wasn't fit to do anything else. I've never passed an examination in my life. I've no brains – that's the trouble.

Q No brains? You've a poor opinion of yourself, haven't you?

LSL No, I've no opinion at all. I'm only stating fact.

Q But to be able to produce work like this you must have brains.

LSL It was dormant in the early days. Every examination I went in for I failed – I couldn't find my name on the lists at all.

Q You never wished to go into education, to pass on your information, your views to people like us?

LSL Well, I'm ashamed to say I haven't.

Q Do you think you've got what you set out to get out of life?

LSL Well, I've got more really. I only set out to try to prove if I could show that there was some real pictorial interest in the industrial scene. But, as I say, Art is an incurable disease and you get carried on and on and on...

Look at me now! I'm 76 and can't stop. It's a terrible thing.

Appendix 2

One man's view

It was John Donne who wrote: No man is an island, entire of itself. And Michael Fitzgerald who added the rider: But Lowry was. He lived in a one-person world.

Nearly thirty years after Lowry's death, when his pictures had come to take their place in the annals of British art as the work of a true original, an eminent Irish psychiatrist produced a disturbing diagnosis of the artist's mental health.

In his book 'The Genesis of Artistic Creativity, Asperger's Syndrome and the Arts', Michael Fitzgerald, Professor of Child and Adolescent Psychiatry at Trinity College, Dublin, placed Lowry among the 'creative talents of genius with Asperger's Syndrome'. The book, he said, was a celebration of such people – a 'revealing exploration of the social behaviour, language, humour and obsessive interests and routine of 21 famous writers, philosophers, musicians and painters'[1] including, among others, Hans Christian Andersen, Arthur Conan Doyle, Spinoza, Mozart, Beethoven, Van Gogh and L S Lowry.

In other words, controversial though Fitzgerald's diagnosis of Lowry might be, he placed him in elite company, among the greats of the arts.

Michael Fitzgerald began his assessment of Lowry by studying his pictures. Noting the eccentricity and individuality of his work, he quite quickly decided that Lowry suffered from Asperger's Syndrome, a milder or lesser form of autism; a high functioning form of autism.

'The first time I saw these bizarre pictures, I thought – he must have Asperger's Syndrome. And that's what set me off…I thought they were revolutionary. They were to me anyhow. Unique and new…lots of people but none of them relating to one another.'

In lay terms, the Syndrome defines a mental disorder that in 93 per cent of cases is genetic. Not only is one born with it but, quite frequently, there are other cases of the disorder evident in the family; in Lowry's case it might well have been his mother.

In the introduction to his book, Michael Fitzgerald states: 'Persons with Asperger's syndrome show signs of an original intelligence. They also develop their own methods. When they are gifted – and this is not infrequently the case – they are often characterised by specific interests.'

He classes Lowry as an Asperger's savant and quotes John Betjeman's description of Lowry as 'a loner', artist Harold Riley's statement that 'he shut himself quite firmly into his own box', dealer Tilly Marshall's observation that he 'had the ability to put a wall around himself.' He refers to Lowry's ability to isolate himself from the crowd, his need to compartmentalise his friends and acquaintances, his lust for art, his difficulty in forming relationships, his dislike of undue emotion and his need for control. And he quotes Lowry's own description of himself as 'a cold fish'.

Fitzgerald does concede, however, that Lowry was possessed of a keen, if quirky, sense of humour which, it seems, is not typical for people with Asperger's.

Asperger's people, says Prof. Fitzgerald, 'are loners, odd, eccentric, relate poorly to the world, and are happier in their own company. A perfect example of Lowry's "aloneness" is the way he left the job he had held for forty-odd years: "I'll not be in tomorrow." And counting the "misfits" he saw from the top of a bus or the drawing pins holding up the paper on his ceiling. Asperger's are massive observers and totally into numeracy.'

At all times, Professor Fitzgerald was anxious that neither his diagnosis, nor his assessment of Lowry's traits, should be taken as critical of him as a person; they are intended to be scientific rather than pejorative. 'I think his art is marvellous. I just adore looking at his paintings. They are absolutely mesmerising, absolutely fantastic. I have utter respect for him, I like him, I find him quirky, I find him interesting, I would have liked to have met him…'

An interview with Professor Michael Fitzgerald, Professor of Child and Adolescent Psychiatry at Trinity College, Dublin. At his home, Dublin, September, 2005.

SR How is it different in an autistic world?

MF Well, it is a one-person world. Our world is a two-person world. We talk to people; we have relationships with people...[...]...I see the autistic world as a one person world, the art as a one-person art, it comes from within; it is not influenced by people outside...

SR All the arts?

MF Yes, true creativity of this nature comes utterly from inside, so the normal world is a social world where people chat and they have coffee and they do this and they do that and they do the other...Now in the autistic world it all happens inside the head, everything happens inside the head....[...]...

I think his art is marvellous; I just adore looking at his paintings, absolutely mesmerising, absolutely fantastic. I have utter respect for him, I like him, I find him quirky, I find him interesting, I would have liked to have met him, I would have been interested in him, etc., etc., so everything I say...(and I don't always feel that for everybody)...I have utter respect for him, even though I am saying these other things...

SR There was a paper written by two psychiatrists, Harold Palmer and Norman Colhoun, which intrigued Lowry enormously. Harold Palmer, who described Lowry as a loner, had done work in the Western desert during the [Second World] War with servicemen who had been shell shocked and he regarded Lowry's attitude to life and the way he stood back from life, even in his paintings, as a state of detachment similar to shell shock...

MF But that is an autistic detachment. He was born with that. He came genetically by it–it's 93 per cent inherited. It is largely a genetic condition–you would find other members of the family with these traits. It would be very common to find other members of the family with these traits. But what they have is the capacity to see detail. Asperger's [people] are massive observers, even though...they have major difficulties with relationship skills, and their capacity to conduct social conversations are poor, their skills are poor, even their social language...[...]...they can't handle chit chat. If they go to a cocktail party they can observe more...than anybody else can observe and they can take away more detail than anybody else, even thought they will usually be there, standing by a wall, maybe with one or two people; they tend to leave early; there will be a lot of avoidance of contact; they won't know what to say–to talk rubbish, because that's what they talk at cocktail parties, rubbish–

SR He didn't have that capacity. For small talk. Or rubbish. Nor the desire actually.

MF No, he didn't have the desire, or the capacity for it. We call it 'weak central coherence'. And that means that you can't see the big picture. You can see the details but you can't see the big picture–some people are pre-occupied with the handles of doors. If you had Asperger's Syndrome and you came in here this morning and you were into this–by this stage you would have every single detail of the door handle in your mind and that would be the big thing about this interview–Now they have the capacity to pick out detail, to see a pin in the ground where I wouldn't see it, you wouldn't see it, so that they are just massive at detail and that is one of the secrets of their success. They don't see the world as the rest of us see it; they see it as bits, as a whole series of bits...[...]... They have very poor capacity to see the big picture. Children have this capacity to see detail...

SR Is that why he got on so well with children?

MF Yes! Oh absolutely. His immature personality–emotionally they are at the level of children.

SR Is it possible to give a lay person's definition of Asperger's?

MF Yes. Yes, it is. They are loners. They are odd. They are eccentric. That's how the lay person describes them. He's odd. He relates poorly. He's in a world of his own.

SR People with these symptoms–doesn't necessarily mean they have Asperger's?

MF Well, a lot of them. Not all

Lewis Carroll didn't marry, Lowry didn't marry–

SR There were always excuses... reasons...

MF They never met the right woman, that's the phrase.

SR Lowry said no-one could have put up with his art...

MF But no, that wasn't it. They all had this anxiety. This terrible anxiety, intimacy anxiety...could you imagine Lowry living with a woman?

SR No.

MF See, you couldn't.

SR He had an interesting relationship with an artist called Pat Cooke and her husband which, unusually, continued after she was a grown woman. But she had a very unworldly, almost naïve attitude to life, you could even say 'childlike'...

MF Was that the heir?

SR No, she is very different. Much more serious. Much more deeply affected by her friendship with him–I once asked her why she thought she had inherited...and she said, because she was at the end of the line...

MF That's it exactly. 'I'll shan't be in tomorrow'. What do you do with your property? You give it to your friend. The one who's there today. You know who did that? George Orwell–he got married on his death bed and I think all the

eccentrics have Asperger's but a higher percentage than the average–it is defined in my book at the beginning but just for the lay person, they are loners, they are odd, they avoid eye contact, they often have a piercing gaze...and they have awkward movements, they walk in a awkward way, they can be clumsy and they are often, usually, happier in their own company. And when he worked–what fascinated me about him [Lowry] was that the last day at work he said: 'I shalln't be in tomorrow'–now that was a complete, utter, absolute and entire

autistic statement. Yes, because there was no relationship to the people. I mean, can you imagine? Forty years–at the very least after forty years you would go to the pub, have pint of beer with the others on the last day. But 'I shalln't be in tomorrow...' The same thing happened with Bartok. He got married in the morning and then in the afternoon he said to his mother: 'She's staying here now, she's my wife.' That's it...[...]...A lot of them couldn't marry. Beethoven didn't marry, Van Gogh didn't marry, Ludwig Wittgenstein didn't marry, royalties went to this woman, that was the same kind of thing. She became his heir—a quite inappropriate thing—

SR Well, with Carol Ann it was very different. She was very appropriate. Absolutely appropriate. She had acquired so much of his feeling that she treats his work as he would have done—

MF And that's even burdensome. That's lack of empathy...

SR What I am interested to know is—Is there a way you could you have told from his pictures?

MF Oh, yes, indeed. That's where I started...because I think they are very odd. The first time I saw these bizarre pictures I thought—he must have Asperger's Syndrome, and that's what set me off—I thought they were revolutionary. They were to me anyhow, unique and new...

SR *(Produces a selection of doodles, mainly the strange figures of the later years, The Man Being Swallowed by Sharks...)*

MF There's something immature about them...it was just the oddness of the shape, they are caricatures in a way...you would be looking for absence of relationships, lots of people but none of them relating to one another...(*He looks at Boy With a Stomach Ache*) Do you know there is none of these looking at each other? That's autistic. Well, this child is looking out. (*He looks at Mother and Child*) That's the same. They are not touching, these are two separate individuals. And

look at this—the child is being held out autistically—what would you do? This child is crying—you'd put it over your shoulder—he has drawn two separate individuals—you would put that child over your shoulder—

SR He always said that this was the way he saw it...he only drew what he saw...

MF No, have you ever seen a parent like that? This is fascinating... they're kind of grotesque figures. They are eccentric...these are all bits of himself...they are outsiders...he was an outsider. They were odd, they were strange, and there isn't a lot of happiness, is there? Is there much smiling in his pictures?

SR He always said there wasn't—'*Never a happy picture of mine you'll see*'—but I think there is a lot of humour in them...

MF You see these are part of his psyche—grotesque is a word I don't like—but these figures are odd, they are strange and they do represent part of his psyche...

SR Psyche? Meaning?

MF Psyche just means mind. It is not a happy world. (Would he be identifying with them? Yes) I mean, he's an outsider and he is painting outsiders and he is autistic and he...picks out little details, novelties, I would say that what the person with autism has is the capacity to pick out odd little details. Vignettes. Because we would see a whole picture, the whole person, but what he would see would

be just that the mouth is slightly skewed—or the hair, he might see little details...(*Prof Fitzgerald is looking at The Cripples*—) Was this a scene he had seen?

SR *(explains about the trip with David Carr looking for odd looking people and had counted 101 or whatever)*

MF Well, that's an autistic phenomenon! They always count things. They are totally into numeracy and numbers, they are mathematically minded very often. Numbers mean an awful lot to them. They like facts and they like numbers. They can't handle intimate personal relationships but they can handle facts, it's a way of controlling the world, it puts an order in the world. You know—a child might do that. In fact a child would do that. You know 'we saw five Jaguars today'. That is very normal for a child. But you, you wouldn't count Jaguars, not unless you had a child in the car. Okay, so he was with a grown man (David Carr) and they were both counting, but they often choose friends with similar traits as themselves—it would be very interesting...with the girls, they were immature, that's the key—Lewis Carroll—Hans Christian Andersen—

SR I thought maybe it was their honesty? Their innocence he liked—they would say, honestly, what they thought of his work...

MF No, no, it wasn't that. It was their immaturity—the autistic person, or the Asperger's person, they're honest, they're innocent, they're naïve, they're immature and they often tell you the truth, so they are relating to someone who is at the emotional age as themselves and who doesn't threaten them, who doesn't make them frightened. You see that classically in Lewis Carroll and Hans Christian Andersen

(We look at The Funeral Party...)

It is bizarre, in a funeral party, people are always huddled around, funerals are liberating, everybody talks, with anecdotes, these are individuals, they are all autistic, nobody is relating...*(It should, perhaps, be mentioned here that Michael Fitzgerald is Irish and we were in Dublin and Irish funeral wakes are probably rather more sociable than English ones!)*...This is brilliant. Each one of these [people] is separate. It's a picture in pieces. It's a picture of individuals...[...]...

(Fitzgerald looks at Head of a Man with Red Eyes)

I am familiar with this–look at the piercing eyes, mad eyes...I've never seen autistic eyes like this before...

(Fitzgerald looks at 'Father and Two Sons')

These [men] are crazy. The three of them are insane. They should be in an asylum...The three of them could be three self portraits...

(Fitzgerald asks to move on to other paintings. He finds the strange heads too disturbing to look at...)

I want to move on, can we look at

some other pictures, I'm even disturbed myself looking at them...I admire them, but I find them disturbing.

(We look at An Island)

SR Lowry said 'These are symbols of my mood, they are myself' –

MF The house represents himself...

SR He would say that he used to stand looking at these empty houses and imagining the happy childhood that went on in them...

MF Yes. Well, you see a non-autistic childhood, a happy childhood, is one in which children are able to relate and where there is fun and where you have the capacity for fun...but he is an island. John Donne said: 'Call no man an Island'. Well, I think now we have got something to counter John Donne...Lowry *was* an island. He was a loner, he was in the world but he was not of the world. He was an individual in the world who passed people in the night...[...]...If you saw him at work, you would think he was part of the group, the group of rent collectors or whatever they were–but he wasn't. He was a sole individual and to think that he was relating to the others in the group–that would be a misconception. In reality Lowry was a rent collector...The amount of social contact you have collecting the rents is minimal, that's why it suited him, and a rent collector wouldn't be necessarily very welcome, he would not be popular...

SR One of his young colleagues at

Pall Mall [Clifford Openshaw] told me that the children in the street would laugh at him but that he, Lowry, used to drop coins, casually, as if by accident, and watch to see them scrabble to pick them up...

MF Yes, children do laugh at autistic people. It's the eccentricity they laugh at–but dropping the money, that would be a way of controlling them. He was controlling them. He was upset, as you or I would be, by their laughing at him...[...]...People with Asperger's Syndrome are *hyper* sensitive, *ultra* sensitive; the most minor little upset will go to their absolute soul. So a mild little hurt, a mild little slight is like putting a knife through the soul, it's utterly devastating...

SR I saw the reason that he compartmentalised his life was because he didn't want people to denigrate his art because he was a rent collector?

MF No. No...

SR Or was it part of the disease–do you call it a disease?

MF No. It's a disorder, we don't call it a disease. It is a developmental disorder, you are born with it, it is probably to do with a migration of the cells in utera, so the brain is not balanced...[...]...it is a huge disorder, a devastating disorder...[...]...it is supposed to be milder than autism but, if one had Asperger's Syndrome one wouldn't say that. It is a huge disorder; it is a devastating disorder or can be...[...]...

SR Would having Asperger's Syndrome make it harder for Lowry to succeed as an artist?

MF He had no choice. Asperger's people are driven by their genes and he didn't have choices...Did Lowry go to college? He did, didn't he?

SR Oh yes, he went to night school for years...

MF But a the end of the day they are usually autodidactic...they teach themselves, the components are self teaching, the autodidact is a thousand times more important than the school...[...]...As a personality he was naïve, his emotional personality was naïve, but his paintings are a work of genius, his art is a work of genius—

SR How would you define 'genius'?

MF Well, genius is something completely new. It has to be innovative, it hasn't been done before. It can't be replicative. It is not modelled on other people, it has to break new ground, it has to be different...[...]....Geniuses are usually dismissed early on—because [what they do] is so new; people think it is crazy and it takes a long time for people to see the novelty. Novelty and originality and, I think the work is usually startling. Because it is new....[...]...I mean, now, he is an iconic painter...

SR He is still not totally accepted by the art establishment...

MF That is appalling because in some ways he is *the* English painter. Of the twentieth century. When I think of art in the twentieth centu-

ry in England—well, there are a few others, I suppose, Hockney—but Lowry is almost the archetypal figure

Asperger's was identified in 1943 in Vienna by Hans Asperger but it was not written about in England (and dubbed Asperger's Syndrome) until 1981. Asperger was working in Vienna during the Nazi occupation and was therefore treated with suspicion, post war.

Fitzgerald looks at some of the hidden pictures...the heavily worked drawings of a girl which have been

described as 'erotic'. He said:'...The last thing that comes to mind is eroticism! I would say robotics—I suppose the bow could be slightly coquettish, even sexual, if you are looking for that kind of thing...'

SR (*in relation to the hidden drawings and the robotic reference*)... Strange you should call them 'robotic' because Lowry's favourite ballet was Coppélia, which tells the story of the puppet master who falls in love with the doll he has created...

MF That's fascinating. That's

MF That's certainly oppressive. She's in a strait jacket. I suppose that is slightly erotic – the skirt – I don't know if dresses were short at that time?
SR They were.

MF Well, then yes. But she's a mad woman. A mad woman in a strait jacket. But it shows a fear of women as well. Women, adult women, are only safe if they are locked up. A safe adult woman is a woman that's in a strait jacket. That's why you can't get involved with an adult woman, because these are very dangerous people...He must have been terrified of sexuality. Completely terrified. Could you imagine him having a sexual relationship? He was a child. Himself and his mother, that was a mother/child relationship. At home, even though he looked after her, he was still the child. And they are often very clingy to mother and they are immature...[...]...He has to compartmentalise himself, to keep himself away from these women, and it's almost phallic – I know these high [heeled] shoes were in fashion at the time but they are slightly phallic. It's just the phallic woman is the most dangerous woman. She's the real dominatrix – or whatever you call them. That's important....[...]...I would say there was a sexual identity diffusion – he was celibate, asexual, but they [Asperger's people] often have sexual identity diffusion. They often seem non-specific, to say that he was heterosexual or homosexual would not be true – I often find that those phraseologies don't work, it's more diffuse than that...

(He looks at the drawing Woman on a Rock...)

hugely important in relation to these. Because an Asperger's man is a robotic man. They have a sense of themselves as robotic and he walked in an odd kind of robotic way which led the kids to laugh at him.

But Lowry wasn't an aggressive man? He didn't do damage to people. But you can have a repressed aggression, a more latent aggression...

SR I thought she was possibly being strangled by it – the bow...

MF Yes. Well, yes, that's right. That is a possible reading because – I didn't see it, but I can see it now, very clearly. That's one reading. The second reading is that she is coquettish. The strangling of course would go with the autistic aggression, but he wasn't an aggressive man, he didn't do damage to people, he wasn't aggressive, but you can have a kind of repressed aggression, a more latent aggression, aggression...

(He looks at another of these drawings.)

That's a safe place for women. That's where they should be. He is phobic of intimacy, so this is where you put them! But look, there–this rock is phallic...these are phallic women–highly dangerous women and the only thing to do with them is put them out to sea where they can't do any damage, where they can't hurt you...But it is also himself. This is the world he lived in. This is the autistic world. He's a man alone, solitary, he's like an island out in the middle of the sea, remember the house earlier...the painting *An Island*...that's him, alone.

(He looks at the drawing of Man Drowning In A Sea Of Sharks)

That's him. That's absolutely him alone...and those? They are human beings...

SR He used to say they were dealers. Art dealers.

MF I think it is more than that. They are art dealers, of course, they are art dealers, but it is more complicated than that. Journalists are sharks as well, but I think it is also his fear of the world. It's too simple to see it like that...as dealers...it's too simple.

But that [picture] is the most profound of all. That summarises everything. He's paranoid. There's quite a paranoid streak in him. He's suspicious. He feels people are out to get him...at a deeper level. Slightly paranoid, that is, it's a paranoid trait, it's not paranoid psychosis. A bit suspicious. Slightly mistrustful and suspicious. He lived in a paranoid world...

But of all the pictures you have shown me today, that is the one that has grabbed me the most. Because that's the key. That's the daddy of them all.

Acknowledgements

As always, when writing about L S Lowry, my debt to his heir, Carol Ann Lowry is incalculable. In the thirty years that have passed since I first enlisted her help, she has been unfailing in her support. Her friendship, expertise, knowledge, interest and above all her eye for a picture have been invaluable–fulsome thanks then to Carol Ann and more recently Bill Stevenson of the Lowry Estate Office for both his help and his patience with my endless queries.

Thanks, and many of them, are also due to:

Professor Michael Fitzgerald of Trinity College, Dublin, for his kindness and hospitality, the hours he gave me expanding on his thesis of Lowry and Asperger's Syndrome, and for allowing me to quote from his book *The Genesis of Artistic Creativity*.

Lindsay Brooks and Ruth Salisbury at The Lowry who are a source of constant support and encouragement; and for ready access to their archive department–a treasure house of information and insight.

Judy Sandling, for many years the Keeper of the Lowry Collection at Salford City Art Gallery, who holds a fund of knowledge in her head and is never anything but willing to share it with those who ask.

Mrs. Margaret Robertson, widow of the late Philip Robertson who, together, were good friends to Lowry; not to mention their daughters who, as young people, entertained Lowry with their chat and, on occasion, obliged him by drawing a horse or two for a current painting. My thanks to them for allowing access to their correspondence with the artist and the use of some of his drawings in their possession.

Michael Howard of Manchester Metropolitan University, with whom I enjoy amicable disagreements on the subject of L S Lowry, but who is never less than willing to share his expertise.

Curator and critic Julian Spalding who allowed me to use an extract of his excellent 2006 Lowry Lecture–the first, it is promised, of a series of such to be held annually at The Lowry on Salford Quays.

Mike Leber, a Keeper of the Lowry Collection at Salford City Art Gallery during Lowry's lifetime, who despite retirement is always willing to search his long memory for some forgotten detail.

Jonathan Horwich, Deputy Chairman of Christie's U K, for his support and help in many areas of Lowry's artistic life–always offered with warmth and a ready smile.

Ann Baxter Wright, and her husband Tom, for sharing the knowledge her father Alick Leggat gained over the long years of friendship with the artist.

Alan May, John Burgess David Hunt and Peter Burnhill all formerly of Stafford College, who were kind enough to offer me their tapes of their interview with Lowry many years ago.

And so many people, now dead who have helped and guided me over the years; their expertise and personal knowledge of the artist creeps into my text so often in these pages that it is impossible to separate one from the other. I am fortunate not only that Lowry made so many friends in his lifetime, but that they have been happy to share their experiences of both the man and the artist. All have been acknowledged in previous books and my appreciation of their co-operation still stands despite the fact that they are not mentioned invidually here.

Barbara Schwepcke and all at Haus, not forgetting our endlessly patient designer Rick Fawcett, and most especially my editor Robert Pritchard for tolerance and understanding, which, as every writer knows, are to be treasured and nourished in an editor.

242

Select Bibliography

Barber, Noel, *Conversations with Painters*. Collins, London, 1964.

Collis, Maurice, *The Discovery of L. S. Lowry*. Alex Reid and Lefevre, London, 1951.

Fitzgerald, Michael, *The Genesis of Artistic Creativity, Asperger's Syndrome and the Arts*, Jessica Kingsley Publications, London and Philadelphia, 2005.

Howard, Michael, *L. S. Lowry: A Visionary Artist*. The Lowry Press, Salford, 2000.

Kalman, Andras, in conversation with Andrew Lambirth, *Conversation Pieces,* Chaucer Press, London, 2004.

Leber, Michael and Sandling, Judith. *L. S. Lowry*. Phaidon Press and Salford Art Gallery, 1987. Published for the L. S. Lowry Centenary Exhibition, Salford Art Gallery.

Levy, Mervyn. *Painters of Today: L. S. Lowry, ARA*. Studio Books, London, 1961.

Levy, Mervyn, *The Drawings of L. S. Lowry*. Cory, Adams and McKay, London, 1963.

Marshall, Tilly, *Life with Lowry*. Robson, Dring Publications, 1987.

Rohde, Shelley. The Lowry Lexicon, *An A to Z of L S Lowry*. The Lowry Press, Salford, 2003.

Rothenstein, John. *Modern English Painters: Lewis to Moore*. Macdonald and Jane's, London, 1976.

Sandling, Judith, *Lowry's City,* foreword by Michael Leber. The Lowry Press, Salford, 2003.

Sandling, Judith, Catalogue notes in the 2002 exhibition, *L. S. Lowry* at Richard Green Galleries, New Bond Street, London.

Seija, Doreen, *The Lowry I knew*. Jupiter Books (London) Ltd., 1983.

Spalding, Julian, *Lowry*. Phaidon Press, 1979.

Spring, Howard, *The World of L S Lowry,* in *The Saturday Book*, No. 17, edited John Hadfield, Hutchinson, London, 1957.

Wraight, Robert, *The Art Game Again!* Leslie Frewin. London, 1974.

Notes to the Arts Council catalogue to the L. S. Lowry Retrospective Exhibition at the Tate Gallery, London, 1966.

'Tributes to L S Lowry',a catalogue to the Royal Academy Exhibition of Lowry's work, 1976.

Footnotes

Prologue

[1] Jonathan Horwich, Deputy Chairman of Christie's, UK, to author, August, 2005.
[2] Jonathan Horwich.
[3] Catalogue notes to Lowry Exhibition, Crane Kalman Gallery, 1987.
[4] Catalogue notes to Lowry Exhibition, Crane Kalman Gallery, 1987.
[5] Harold Riley to author.
[6] Michael Ayreton, writing in the *Evening Standard*, 1945.
[7] Lindsay Brooks, *The Independent*, February, 2006.
[8] Mike Leber to author, 2006.
[9] Julian Spalding to author, 2006.

Chapter 1

[1] The late May Eddowes, née Shephard, to author.
[2] Rowley Fletcher, nephew of Charles Rowley, Chairman of the Trustees of Bennett Street Sunday School, to author.
[3] The late Lucy Holmes, nee Snarr, to author.
[4] The late May Eddowes to author.
[5] Tyne Tees Television, documentary film *Mister Lowry,* Produced by Robert Tyrrell. Made in 1968, it was not shown until 1971.
[6] The late Pat Cooke to author.
[7] L S Lowry to a group of students from Stafford College of Art, 1964.
[8] L S Lowry, *Mister Lowry*, Tyne Tees Television.

Chapter 2

[1] L S Lowry to Prof. Hugh B Maitland at Burton-on-Trent, on tape during a period of several weeks during the winter of 1970, when Maitland was preparing a (unpublished) biography of Lowry.
[2] Maitland tapes.
[3] Interview given by L S Lowry to students of Stafford College of Art, at home in Mottram on tape, 1964.
[4] *'Lancashire made them'* by Frank and Vincent Tilsley, *News Chronicle* and *Daily Dispatch*, 1st December, 1955.
[5] The late Mrs. May Eddowes to author.
[6] The late H H Shephard to author.
[7] Clifford Openshaw to author.
[8] Maitland tapes.
[9] Clifford Openshaw to author.
[10] Maitland tapes.
[11] The late Mrs.May Eddowes, daughter of Tom Shephard, to author.
[12] The late Sam Rabin to author
[13] *'Mr. Monsieur':* Adolphe Valette in Manchester' by Sandra A. Martin, *Lancashire Life*, November, 1976.
[14] Clifford Openshaw to author.
[15] The late James Fitton, R A, a fellow pupil in Valette's life class, to author.
[16] Martin, *'Mr. Monsieur'.*
[17] *Modern English Painters, vol.2, Lewis to Moore,* by John Rothenstein, Macdonald and Jane's, London, 1976.
[18] L. S. Lowry to the late Monty Bloom, on tape (undated).
[19] Maitland tapes.
[20] *L S Lowry: the artist* by Frank Mullineux, Catalogue to the Lowry Collection at Salford City Art Gallery, 1977.
[21] L S Lowry to the late Gerald B Cotton, Chief Librarian of Swinton and Pendlebury and later Salford, and the late Frank Mullineux, Keeper of Monks Hall Museum, Eccles, on tape (undated).
[22] *L S Lowry* by Margo Ingham, Fine Art Editions, No.2, Aquarius publications, 1977.

Chapter 3

[1] *Eccles Journal,* Friday 7th May, 1909.
[2] The late Ethel Ridgeway, general maid at 117 Station Road from 1916 to 1920, to author.
[3] Maitland tapes.
[4] BBC Television documentary film L S Lowry, produced by John Read, 1957.
[5] Cotton/Mullineux tapes (undated).
[6] Robert Wraight in catalogue notes to the Crane Kalman Gallery's Lowry Exhibition, November 1966 to January 1967.
[7] *English Painters, vol.2. Lewis to Moore* by John Rothenstein, Macdonald and Jane's, London. 1976.
[8] Tyne Tees Television documentary film *Mister Lowry,* produced by Robert Tyrrell, 1968.
[9] Cotton/Mullineux tapes.
[10] *The Discovery of L S Lowry* by Maurice Collis, Alex Reid and Lefevre, London, 1951.
[11] Mullineux/Cotton tapes (undated).

[12] Lowry on tape to students from Stafford College of Art, 1965.
[13] The late Clifford Openshaw, Rent Collector and Clerk at Pall Mall Property Company, to author.
[14] Clifford Openshaw to author.
[15] Clifford Openshaw to author.

Chapter 4

[1] Clifford Openshaw to author.
[2] BBC Television documentary film 'I'm Just a Simple Man', produced by John Read, 1977.
[3] The late Philip Robertson, a frequent companion of Lowry's at the Seaburn Hotel, Sunderland, to author.
[4] The late Sheila Fell to author.
[5] L S Lowry to Monty Bloom, one of his most addicted collectors, on tape (undated).
[6] Clifford Openshaw.
[7] Sir John Rothenstein, *Mister Lowry*, Tyne Tees Television.
[8] Cotton/Mullineux tapes.
[9] Rothenstein, *Modern English Painters*.
[10] Rothenstein, *Modern English Painters*.
[11] Maitland tapes.
[12] The late James Fitton, R A, to author.
[13] Margaret Robertson to author.
[14] James Fitton, R A.
[15] James Fitton, R A.
[16] Rothenstein, *Modern English Painters*.
[17] The late H H Shephard to author.
[18] *Mister Lowry*, Tyne Tees Television.

Chapter 5

[1] *Life with Lowry* by Tilly Marshall, Robson Dring Publications, 1987.
[2] *Mister Lowry*, Tyne Tees Television.
[3] Cotton/Mullineux tapes.

[4] Lowry to students of Stafford College of Art, on tape, 1964.
[5] Clifford Openshaw.
[6] Hal Yates, author of *A Short History of Manchester Academy of Fine Art*, 1973, to author.
[7] *Shabby Tiger* by Howard Spring, published by Collins, London, 1934.
[8] BBC Television documentary, *I'm Just a Simple Man,* produced by John Read, 1977.
[9] The late Pat Cooke to author.

Chapter 6

[1] Maitland tapes.
[2] Maitland tapes.
[3] *Manchester Guardian,* 31st October, 1921.
[4] The late Eric Newton in 'For Your Leisure', BBC Radio, 14 November 1948.
[5] Maitland tapes.
[6] Letter to L S Lowry from Howard Spring, 21st May, 1942.
[7] *Mister Lowry,* Tyne Tees Television.
[8] Cotton/Mullineux tapes.
[9] Maitland tapes.
[10] Bloom tapes.
[11] Bloom tapes.
[12] Letter from L S Lowry to A S Wallace, Literary Editor of the *Manchester Guardian*, 9th November, 1926.
[13] *Mister Lowry*, Tyne Tees Television.

Chapter 7

[1] The late Edith Timperley to author, 1977.
[2] Edith Timperley.
[3] Lowry to students of Stafford College of Art, 1965.
[4] Edith Timperley.
[5] Letter from L S Lowry to Harold Timperley, 14th June, 1929.

[6] Edith Timperley.
[7] Letter from L S Lowry to Harold Timperley, 28th October, 1929.
[8] Letter from L S Lowry to Harold Timperley, 5th December, 1931.
[9] 'My Lonely Life' by Robert Robinson, *Sunday Times,* 11th September 1962.
[10] Letter from L S Lowry to Harold Timperley, 10th September 1931.
[11] *The Lowry I Knew* by Doreen Sieja, Jupiter Books, London, 1983.
[12] The late Rev Geoffrey Bennett to author.
[13] Maitland tapes, 1970.
[14] *Fifty Years of the New English Art Club: 1886–1935* by Alfred Thornton, Curwen Press, London, 1935.
[15] *Fifty Years of the New English Art Club.*
[16] *Méditerranea,* June 1928.
[17] Letter from Harold Timperley to L S Lowry, 29th November, 1942.
[18] Letter from Lowry to Lawrence Haward, Curator of Manchester City Art Gallery, 3rd April, 1930.
[19] Letter from Lawrence Haward to Lowry, 23rd July, 1930.
[20] Letter from Lowry to Lawrence Haward, 28th July, 1930.
[21] Letter from Lowry to Lawrence Haward, 18th September, 1930.
[22] Maitland tapes.
[23] *Conversations with L S Lowry* by Hugh Maitland, unpublished.
[24] 'Lowry revisits his landscape' by Arthur Hopcraft, *Illustrated London News,* 9th July 1966.
[25] Letter from Gordon Phillips 'for the editor', *Manchester Guardian,* to L S Lowry, 5th March, 1939.
[26] Cotton/Mullineux tapes.

Chapter 8

[1] L S Lowry to Carol Ann Lowry, thence to author.
[2] L S Lowry to Carol Ann Lowry,

thence to author.

3L S Lowry to Monty Bloom, on tape (undated).

4Letter to L S Lowry from Mary Fletcher Shelmerdine, 9th May, 1932.

5The late Doris Jewell, sister of the late Daisy Jewell, to author.

[6] Letter to L S Lowry from Major Armand Blackley, Director of James Bourlet and Sons, Ltd., 25th April, 1955.

[7] Letter to Major Armand Blackley from L S Lowry, published in the Bourlet brochure.

[8] Tommy W Earp writing in the *Daily Telegraph*, 14th January, 1935.

[9]Letter from L S Lowry to Harold and Edith Timperley, 25th April, 1937.

[10] The late Bert Jones of James Bourlet and Sons to author.

[11]Letter from Daisy Jewell to L S Lowry, 23rd March, 1937.

[12]Bert Jones to author.

[3]The late A J McNeill Reid in Tyne Tees Television documentary film Mister Lowry, produced by Robert Tyrrell, 1968.

[14]"*L S Lowry Sees Beauty Through the Smoke*' by Harry Hopkins, John Bull, 16 November, 1957.

[15]*The Discovery of L S Lowry* by Maurice Collis, published by Alex Reid and Lefevre Ltd., London, 1951.

[16]The Discovery of L S Lowry by Maurice Collis.

[17]Quoted in *The Arts Review*, January 1968.

[18]Brian Sewell, writing in the *Evening Standard*, 25th August, 1988.

[19]Letter from Daisy Jewell to L S Lowry, undated.

[20] *Brave Day, Hideous Night* by John Rothenstein, Hamish Hamilton,

1965.

[21]ibid.

[22]Sir John Rothenstein in Mister Lowry', Tyne Tees Television.

[23]Letter from A J McNeill Reid to L S Lowry, 22nd June, 1940.

Chapter 9

[1] Tilly Marshall of The Stone Gallery, Newcastle upon Tyne, to the author, 1976.

[2] Notes made by the late Tony Ellis, Curator of Salford City Art Gallery, of conversations with L S Lowry in preparation for a biography (unpublished) of the artist.

[3] James Fitton R A to the author, 1977.

[4] James Fitton R A to the author, 1977.

[5] *Mister Lowry,* Tyne Tees Television.

[6] *'My Lonely Life'* by L S Lowry as told to Edwin Mullins, *Sunday Telegraph*, 20th November, 1966.

[7] Edith Timperley to author.

[8] L S Lowry to Edith Timperley, to author.

[9] Edith Timperley to author.

Chapter 10

[1] Kathleen (née Leatherbarrow) to author.

[2]The late Margo Ingham of the Mid-day Studios to the author.

[3] Margery Clarke (née Thompson) to author.

[4]Doreen Sieja (née Crouch) to author.

[5] The late Pat Cooke (née Gerrard) to author.

[6]Frederick May in an introduction to the Heinemann Drama Library Edition of Pirandello's *Six Characters in Search of an Author.*

[7] The late Sheila Fell to author.

[8] The late Sheila Fell to author.

[9] Doreen Sieja (née Crouch) to author.

[10] Lowry to Carol Ann Lowry, his heir.

[11] Mervyn Levy in the Royal Academy of Arts catalogue to the Lowry Exhibition 1976–77.

[12] *'A Pre-Raphaelite Passion'* by Sandra A. Martin, catalogue notes in the Manchester City Art Gallery exhibition of Lowry's private art collection, 1977.

[13] L S Lowry to Monty Bloom on tape (undated).

Chapter 11

[1] The late Alick Leggat to author.

[2] Carol Ann Lowry to author.

[3] Carol Ann Lowry to author.

[4] Prof Michael Fitzgerald, Trinity College, Dublin, to author.

[5] The late Pat Cooke to author.

[6] The late Sheila Fell to author (on tape).

[7] Mrs Tilly Marshall to the author (on tape).

[8] Professor Michael Fitzgerald. Trinity College, Dublin, to author.

Chapter 12

[1] 'The Discovery of L. S. Lowry', a critical and biographical essay by Maurice Collis published by Alex Reid and Lefevre Limited, 1951.

[2] *Time and Tide*, 27th February, 1943.

[3] L S Lowry to Prof Hugh Maitland, on tape, 1970.

[4] Granada Television documentary film, *Mr Lowry*, produced and directed by Leslie Woodhead, 1965.

[5] Letter from L A Lowry to David Carr, 1st November, 1949.

[6] *Journal of Mental Science*, vol 99, pp136-143.

[7] Letter to L S Lowry from Harold Palmer, MD, Medical Superintend-

ent, Hill End Hospital, St Albans, 5ᵗʰ July, 1951.

⁸ Harold Palmer to author.

⁹ Michael Fitzgerald, Professor of Child and Adolescent Psychiatry at Trinity College, Dublin, author *The Genesis of Artistic Creativity*, published by Jessica Kingsley, London and Philadelphia, 2005.

¹⁰ Article by Jessica W. Stevens in *The Studio*, Vol. 95, No 48, January 1928.

¹¹ Harold Palmer to author.

¹² Prof Fitzgerald to author, Dublin, 2005.

¹³ Letter from L S Lowry to David Carr, 1ˢᵗ November, 1950.

¹⁴ Maitland tapes.

¹⁵ Letter from David Carr to L S Lowry, 5ᵗʰ December, 1943.

¹⁶ Letter from L S Lowry to David Carr, 9ᵗʰ December, 1943.

¹⁷ L S Lowry to the late Gerald B Cotton, Chief Librarian of Swinton and Pendlebury and later Salford, and the late Frank Mullineux, Keeper of Monks Hall Museum, Eccles, on tape.

¹⁸ Cotton/Mullineux tapes.

¹⁹ Letter from L S Lowry to David Carr, 14ᵗʰ September 1949.

²⁰ '*My Lonely Life*' as told to Edwin Mullins by L S Lowry, *Sunday Telegraph*, 20ᵗʰ November, 1966.

²¹ Cotton/Mullineux tapes.

²² L S Lowry to Monty Bloom on tape, undated.

²³ The late Monty Bloom to author, 1976.

²⁴ Letter from L S Lowry to Monty Bloom, undated.

²⁵ Maurice Collis in the catalogue notes to the exhibition of the Bloom Collection of L S Lowry's works at the Hammett Gallery, London, 21st September to 21ˢᵗ October, 1972.

²⁶ Mrs Phyllis Marshall to author.

²⁷ ibid.

²⁸ The late Monty Bloom to author.

Chapter 13

¹ Jonathan Horwich, Deputy Chairman of Christie's UK.

² L S Lowry to author.

³ Fitton to author.

⁴ Letter from L S Lowry to Sally Vickers, Invitations Secretary at 10 Downing Street, undated draft reply found in Lowry's private papers after he died.

⁵ L S Lowry in a letter to the Prime Minister, draft in his private papers, undated.

⁶ Letter from L S Lowry to the late Percy Warburton, 2ⁿᵈ June, 1962.

⁷ L S Lowry to Hugh Maitland, on tape, undated.

⁸ Mervyn Levy on BBC Television.

⁹ '*Hip Hip R A*' by Robert Wraight (Leslie Frewin, London, 1968).

¹⁰ James Fitton to author.

¹¹ Pat Cooke to author, on tape.

¹² Lowry to Pat Cooke.

¹³ L S Lowry to author.

¹⁴ Review by Norbert Lynton in *The Guardian*, 26ᵗʰ November, 1966.

¹⁵ Andras Kalman of the Crane Kalman Gallery, London, to author.

¹⁶ Andras Kalman to author.

¹⁷ Pat Cooke to author.

¹⁸ Monty Bloom to author.

¹⁹ Ian Stephenson to author.

²⁰ Granada Television documentary film by Leslie Woodhead.

²¹ '*Why Lowry politely refused a Knighthood*' by John Dunsford, *Daily Telegraph*, 31ˢᵗ October, 1974.

Index of Paintings

Gallery of Modern Art, Edinburgh © the Estate of L S Lowry 2007
View from a Window of the Royal Technical College, Salford (1924) 78 *The Lowry Museum © The LS Lowry Collection, Salford*

Woman in a Hat (1924) 45 *The Lowry Museum, Salford © the Estate of L S Lowry 2007*

Yachts at Lytham (1924) 82 *The Lowry Museum, Salford © the Estate of L S Lowry 2007*
Yachts (1959) *152 The Lowry Museum © The LS Lowry Collection, Salford*

The Index of Names

Note: Family relationships are to L S Lowry